The Queerest Art

SEXUAL CULTURES: New Directions from the Center for
Lesbian and Gay Studies
General Editors: José Esteban Muñoz and Ann Pellegrini

The Queerest Art
Essays on Lesbian and Gay Theater

Edited by
ALISA SOLOMON AND FRAMJI MINWALLA

NEW YORK UNIVERSITY PRESS
New York and London

NEW YORK UNIVERSITY PRESS
New York and London

© 2002 by New York University

Library of Congress Cataloging-in-Publication Data
The queerest art : essays on lesbian and gay theater / edited by Alisa Solomon
and Framji Minwalla.
p. cm. — (Sexual cultures)
Includes bibliographical references and index.
ISBN 0-8147-9810-1 (alk. paper) — ISBN 0-8147-9811-X (pbk. : alk. paper)
1. Gay theater—United States. 2. Gay theater. I. Solomon, Alisa, 1956–
II. Minwalla, Framji. III. Series.
PN2270.G39 Q44 2002
792'.086'640973—dc21   2002000728

New York University Press books are printed on acid-free paper,
and their binding materials are chosen for strength and durability.

Manufactured in the United States of America

10 9 8 7 6 5 4 3 2 1

for our beloveds
marilyn kleinberg neimark
and
evan zelermyer

Contents

Preface

Alisa Solomon and Framji Minwalla

Some years back, the two of us had a few ideas about issues we thought were important, a go-ahead from the board of the Center for Lesbian and Gay Studies (CLAGS) at the City University of New York to put together a conference on lesbian and gay theater, and a conference date set for April 1995. Much has transpired since then that has given life to those ideas, and expanded, deepened, and reshaped them in countless fruitful ways. First, thanks to a working committee notable for its vast scholarly knowledge and professional theater experience, as well as for its dogged labor, CLAGS did put on a Queer Theater Conference that April, the first-ever organized gathering of more than two hundred queer theater scholars, practitioners, and audiences talking about the past, present, and future of their work, about how and why theater has been one of the foundations on which we've built our queer lives. (The extraordinary working committee included Ellie Covan, Jill Dolan, Martin Duberman, Randy Gener, James Hannaham, Holly Hughes, Joe E. Jeffreys, Morgan Jenness, Carol Kaplan, James Leverett, José Muñoz, Ken Norz, and David Román.)

And now, after a lengthy but rewarding process, we have, we hope, captured the scope and energy of that exhilarating event in this volume. Though this book is by no means a record of the conference—indeed, presenters did not prepare papers for it, as we preferred roundtable discussions among panelists—the diverse essays gathered here were certainly inspired by it.

In bringing together works addressing same-sex desire in Restoration comedy, the racialized impact of colonial Shakespeare, the *cuerpo politizado* of a performance artist in today's Los Angeles, and the nitty-gritty details of getting a queer show presented in Peoria, we want *The Queerest Art* both to reflect the vast range of queer research coursing through Theater Studies these days, and to evoke the debate that took place at the conference (if sometimes only tacitly) as scholars focusing on disparate places and periods claimed *queer* for their findings—or rejected it. We certainly don't mean the sweep of this volume to imply that *queer* is a stable transhistorical, transcultural term—heavens forfend!—nor to erase *gay* nor, particularly, *lesbian*. Rather, we're eager to replicate both the giddying and grounding nature of a discussion that, with apt contradictory impulses, continually sought to place that decentering term at the center of a slippery analytical project.

While collecting completed essays here, we have also sought to sustain the all-important sense of humor, open exchange, and downright disputation that the roundtable format afforded. We have also wanted to keep the voices of theater makers, so crucial to the conference, audible in the book. We are publishing virtually verbatim the keynote talks by Jill Dolan and Brian Freeman and also including among the academic essays some transcripts of panel discussions.

Just as Dolan began the conference, her piece begins this volume, setting forth a number of incisive questions that pointedly frame the issues of this book. "We might think about what we *use* our theater for," she suggests, "how it provokes us to investments of fantasy and desire." That is certainly the spine running through the essays here.

The Queerest Art goes on to look, first, at the classical canon, beginning with pieces by Alisa Solomon and Laurence Senelick that themselves leap across geography and time to ask, from different perspectives, what it is about theater as a form that has long associated it with dissident sexualities, and vice versa. As Senelick puts it, "Theater is most truly itself when it is most queer," and both writers consider the consequences: Solomon by way of the abiding sex-panic of antitheatrical prejudice, and Senelick by surveying an astonishing range of same-sex scenes over several centuries.

The volume then focuses in on English drama in the early modern period and the eighteenth century. Ania Loomba forcefully argues that "The postcolonial critic today who claims the racial other in Shakespeare as her sister, or the queer theorist who studies Renaissance same-sex relations, have both to admit that those histories are not theirs, except insofar as we choose to make them so, and for purposes that we must specify." Valerie Traub widens the raging currents of queer Shakespeare scholarship by asking "what happens when female-female desire is granted a cultural presence on Shakespeare's stage?" while in his discussion of Restoration drama, George Haggerty shows how "the heroic spectacle of male friendship resists the explanatory power of the libertine model and offers a different understanding of male-male desire in early modern culture."

The next set of essays and conversations carries such questions fully into the contemporary United States. A personal essay by Don Shewey introduces a panel from the Queer Theater Conference called "From the Invisible to the Ridiculous: The Emergence of an Out Theater Aesthetic," which grounds some of the issues raised by the critical essays in the practical experiences of lesbian and gay theater artists. Their testimonies remind us of the power of theater as a place where many of us have become emotionally and intellectually aware of our queerness, learned to represent ourselves for ourselves, and learned to look at ourselves critically—and thus, to become politicized.

Drawing from some of the work these artists have helped to forge, David Savran reconsiders some of the theoretical questions often raised in the context of canonical theater in light of the "ascendancy of a deconstructive queer theater in the United States and of a universalized queer subject." The transcript from the panel, "Out across America: Playing from P.S. 122 to Peoria" ties such concerns more concretely to practical matters of presenting queer work in a homophobic world. The tales of the artists in this panel powerfully remind us that creating queer theater still faces considerable obstacles, from the mundane to the mendacious.

In her essay on a lesbian-feminist community theater in the Midwest, Stacy Wolf looks at such issues from the other side of the performer-audience divide, making an ethnographic inquiry into the connections among performance, politics, and lesbian identity. Her questions about the relationship between spectacle and spectator, especially when the audience is a self-identified community, are extended in David Román and Tim Miller's essay; writing antiphonally as performance artist and critic, the two unpack the pejorative charge that queer theater "preaches to the converted," asking, most seriously, converted from and to *what*? José Muñoz ponders another sort of collaboration between performer and critic in his discussion of Luis Alfaro, a contemporary artist with whom he is in conversation both literally and through his writing. "Queer Latino selves are called into existence through *Cuerpo Politizado*," Muñoz writes. "Social space is reterritorialized through queer theater's demand for change."

Brian Freeman's rich reverie on the "cultural warriors" of the nineties and the new millennium muses precisely on the promise of such change, as he dreams that the next generation might create its own "new Caffe Cinos." Finally, in his chronicling of the multimedia spectacles of the youth company, School's Out: The Naming Project, Randy Gener shows us how young people are already doing just that.

The sublime, the Ridiculous, the celebratory excesses, and the deadly waste that coexist in queer theater-making nowadays are brought forth in a poignant endnote by Carmelita Tropicana. Taking us backstage at the performance that closed the Queer Theater Conference, she reveals how collective memory is forged in performance. Jill Dolan says in her introductory essay, "Our theater is our historiography; it encompasses our past, present, and future; our practice writes our history, in sedimented forms that converge in our cultural productions. Theater is our cultural memory." As Carmelita Tropicana muses about the early plays of Maria Irene Fornes at the Judson Memorial Church, murmurs lines from *Hamlet* to herself in mourning for a performer who has died of AIDS, summons her audience to swish and sashay boldly into the future, she demonstrates how such memory is both made and put to use. Offering a glimpse of what makes queer theater, she returns us eagerly to the question of what makes theater queer.

Introduction

Building a Theatrical Vernacular: Responsibility, Community, Ambivalence, and Queer Theater

Jill Dolan

I see my role here as setting out some ideas with which I hope to provoke some quarrels. If queer means anything at all, especially as an adjective for theater, it means multiplicity. It can't be anything as stable or coherent as agreement over what we're about here. And that's good. So I'll frame some issues, ask some questions, share some of my own musings about the state of queer and gay and lesbian theater and performance as it's practiced, consumed, and discussed today.

I describe myself and my work, these days, as lesbian and feminist and sometimes queer. I say that I am a theater and performance critic who also teaches in state and city university systems. So my perspective on the questions that might frame this volume and the conference that generated it come from at least two directions: One, I've watched lesbian and gay and queer studies become visible (even fashionable) in the academy. Two, for the last fifteen or more years, as a critic and a *very* enthusiastic spectator, I've watched gay and lesbian and queer theater build its own history and future, its own vocabulary, and multiple audiences. My position within this always shifting description of my location and my work is not, I'm sure, unique to me at this gathering. But I do think it will be interesting and important to see how we put our various perspectives, locations, and identities (however provisional or suspect or indeterminate we might desire them to

1

be) into conversation around the questions raised by the practice, production, study, and proliferation of something we're now calling "queer theater."

If I were going to do a more standard keynote that presumed to frame the story of the rise of gay and lesbian and queer studies, and gay and lesbian and queer performance and criticism, I would dissemble a bit, and insist that there are many ways to organize such a narrative. I would resist chronology. I wouldn't want to install a progress narrative in which gay and lesbian theater and performance is closeted, then comes out, then gets avant-garde, then looks queerly, then goes Vegas, or something. One thing that interests me in this field is that many *modes* of gay and lesbian and queer theater production continue to exist side by side, in New York and across American geography. Our history, too, resides next to our present. So, for instance, the realism and populism of *Love! Valour! Compassion!* might be the contemporary inheritor of *Boys in the Band*, in terms of form and genre, and the ways in which the larger culture adopted these representations, as an index to certain kinds of gay male experience, within their particular moments in history.

But while the media and audiences—gay and mainstream—debate Terrence McNally's play as representative of a theater style or a lifestyle, other modes of queer and gay and lesbian production happen simultaneously, and belie the apparent centrality of the Broadway stage or the identities, histories, and experiences that *LVC!* encompasses. While the men in McNally's play exchange rings and repartee about Broadway musicals or modern dance performances, and offer their bodies to each other and to the audience as aestheticized love objects, Tim Miller could be downtown at P.S. 122. He would be performing his personal-political-historical narratives, and offering *his* body as a referent for a collective reading of the events the last fifteen years have wrought. Miller's theater style and lifestyle, his analysis of the political as something that writes him, as well as something he writes, seems to form itself in a different galaxy than McNally's. And yet not really. Differences, multiplicities, gaps, contradictions, desires, sexualities—that is, the stuff of queerness—arch like a gay rainbow from 42nd Street to First Avenue— if that's not too unifying or idealistic an image (although I'm not really afraid of trading in those, sometimes). Let's leave it as an image that shimmers for a moment, then disappears. Or let's call it an image of unity into which holes are poked, perhaps, by the lesbian theater workers who somehow remain on the streets below the rainbow, agitating.

But not just on the streets: WOW's series of lesbian performances, now well over ten years old, continues in the East Village. And Dixon Place, on the Bowery, offers a regular bill of performance work by queers, lesbians, and others. The situation of queer theater produced by lesbians mirrors the typical situation of the lesbian bars which historically have organized our communities; geographically marginalized, in neighborhoods colorful, eclectic, and maybe just a little scary to walk to by yourself at night, if the culture still reads you as a woman on the street. This compared to the easy access to 42nd Street, to Broadway, to subscription houses like Manhattan Theater Club that are somehow centered in their touristy neighborhoods, just as gay male bars tend to be centered in their communities. Money makes access easy. And access, to queer theater, and not just for queers, is key here.

Lesbian and gay and queer theater, then, happens across geographies, accessible only variously and particularly, although those terms, too, change with history. The audiences at WOW are now very different from what they were when the Café started on East 11th Street, and their difference is a good thing. New audiences at WOW implies that the history of theater and performance with which we're engaged isn't static, isn't even predictable, can't claim us all in some monolithic description of our past, present, or future. The fact that this conference is happening at and is sponsored by theater-producing organizations like the New York Shakespeare Festival and the New York Theater Workshop is enormously important. Whether you read this placement as a subversion of dominant cultural production or an affirmation of how queer these spaces already are, our discussions and performances for these three days are located in the places where they come from, where they move toward, and/or with which they're in dialogue, simply because of the structure of theater production in New York and in the United States.

So here we are, talking about queer theater and performance that we've created, written about, consumed, diss'd, dished, digested, and debated. I don't think we can really say that this work has progressed formally (or politically) in some linear fashion. But we can perhaps productively say that different forms and contents and contexts of queer theater production and reception coexist, and that they're differently useful to different audiences in different locations, whether they're straight, gay, lesbian, queer, of color, of money, of ability, all of these at once and more, many more. What would it mean, in fact, if queer production and consumption weren't ontologically queer at all, but simply a position of art practice or reading that anyone so inclined or so desiring could assume?

Alexander Doty, in his book, *Making Things Perfectly Queer*, describes such a strategy for engaging with popular culture, of which we might consider theater, *our* theater, a part. Queerness becomes a place to which people can travel, to find pleasure, and knowledge, and maybe (or maybe not) power. Anyone in the audience of *Belle Reprieve*, for example, might experience a queer pleasure, because the performance structures its references to popular and high cultural icons—burlesque, vaudeville, drag, Tennessee Williams—as insistently queered, as only meaningful through the queer, postmodern appropriations of a performance group that's queered itself through its own affiliations across gender, sexual practices, class, access to production. The melding of Peggy Shaw and Lois Weaver and Bloolips into the cast of *Belle Reprieve* perhaps represents the hopeful, coalitional politics that queer theater might set as a standard for the larger activist movement.

So we have a history, and a couple of articulated examples, and more examples that we hold in our collective memories of theater work that might or might not fit under the banner we're waving of "queer." Is queer more radical than gay or lesbian? Can we say that gay and lesbian theater in the sixties, for instance, was more or less radical than queer theater and performance in the nineties? Or than performance in the nineties that still calls itself lesbian or gay? What kind of yardstick are we using to judge radical or political and why is this an important standard to bring to theater (if you agree that it is)? Is all gay and lesbian and queer theater political because of its identity politics, its insistence on visibility (or its more covert generation of meanings that subvert dominant systems)? Or, in the age of queer, is this theater political because it proliferates meanings not necessarily linked to identity politics or visibility, but tied more squarely to sexual practices and gender rebellion and social performances of the mutability of race and ethnic categories? Is sexuality enough of a category here, when we know now, through theory and experience, that sexuality never stands alone? Is sexuality all we mean by queer anyway? What tools are we all using to critique or to make plays and performances we see and create, according to what presumption of political effectiveness?

Is it desirable to look at history as a progress narrative, always assuming that now is better, even if we're wistful and nostalgic for an unrecoverable past? Or is it more important to give history and local contexts their due, and assume that while New York generates "queer" as a new category of activism and performance, people in smaller, more isolated communities are still risking maybe even their lives by producing a lesbian play like *Last Summer at Bluefish Cove*? With the new hegemony of queer as an identity, "gay" and "lesbian" have been made essential, ontological, fixed spaces and have been thrown into apparent disrepute by contemporary queer theorizing. What happens to gay and lesbian drama now? Does it get "queered"? It seems easy enough to "queer the canon," or "queer Shake-speare," but can we or should we queer our more recent past? Can we queer feminism, from which lesbian theater derived much of its initial energy? Should we?

Queerness has come to encompass numerous strategies, all of which carry the charge of multiplicity, openness, contradiction, contention, the slipperiness of sexual practice seeping into discourse, into fashion, into style and politics and the-ater. Queer skids on the slipperiness of its investments, its identities, its human composition, the multifacetedness of its interventions in culture. To be queer is not who you *are*, it's what you *do*, it's your relation to dominant power, and your relation to marginality, as a place of empowerment. "Queer" opens spaces for people who embrace all manner of sexual practices and identities, which gives old-fashioned gays and lesbians a lot more company on the political front lines, as well as in capital consumption, and, of course, in bed. That's the beauty and the flaw of "queer," depending on how you look at it.

I'm insistently using the words gay and lesbian along with queer in relation to theater to remind us of history, to remind us of differential power, to remind us that however fluidly we might practice and perform our identities, regulatory systems tend to fix them and to legislate against them, through juridical, medical, and educational discourses in which the theater we make and write about must intervene. And gay and lesbian theater has a hard-fought history, as a genre, as a renegade style of wresting the power of representation from dominant voices, of insisting on our right to imagine ourselves, to take pleasure from displaying and receiving each other's bodies through the representational frame. I hope that at this conference we'll celebrate the achievements of gay and lesbian theater and performance, along with the queer version, so that we can remember our history.

In the framing narrative I would tell, were I telling this story, I would insist on the importance of history for all of us, regardless of how we define our selves or our sexual practices, regardless of whether or not we believe there is anything there, on the stage or in our homes, to define. This, of course, comes now, in an age of poststructuralist theorizing and postmodern style that privileges surfaces and their transformations, their subversions, perhaps, over depth, soul, spirit—sometimes, at least. Joan Nestle remains my guide here, always my inspiration. In *A Restricted Country*, she writes,

[F]or gay people, history is a place where the body carries its own story. . . . If we are the people who call down history from its heights in marble assembly halls, if we put desire into history, if we document how a collective erotic imagination questions and modifies

monolithic societal structures like gender, if we change the notion of woman as self-cho-
sen victim by our public stances and private styles, then surely no apologies are due. Being
a sexual people is our gift to the world.

Being a sexual people is our gift to the theater, as well, where in our own representations, in our revisions of the relation between performer and spectator and
among audiences, in our rewritings of the relation between art and culture, we insist on the importance of desire as history, desire as future, on our import as bear-
ers and shapers of different, necessary cultural meanings, through the presence of
our desire. Our theater is our historiography; it encompasses our past, present, and
future; our practice writes our history, in sedimented forms that converge in our
cultural productions. Theater is our cultural memory.

Desire is our legacy to theater and, probably, theater's past and its future. I hope
we'll indulge ourselves at this conference in describing the pleasure we take in
queer performance, because on some level, our pleasure *is* our resistance. I hope
that together we'll chart the thrill of being in audiences charged with overt erotics,
of consuming and writing about and making performances that are enormously
seductive on multiple levels, from the aggressive presentation of queer bodies to
the embodiment of texts that are smart and wry and irreverent, back to bodies,
dressed or not in unpredictable, incongruent ways in the accoutrements of gendered, raced, classed, eroticized culture, switching codes for each other and for us.

I hope we share the pleasure of going to WOW with other lesbians and with
straight women and with men of all stripes, and being so proud on some level of
the different pleasures we could offer in this space. I hope we share the pleasure of
seeing Carmelita Tropicana develop as a character and as a performer who gives so
much to our communities; of seeing Holly Hughes grow from a manic, barely con-
trolled bombshell in *The Lady Dick* at WOW to the mistress of queer language, the
performer who can wrap her tongue around discourse and queer it by drenching
it with juices (and I don't just mean saliva); of seeing Peggy Shaw and Lois Weaver
sing "I Like to Be in America" in Yiddish with Deb Margolin in *Upwardly Mobile
Home* and seeing them deconstruct marriage in *Anniversary Waltz.*

If Roberta Sklar and Sondra Segal, Jane Chambers, Karen Malpede, Mart Crow-
ley, and Terrence McNally offered me a new ancestry, one different (and yet
strangely similar) to the Jewish one I brought with me to New York, packed in my
baggage, I feel like I grew up with Carmelita, and Holly, and Peggy, and Lois, and
Deb, and Lisa Kron, Babs Davy, Moe Angelos, Dominique Dibbell, and Peg Healy—
separately and as the Five Lesbian Brothers—whose name alone, when I describe

6

their work in places removed from the downtown New York context, inspires gasps of wonder and either dismay or delight. I *did* grow up, watching their work, learning new genre conventions, and how to queer the old ones, thinking about the radical potential in the expression of lesbian desire in these out-of-the-way spaces. I'm noticing, now, that we're all getting older, I see it on our faces, and this persuades me that as critics and practitioners, as theorists and producers, we have to teach ourselves how to incorporate our past with our present.

At the organizing meetings for this conference, we seemed continually excited about work that looked forward, but unsure how to approach work from even the recent past. Likewise, "downtown," "off-center," "marginal," or more positively described, community-oriented work for constituent audiences, captured our imaginations and our commitments, and we weren't quite sure what to do with work that we could determine more "successful" in predictably traditional, mainstream terms. Does a play or performance lose a queer credential when you can buy a ticket for it in Duffy Square on the TKTS line? I don't *think* it does, I think in fact it *can't*, but something about the presumed outlaw status of "queer" made us stumble over the question of "midtown" success at our planning meetings.

I think what we came up against in our contentious, productive discussions was what Kobena Mercer describes as the burden of responsibility placed on marginalized work that seems to gain access to wider audiences or distribution systems. Mercer suggests that we consider gay, lesbian, queer representations as speaking *from* community or identity positions, rather than speaking *for* them. This might help us navigate the roiling waters of political responsibility and accountability at this conference: an understanding that dominant media burdens queer producers with speaking *for*, and that those of us who locate ourselves in relation to queerness in one way or another might read queer productions as speaking *from* multiple, always partial places within constantly changing definitions of queer community. This might offer us a strategy for speaking at this conference.

We might think about what we *use* our theater for, how it provokes us to investments of fantasy and desire, how it employs what Cindy Patton calls a "sexual vernacular" or how it might use several vernaculars, to speak differently to the specific, local communities with which it would affiliate. I recall reading Patton's description in *How Do I Look?* of a group of queer activists carefully watching a porn film to decide questions of representational efficacy around condom use. How might queer theater inspire the same kind of close looking, not necessarily to find an unmediated relationship to the real, not necessarily to secure a too direct link between cause and effect, but because performance and theatrical representation had become an intervention in matters of life and death? Richard Schechner once made a distinction between theater and ritual that hinged on need. Participants *need ritual* to sustain them, he suggested, but theater *needs audiences* to sustain it. How might *queer* theater become a kind of social ritual that *audiences* need for sustenance?

Finally, we work at many different sites. We write and make theater and performances for an activist movement; to offer pleasure to our communities; and to circulate our cultural practices, our art, widely through various social geographies. We write about performance in academic journals and the popular press. Queer theater and performance have been buffeted and bolstered by academic criticism, by academic residencies, by critics and performers very clear about how we mutually support and need each other. Queer theater has been brought to wide attention by gay and lesbian and queer cultural critics in the wildly proliferating gay press, and in established presses like the *Village Voice* and even the *New York Times*, as well as in weeklies and dailies in large urban areas around the country. Gay-lesbian-queer journalism has critically engaged our performance work, and has insisted that others look closely at the new forms, styles, meanings, pleasures we're producing in the theater.

There are many questions to pose here, many disagreements to have, many remembrances to be made for those who have died and can't be here to mark their contributions to our theater history, and much pride to be shared in the fact that we're here together at all. We can't rest on our laurels, even if we're surprised to find that we've accumulated any. We have to push forward into the future and backward into the past, knowing all we know and wanting to know more as we work under the risk of erasure, of vilification, of further political and artistic disenfranchisement as the spaces that produce our work watch their finances becomes more and more precarious. The inhospitable political climate under which we're working is the one under which gay and lesbian and queer work has always been produced. It shouldn't seem worse now, but somehow it does.

To counter the political machinery of the Right, we should transmit our knowledges. We should form sexual and theatrical apprenticeships, to teach each other and others what we know and what we don't. We should transform consciousness with our theaters and our performances, offering our multiple representations of desire up for what Doty calls "sexually transmutable" responses. Our theater can bridge theory and activism by offering a sexual vernacular for speaking desire in performance, and invite the world to partake with us in the politics of our pleasure.

1 Great Sparkles of Lust

Homophobia and the Antitheatrical Tradition

Alisa Solomon

Theater is the queerest art. That's not merely to say that there have always been lots of gay and lesbian people in the theater, nor even that it's probably no coincidence that in New York, at least, June is both Gay Pride month and Celebrate Broadway month. Rather, it's to take pleasure in the possibility that the antitheatrical Puritans were right when, like William Prynne, they ranted against theater as "sinfull, heathenish, lewde, ungodly Spectacles and most pernicious Corruptions."[1] In the same twisted way, it's tempting to regard even Jesse Helms as correct when he sputtered on the floor of the U.S. Senate against the insurrectionary power of queer performance art. What they're all right about—when we're lucky— is that the kind of mimetic experience offered in the theater can by its very process disrupt conventional patterns of seeing, of knowing, and, especially, of seeing and knowing bodies.

That theater should be the art potentially most offensive to social order makes obvious sense: onstage the human body is absolutely present in all its sweating, spitting specificity. Antitheatrical railers recoiled especially from this unavoidable, bodily fact—and from the theatrical suggestion that the factness of the body doesn't imply everything about the identity of the self. The Puritans, of course, were particularly peeved by the convention of boy-actresses on the early modern stage, a threat, they warned, to the very category of gender. In 1990s America—a period that, by many accounts, shares some preoccupations with the early modern era—performance art would become the most fractious site of gender and sexual insubordination, and of attacks on art as a despoiler of the state.

What is it about theater, as a form, that provokes (homo)sex panic? And, as a corollary, one well might ask, what is it about homosexuality that steers queer theory inevitably toward theatrical metaphors? Why, in different historical moments and distant locations, does theater consistently collide with queer? And how might understanding that relentless confrontation help explain the mobilization of hoary homophobic tropes in the attacks on the National Endowment for the Arts in the early 1990s—and in the legislation that enabled and resulted from those attacks? To get to the heart of these abiding questions, I want to offer three disparate snapshots of theater's connection with queerness: the appalling attacks on the early modern playhouses of England; the affinity between performance and performativity that animates contemporary queer theory; and the legislative achievements of America's antiabortion movement, which set the stage for the homophobic attacks on the National Endowment for the Arts in the early 1990s. These are disjointed images, to be sure, but I hope that laying them alongside each other as a triptych will prove them to be mutually revealing.

Playing the *Sodomits,* or *Worse*

That homophobic panic throbs at the heart of the age-old antitheatrical prejudice hardly needs documenting. Recent research by Renaissance scholars and queer theorists alike has amply demonstrated the ease with which arguments against the theater slid quickly into horror-struck warnings about sexual activity that exceeded legal and customary limits, and indeed, how any expression of sexuality that violated the proprieties of heterosexual marital relations was regarded as *sodomy.*[2] As Phillip Stubbes famously put it in *The Anatomie of Abuses:*

Marke the flocking and running to Theaters & curtens, daylie and hourely, night and daye, tyme and tyde to see Playes and Enterludes, where such wanton gestures, such bawdie speaches: such laughing and fleering: such kissing and bussing: such clipping and culling: Suche winckage and glancinge of wanton eyes, and the like is used, as is wonderfull to behold. Than these goodly pageants being done, every mate sorts to his mate, every one bringes another homeward of their way verye freendly, and in their secret conclaves (covertly) they play the Sodomits, or worse.[3]

The theater, according to this aghast perception, was a place of limitless debauchery. Of course, it wasn't just onstage that audiences were roused by such wanton sights. Part of the objection to theaters as dens of depravity came from their location in the "liberties" of London—the liminal outskirts to which illicit activities were banished, prostitution chief among them. Thus, as Puritans frantically warned, in attending theater, men entered a territory where leering was their primary means of social engagement, and otherwise respectable women associated themselves with whores by venturing out in public where they could be the object of men's lascivious gaze. More subversively, as Jean Howard has argued, women could themselves take up the role of spectator.[4] They, too, could look with desire. Thus, they too, in even thinking beyond the marriage bed, entered the realm of sodomy.

Like many of his anxious colleagues, John Rainolds considered the convention of boy-actresses particularly culpable. Their very presence, he warned, ignited "great sparkles of lust." He explains:

The apparel of wemen . . . is a great provocation of men to lust and leacherie: because a womans garment being put on a man doeth vehemently touch and move him with the remembrance and the imagination of a woman: and the imagination of a thing desirable doth stirr up the desire.[5]

There's an apparent, superficial literalness to Rainolds's suggestion: he seems to think that it's the apparel, not the body wearing it, that incites lust. But the dress is just the trigger. The real culprit in Rainolds's formulation is the spectator's imagination. And most of all, the experience of nonillusory theater is an experience that vigorously stirs up the imagination. Underlying the antitheatricalists' overheated claims, then, is a deep suspicion of the nature of spectating itself.

It's no accident that the sort of theater that riled England's early modern scolds was nonillusory—that is, it called directly, brazenly, on the spectator to complete the play by engaging her or his imagination, often calling attention to the ironic gap between what is said on stage and what is shown. No light technician, for example, executes a series of light cues to suggest how "the morn in russet mantle clad / walks o'er the dew of yon high eastward hill" (*Hamlet* I, I, 171–72). Rather, the language asks spectators to see such colors in their mind's eye—much as the spectator is asked to recognize "this place," a bare stage, as Illyria or to take Burbage for Hamlet—and a teenaged boy for Ophelia. In other words, on the nonillusory stage, language is performative in J. L. Austin's original sense: Utterances are enactments. Words call scene, character, and action into being. Meanwhile, the spectator is reminded of her or his role in producing the spectacle, and invited to take pleasure in this imaginative complicity. Theater itself, then, enacts a kind of seduction—not one in which the audience is swept out of their senses, as critics of the later naturalistic theater complained, but all the more dangerous precisely because they *weren't* completely swept away. Frequently reminded of the mechanisms of theatrical mimesis, early modern spectators engaged knowingly and willingly in the construction of the event of theater.

The dangerous organ, then, is not simply the eye (through which, it was thought at the time, love struck directly into the liver), but also the ear. Like Hamlet's father, we're poisoned in the theater by what pours into that orifice. For it's the imaginative link the spectator makes between what s/he sees and what s/he hears that constitutes the action of engaging theater. Indeed, the spectator is most emphatically enlisted when the seen and the shown contradict each other. Unlike film, which invites its audience to enter a closed, finished fantasy, nonillusory theater calls upon the spectator to complete the fantasy. Without his or her polymorphously perverse engagement, there is no play. What is more, the physical presence of both actors and spectators casts them, in the film theorist Christian Metz's provocative phrase, as "the two protagonists of an authentic perverse couple."[6]

The most potent emblem of this process is the boy-actress, and thus his danger exceeds the breaching of biblical and royal sumptuary codes or the striking off of the "remembrance and imagination of a woman." The boy-actress's "provocation to lust and leacherie" stems more subtly from his position as an overdetermined icon of the nonillusory theater. Contemporary texts often call attention to his both-at-once status, with jokes about not-quite-breaking voices, or whiskers beginning to peep through damask cheeks, and even, at times, the flirtatious, fetishizing promise to reveal a breast. This is an erotic incitement, to be sure, but different only in its literalness from the erotics of engaging any moment of a play. As the antitheatrical Puritans understood it—in an inchoate Foucauldianism, if you will—the confluence of actors' and spectators' bodies and the nature of nonillusory theatrical stimulation aroused a confusion of sexual (and other) categories: in a word, nonillusory theater featuring boy-actresses could not help but produce *sodomy*.

The Theatricality of Queer

One consequence of "playing the *Sodomits*" and erasing borders of sexual categories was losing *all* sense of boundary and propriety, all sense of self. That is

Stubbes's idea of the *worse* result: *becoming* the sodomite. Theater threatened this too, through the shameless display of the actor's skills at changing, apparently, his very nature. His abilities called into question the notion that anyone actually has a nature.

In one of the most vitriolic and oft-quoted antitheatrical tracts, *Histriomastix*, William Prynne excoriates theater for contravening God's act of having given a "uniforme, distinct and proper being to every creature." As Laura Levine notes in her influential essay, "Men in Women's Clothing: Anti-Theatricality and Effemi- nization from 1579 to 1642,"[7] Prynne and compatriots must have had their own doubts about this divine gift since they protest so much. After all, if every creature were so endowed, why were these pious men so hysterical about the capacities of costume, acting, and theater watching to *change* that distinct and proper being? Levine draws some useful conclusions about what theories of the self prevailed in that era; what's important here is how theater provokes or stirs up the anxiety it- self—in this instance, an anxiety born in an age of new social mobility, spurred by an emerging market economy. Theater, by *its* nature, reveals and revels in the very angst the antitheatricalists were frantically trying to quell: the notion of identities as contingent and malleable and the suggestion that categories can be playfully transgressed—*queered*.

As several critics have noted, it's a particularly postmodern point too. Barbara Freedman, for one, explains how "both Renaissance and postmodern models of representation undermine the humanist impulse to 'stand / As if man were author of himself' (*Coriolanus* V, 35–36)."[8] Queer theory, of course—among other post- modern critical stances—assumes, indeed celebrates, the centrality of representa- tion in the formation of social identities, shooting a campy, appreciative glance at the self-conscious ways in which queers represent our identities in the social world. Going beyond sociological theories of role-playing in everyday life, queer theorists ask who is home—and who has built that home—when the roles are stripped away. As in theater, such a question is particularly compelling when ad- dressed to identities whose social construction is demonstrable, but that feel as though they are as unshakable as our skins.

Here lies the deepest source of queer tropism toward theater. Certainly, as many have argued, gay men and lesbians may have long found some pleasure and sol- ace in theater as a place where the acting they employed in everyday life to hide their sexuality enjoyed more productive expression. Not only was the theater hos- pitable to those bound up in impersonation; it also acknowledged and made space for gender ambiguities that mainstream society labored vigorously to suppress.

But more keenly, in the theater, heteronormative master plots could be undercut and questioned through self-conscious performance styles, even as they were played out in the stories staged. Theatrical irony enables theater to attract sexual outlaws through its sodomitical tendencies to disrupt category and make hash of convention.

Irony—the capacity to hold contradictory ideas at the same time, and more specifically in theater, the gap between what audiences know but characters in a play don't—drives a wedge between representation and reality, throwing their relationship into question. Thus like queer theory, which examines how representations of all kinds shape sexualities, theater—in Bruce Wilshire's words, "the art of imitation that reveals imitation"[9]—unmasks representation's effects *qua* effects. As Herbert Blau explains, "Theater implies no *first time*, no origin, but only recurrence and reproduction."[10] The uncanny echo is telling when Judith Butler states, "the original identity after which gender fashions itself is an imitation without an origin . . . it is a production which . . . postures as an imitation."[11]

Theater and queer theory challenge ideas of fixed identities. Both break through the seemingly impermeable walls of gender and sexual categories by unmooring them from the idea that they derive absolutely and inevitably from an original objective source. Much as the boy-actress (synecdochically for the theater generally) was the signifier of instability for the Puritan antitheatricalists, *queer* has proudly proclaimed itself the signifier of instability in postmod America.

Helms's *Histriomastix*: Legal Legacies[12]

To the extent that instability breeds anxiety and crusades of containment, queerness and theater collided once again in America's "culture war" of the nineties, particularly as it played out in the battle over the National Endowment for the Arts. Conservative efforts to defund the NEA—and indeed, to undermine the very principle of public spending—self-consciously mobilized homophobia and its age-old link to antitheatricalism. Conservatives didn't have to search hard for these tropes, of course. The Puritan legacy pervades American politics. One can hardly forget that the United States was founded by the very folks who closed the theaters in London from 1642 to 1660. Colonists in Virginia enacted a law that forbade public acting (as we know from court records of the arrest of actors playing in *Ye Bare and Ye Cub* in Accomac County in 1665).

As the theater historian Gary A. Richardson notes, with the exception of Maryland, all the American colonies at one point or another had laws to discourage, or even prohibit, theatrical activity in America. The most stringent were in New England, but even the Quakers of Pennsylvania enacted a statute in 1682 asserting that anyone found guilty of introducing or attending "such rude and riotous sports and practices as prizes [fights], stage plays, and masques" would be sentenced to hard labor.[13]

If antitheatrical prejudice has long burbled beneath the surface of American culture, the parallel disgust with nonmarital, nonreproductive sex has erupted with dangerous frequency. If the two streams merged once again in the NEA debates, it's important to trace the role of antiabortion legislation in directing the flow of sentiment against the expression of sex beyond the bounds of marital bonds.

Both crusades center on regulating the body, and especially, the body's inexorable association with sex. At the height of the NEA fracas, merely mentioning that Holly Hughes, Tim Miller, and John Fleck are openly gay, and that Karen Finley is a feminist, was enough to raise the specter of the unruly body—not in the acceptable sense of sex object or commodity on display for straight men, nor the body purified of its passions, cleaved, in Cartesian manner, from the soul for which it provides a residence. (As then NEA chairperson John Frohnmayer famously said: "Holly Hughes is a lesbian and her work is heavily of that genre."[14]) The great sin of these artists was their presentation of the sweating, secreting, excreting, ecstatic body as a site of self-defined meaning, not subject to the regulations of church or state.

This notion of the body as a playful ground of pleasure, exploration, and self-definition is exactly what the fundamentalist right objects to when it rails against abortion (and against safe-sex education in high schools). Claims to "rescuing the unborn" notwithstanding, the right makes no secret of its contention that women should remain at home raising babies instead of thwarting their "natural" roles by entering the workforce. Unwanted pregnancy, in their view, is God's punishment for recreational sex (just as, in their view, AIDS is God's punishment for the "perversion" of gay sex). This principle is important to recognize in the context of the arts debate because the regulations and litigation tactics employed to clamp down on the arts were developed and tested around the issue of reproductive freedom. The anti-NEA argument—No one's saying they can't express themselves, taxpayers just don't have to pay for it—scored its first success with the Hyde Amendment of 1977, and was soon after upheld by the Supreme Court. That regulation prohibited abortions in federally funded health services. Thus women on Medicaid as well those in the military, on Native American reservations, and in the Peace Corps were denied access to abortions in the health facilities they relied on. The reasoning went: No one is saying these women can't have abortions, it's just that the government shouldn't pay for what it doesn't endorse. But of course, given the uneven availability of affordable health care in this country, canceling services in federally funded health programs effectively made them unavailable to anyone without the means to pay for, and often to travel to, a private physician.

It's not a large logical leap to the "gag rule," the controversial 1991 Supreme Court decision in *Rust v. Sullivan*, which prohibits counselors and other personnel in federally funded health facilities from even mentioning abortion. But the most blatant connection between the narrowing of reproductive rights and attacks on the NEA was made by the Department of Justice itself, when, in Senate hearings on First Amendment implications of *Rust* v. *Sullivan*, a Department of Justice representative stated, "when the government funds a certain view, the government itself is speaking. It, therefore, may constitutionally determine what is to be said." Later, he specifically cited the application *Rust* has to the NEA, an application that could have grave repercussions in decisions about the selection of library materials or scientific research projects.

Meanwhile, following rulings on abortion, Congress enacted antifunding provisions directed specifically against gay men and lesbians and against gay and lesbian expression. Shortly after the Hyde Amendment was passed, for instance, came the McDonald Amendment, which forbids legal services lawyers—that is, lawyers paid with government funds—from taking on any cases having to do with gay rights. Around the same time, the Oklahoma legislature adopted a statute that called for the firing of public employees who "promoted homosexuality." (A similar initiative was narrowly defeated in California.) This law was challenged and litigated by the American Civil Liberties Union on the basis of a freedom of expression argument, since the provision basically made it illegal for anyone working in, say, a public school or a public health agency, or any other government-subsidized institution (perhaps even an NEA-supported theater) to say anything in public that could be construed as advocating—which is to say, not condemning—homosexuality. Violation of this rule would cost the worker her or his job, even if the offending remark were made on the employee's own time. A high school teacher under this law might, for instance, be prevented from nonjudgmentally pointing out that Walt Whitman addressed love poetry to men; a road repair worker could be barred from marching in a gay pride parade.

The U.S. Court of Appeals ruled that the law was, indeed, unconstitutional, but when the case moved on to the Supreme Court, no majority decision was reached. With Justice Powell absent due to illness, the Court was divided four-to-four, which meant that the ruling reverted to the appeals court decision and was therefore thrown out. Echoing one of the antitheatricalists' biggest objections to actors, arguments supporting the statute focused heavily on the specious notion that spectators unwittingly imitate what they see; advocates of the Oklahoma law worried that progay teachers, straight and gay alike, might give innocent pupils wicked ideas that would otherwise never occur to them.

A year later, in 1986, in *Bowers* v. *Hardwick*, the Court, in upholding Georgia's antisodomy laws, ruled that the right to privacy does not extend to gay men and lesbians. Indeed, the Court opinion explicitly stated that certain sexual acts were no business of the state when performed by consenting heterosexual adults, but could be deemed illegal when engaged in by partners of the same sex. Thus gay and lesbian expression of the most intimate kind was officially excluded from constitutional protection. Describing or depicting such relationships, then, could easily be banished to a realm beyond the compass of the First Amendment.

Certainly, the AIDS epidemic brought these issues to the surface, as it increased the visibility of gay men, for better and for worse. If a centuries-old association has linked gays to the arts, a simple syllogism of popular understanding soon linked the arts to AIDS. Crudely put, the reasoning runs: Arts=Gays; Gays=AIDS; therefore, Arts=AIDS. Never mind that this hysteria-driven logic is based on stereotypes and incomplete information, it goes a long way toward explaining the rancor toward art that deals with sexuality.

Antitheatrical tirades of centuries past often used disease imagery to denounce the dangerous contagion of the stage. The seventeenth-century English Puritans railed against playhouses as hotbeds of impurity and contamination, both literal and figurative. As illness itself was considered a moral sentence, a sort of physical manifestation of evil inclinations, disease and blasphemy were wrapped up together in harangues against the theater—thus Prynne's venomous and voluminous diatribe against the "most pernicious Corruptions" of the stage.

Some three hundred years seemed to vanish when Jesse Helms stood on the Senate floor waving this or that federally funded "abomination" or "obscenity," instructing women to leave the room, describing how ill he feels at even contemplating the "filth" he waved overhead. One of the first props Helms brandished in these performances of outrage, was a safe-sex comic book published by Gay Men's Health Crisis. In the battle over this audience-specific manual, AIDS and gay expression converged, and the question of government funding for "objectionable" material was played most blatantly in this double context.

In debates on every AIDS education funding bill that followed, Helms was able to attach riders prohibiting federal funding of any material that "promotes homosexuality or promiscuity"—a goal he successfully labeled as "pornographic." Soon the panic-mongering epithet could be applied to *any* expression of nonnormative sexuality. Redundantly, theater by queers—and by syllogistic extension, theater in general—was officially branded, once again, as "sinfull, heathenish, lewde, ungodly Spectacles and most pernicious Corruptions."

Postscript: Coming Home to Roost

If there's a solid tradition of attacking theater as queer as a way of asserting normative sexuality and social mores generally, it stands to reason that the emergence of conservative gay politics has deployed the old tropes to claim a place in the mainstream. Gay conservatives have attacked theater, or the idea of theater, to mark their distance from queerness and to display their acceptability to straight power elites. Early in his career as the star gay conservative, Andrew Sullivan dismissed ACT UP's tactics as "exercises in theater and rhetoric."[15] And in San Antonio, Texas, in 1998, a small group of conservative gay men joined the local attacks on the Esperanza Center, a community-based arts organization, after it presented a gay and lesbian film festival and series of queer performances. Fundamentalist Protestants spearheaded efforts to revoke city funding to the organization, claiming that it was presenting "pornography," and local gay conservatives jumped at the opportunity to distinguish themselves as *respectable* gay citizens, far more worthy of the city's embrace. As a letter to Mayor Howard Peak and the City Council from a founding officer of the San Antonio [gay] Equal Rights Political Caucus put it, "the gay community in San Antonio in no way supports the sort of filth seen at these publicly funded events." The Esperanza Center, the letter added, "is an embarrassment to San Antonio's gay community and should not be receiving funding from the City."[16]

The author of that screed, Ted Wesley Switzer, M.D. (also the publisher of the local gay newspaper), was also a signatory to a memo sent around their circles for endorsements.[17] That letter attacks the Esperanza Center for being "obsessed with victimhood and using 'sexism, racism, classism and homophobia' as rhetorical and political ploys to extract guilt money from individuals and organizations, including the City." It echoes Switzer's solo charges that Esperanza programs "have consistently been anti-Anglo, anti-male and in many cases have been pornographic if not obscene," and it adds that the center "has taken its cues from the national 'victim art' movement" (as if there were such a thing). Indeed, the letter chides the Esperanza Center for "damaging the cause of equal rights for gays and lesbians in San Antonio." In sum, they charged, the group's presentation of lesbian "pornography" was evidence of its commie predilections (and vice versa), and thus a scourge to the civilized (that is, white, male, Protestant, American-born, and well-to-do) gay community that didn't want to be tarred by any association with the immigrants, poor folks, and women of color who attend Esperanza's various programs.

In this sordid story, conservative gay men attempt to escape the queer undertow of sexual difference by distancing themselves from the currents surging away on the other side of town. It makes good queer sense that they'd do so by attacking a theater space. As these assimilationist, conservative gay men well understand, theater is precisely where queerness can't help but thrive.

Notes

1. William Prynne, *Histrio-Mastix: The Player's Scourge or Actor's Tragedy* (New York: Garland, 1974).

2. See, for example, Jonas Barish, *The Anti-Theatrical Prejudice* (Berkeley: University of California Press, 1981); Jonathan Goldberg, *Sodometries: Renaissance Texts, Modern Sexualities* (Stanford: Stanford University Press, 1992); Laura Levine, "Men in Women's Clothing: Anti-Theatricality and Effeminization from 1579 to 1642," *Criticism* 28.2, Spring 1986: 121–43; Stephen Orgel, "Nobody's Perfect: Or Why Did the English Stage Take Boys for Women?" *South Atlantic Quarterly* 88:1, Winter 1989:7–29.

3. Phillip Stubbes, *The Anatomie of Abuses* (1583), facsimile, ed. Arthur Freeman (New York: Garland, 1973), N8r-v.

4. Jean Howard, "Scripts and/versus Playhouses: Ideological Production and the Renaissance Public Stage," in *The Matter of Difference: Materialist Feminist Criticism of Shakespeare*, ed. Valerie Wayne (Ithaca: Cornell University Press, 1991), 221–36.

5. John Rainolds, *Overthrow of the Stage-Plays* (New York: Johnson Reprint Corp., 1972), 96–97.

6. Christian Metz, *The Imaginary Signifier: Psychoanalysis and the Cinema* (Bloomington: University of Indiana Press, 1977), 63.

7. Levine, "Men in Women's Clothing," 121–43.

8. Barbara Freedman, *Staging the Gaze: Postmodernism, Psychoanalysis, and Shakespearean Comedy* (Ithaca: Cornell University Press, 1991).

9. Bruce Wilshire, *Role-Playing and Identity: The Limits of Theatre as Metaphor* (Boston: Routledge & Kegan Paul, 1981), x.

10. Herbert Blau, "Universals of Performance; or, Amortizing Play," *Substance* 37–38, 1983:148.

11. Judith Butler, *Gender Trouble: Feminism and the Subversion of Identity* (London: Routledge, 1990), 138.

12. Much of this argument was first developed in, and is in part excerpted here from, "Art Attack: What Do Plato and Pat Buchanan Have in Common?" *American Theater*, June 1992:18–24, 57.

13. Gary A. Richardson, *American Drama from the Colonial Period through World War I: A Critical History* (New York: Twayne Publishers, 1993), 6.

14. John Frohnmayer said this at a National Council meeting in Winston Salem, N.C., in May 1990, which was convened specifically to talk about grants that had been recommended to the four performance artists who became known as the NEA Four (Hughes, Karen Finley, John Fleck, and Tim Miller), who sued when their grants were revoked. The transcript of that meeting was made available to the plaintiffs in the discovery segment of the lawsuit. I am grateful to Hughes for sharing the material with me.

15. Andrew Sullivan, "The Politics of Homosexuality," in *Taking Liberties: Gay Men's Essays on Politics, Culture, and Sex*, ed. Michael Bronski (New York: Richard Kassak, 1996), 32.

16. Letter from Ted Wesley Switzer, M.D., dated September 10, 1997, to Mayor Peak and City Council Members. I am grateful to the Esperanza Center for furnishing me with a copy.

17. This undated memo to Mayor Peak and "All City Council Members" is signed by Switzer and Rob Blanchard, Dan Castor, Michael McGowan, Glenn Stehle, and Byron Trott, all active in local gay organizations such as the San Antonio Gay and Lesbian Community Center, the San Antonio Equal Rights Political Caucus, and the San Antonio Log Cabin Republicans. I am grateful to the Esperanza Center for furnishing me with a copy.

2 The Queer Root of Theater

Laurence Senelick

Queer theater is in the making. Identifying its antecedents means first identifying its characteristics, and the phenomenon is still too recent, too much in flux, for any simple definition to serve. Since I am a frequent contributor to encyclopedias, I am afraid that some day I shall be called upon to provide such a definition. So I might as well make a stab at it now. To speak in general terms, queer theater is grounded in and expressive of unorthodox sexuality or gender identity, antiestablishment and confrontational in tone, experimental and unconventional in format, with stronger links to performance art and what the Germans call *Kleinkunst*, that is, revue, cabaret, and variety, than to traditional forms of drama.

Let this definition serve as an academic stopgap until something better is devised or until the genre itself is defunct and ready for taxonomy and taxidermy. What it does omit is the symbiosis between the performers' private lives and sensibilities and the performance. Queer theater cannot be created from without: the status of its creator as a "queer" within a "straight" society is, at some level, its raw material. In view of the theater's past indentures to society, "queerness" was more easily come by in the fairground or the nightclub than in the playhouse. Even so, some analogues can be offered as forebears, more or less remote, of queer theater.

Kabuki Means Queer

In modern Japanese, *kabuki* is written with two charactergraphs *ka-bu*, meaning "song and dance" and *ki*, meaning "skill or skilled persons." This, however, is latter-day rationalizing, an attempt to lend respectability to what had originally been a disreputable entertainment. The word *kabuki* derives, in fact, from a native verb, *kabuku*, which originally meant "to slant" or "to tilt." By the Tokugawa era, it had acquired a slang meaning, defined by a Japanese-Portuguese dictionary of 1603 as implying excess, dissolute overindulgence, and taking liberties. The usage began to be extended to any eccentric behavior or appearance or any action viewed as unconventional or antiestablishment. *Kabuki-mono*, "*kabuku* people," was a derogatory term describing nonconformists whose challenge to the established order might range from outlandish costumes and hairdos to the display of outsized swords and tobacco pipes. Benito Ortolani has compared them with motorcycle gangs, but, since many of them were masterless samurai and the offspring of important officials, their random acts of violence and rioting in the streets more closely resemble those of the Mohocks of Augustan London.[1] The Tokugawa government read these acts of defiance as heretical and potentially revolutionary, and punished the more egregious infractions of well-born *kabuki-mono* with death.

For the common people, however, such daring was heroic, and they spun yarns about these libertines. *Kabuki-mono* came to cover hoodlums and ruffians, prostitutes of both sexes, wantons and profligates, and, naturally enough, actors. The preexisting terms for actors, *kawaramono* (people of the riverbed) and *kawara kojiki* (riverbed beggars), referring to their place of playing, had lumped them together with other outcasts subject to humiliating residential, sartorial, and travel restrictions. The new appellation, classifying them as *kabuki-mono*, associated them with extravagant and debauched fantastics rather than with common or garden pariahs.

Sixteen hundred and three, the year the Portuguese lexicographer recorded the new slang meaning of *kabuki*, is also the date assigned to the legendary first *kabuki* performance, the dance pantomimes of the temple dancer and prostitute Okuni. According to the Confucian scholar Hayashi Razan writing in 1621:

She dressed as man, wore a sword at her side, and sang and danced. . . . The men wear women's clothing; the women wear men's clothing, cut their hair and wear it in a man's topknot, have swords at their sides and carry purses. They sing base songs and dance vulgar dances; their lewd voices are clamorous, like the buzzing of flies and the crying of cicadas. The men and women sing and dance together.

"This," he informed his readers, "is popularly called *kabuki*."[2] In other words, over the course of a generation, both the audience and the authorities had come to see this new style of transvestic performance as yet another cause for outrage.

The subsequent history of the *kabuki* involves a gradual disentanglement of the arts of the theater from the allurements of the brothel (without ever repudiating the seductive quality of *iroke* or sensual beauty). Even when the leading actors were, like rock stars, the objects of cults, they still bore the stigma of their origin and its connection with flesh-peddling.

My point in going over this history is to suggest that *kabuki*, etymologically and practically, is a paradigm of queer theater. The word itself, both in its primary meaning of "off-kilter," "off-beat," and in its slang overtones of a violence and sexuality that are over-the-top and in-your-face, could easily be translated as "queer," in our special sense. In particular, the all-pervasive atmosphere of male homosexuality that informs the first centuries of *kabuki* boy actors serving as catamites in teahouses attached to the theaters, the same-sex love affairs that make up the plots of the early repertory, the evolution of the *onnagata* or female impersonator, the close-knit relationships between fan and idol—provide a neat analogy with the gay-lesbian ambience of what we call "queer theater."

The Queer Avant-Garde

One of the examples of objectionable behavior cited by the seventeenth-century authorities against the *kabuki-mono* was playing a flute with one's anus. This scandalous musicianship with an ill-wind instrument seems to have aroused ire in the West as well: besides the lesser devil in Dante's *Inferno* who "made a trumpet of his arse,"[3] the infernal practice of rectal piping appears frequently in demonological imagery, particularly the paintings of Hieronymous Bosch. In Christendom, the metaphor for disharmony—flatulence in lieu of concordance—is compounded with the sin of sodomy: the thrusting of a hollow tube up the fundament is interpreted as horrendous sacrilege of the act of procreation. The image is long-lived. In Yury Olesha's Soviet play *A List of Benefits* (1931), it graphically illustrates how capitalism degrades art: the heroine, a classical actress who deserts the Soviet Union for the allegedly greater advantages of the West, is humiliated to find that the first job offered her in Paris is to play a flute with her anus in a nightclub. (Since the actress has been famous for her Hamlet, his line "Though you can fret me, you cannot play upon me" seems to be the burden of the symbolism here.)

23

This scatalogical stunt may have appalled Tokugawa censors, Christian moral-ists, and Soviet ideologues—in short, the establishment; but playing a flute with one's anus could easily be part of a World War I Dada concert of *bruitisme* (noisis-tics). Its grotesque topsy-turvydom fits neatly into a performance that deliberately rejects and parodies traditional art forms. In this respect, queer theater by its very nature has to be "avant-garde," "alternative," "fringe," with an appeal to special-ized tastes. Anal virtuosity would be welcomed in it.

Theater is most itself when it is most queer, when it most resembles Tokugawa-era *kabuki* and is, like Dr. Johnson's description of opera, "an irrational and exotick entertainment."[4] Japanese *kabuki* has, unfortunately, lost most of its outrageous-ness. By means of adapting while retaining its primordial conventions, it became institutionalized, a "national treasure," and is now a highly subsidized example of establishment art, with little appeal to the average Japanese, though it retains a semblance of outlandishness for tourists. Its homoeroticism still survives in an eti-olated way and even enjoys a resurgence when a homosexual star such as Tamasaburo Bando emerges, but the plays of same-sex love are rarely revived[5] and the official line taken by Japanese scholars and performers mutes any association with a twentieth-century notion of gayness.

In the West, the establishment theater is a middle-class entity, with certain pre-tensions to high art. I would argue, however, that the trend to greater naturalism in drama and stagecraft and the drive to greater respectability in the acting pro-fession over the past century were essentially wrongheaded movements. They managed by the 1950s to turn the mainstream theater into a constricted, gray clinic for post-Freudian mystery solving. For all its predominance, it was con-stantly challenged by the "theatrical theater," most often in evidence in the works of the so-called "avant-garde."

The play invariably cited as common ancestor of the modern theatrical van-guard, Alfred Jarry's *Ubu Roi*, may deserve the honorific of first "queer" play as well. Whatever Jarry's own sexuality (which seems to have been amorphous, free-float-ing, and probably unacted upon), the whole ethos of the Ubu cycle is "queer" in its refusal to play by the rules of the universe. Like Peter Pan, Jarry refused to grow up; he gradually merged with his creation Père Ubu. The need for the queer performer to inform the work with personal experience reached its logical conclusion here.

Jarry's writing is infused with *fumisterie*, a term difficult to translate into Eng-lish, although the French themselves thought it a peculiarly English style of humor. It might be rendered by the contemporaneous "spoof," coined by the music-hall comedian Arthur Roberts. It suggests a deadpan hoax, an elaborate practical joke or shaggy-dog story pulled off with the driest of humor, but entirely subversive in intent. Jarry's *Ubu*, though grossly overcolored and hyperbolic when compared with the writings of his *fumiste* colleagues, knew that it took just such exaggeration to make *fumisterie* work onstage.[6]

I'm not eager to join the increasingly tiresome debate over what is meant by camp. As the Supreme Court Justice said of pornography, I know it when I see it. No one would argue whether or not camp is queer (or would they? Susan Sontag strove to avoid the queer label, whereas Moe Meyer suggests that camp is nothing if it is not queer).[7] Is *fumisterie* camp and therefore queer? Except for Jarry and possibly Charles Cros, all the French practitioners were entrenched heterosexuals and even family men. Their playful diversions were the self-protection of the bourgeois against his own claustrophobia. Jarry's living out the role of Père Ubu in real life seems to put something else at stake, and move it away from *fumisterie tout pur* into the realm of the queer. The *animateur* of queer theater has something personal to lose.

Revivals of *Ubu*, no matter how modernized, smack of the antiquarian; they invariably lack the shock effect of its first performances. To recreate *Ubu*, one must concoct one's own attack on the sacred cows of one's own society. Queer theater has an advantage in that its most essential component, sexual unorthodoxy, still packs a considerable punch, for all the commercialization of the gay image. Even when performed in a properly *fumiste* spirit, the enactment of sexual scenarios and gender metamorphosis still aims for the viscera.

To be queer, therefore, queer theater has to be irreverently *fumiste*, never taking itself too seriously, as well as highly sexualized. All the avant-garde movements of the twentieth century launched programmatic assaults on the preexisting social or artistic establishment. What began as *jeux d'esprit*, however, soon became overearnest: with a kind of will to power, the vanguards exhibited an eagerness to become the establishment. The surrealists' surrender to Marxism and their ostracism of homosexuality; the futurists' kowtowing to fascism; and the constructivists' implementing of communism are the most obvious examples. Dalí might have played the rectal flute, but Louis Aragon never! Ideological revolt is always in danger of being co-opted. Sexual revolt, however, tends to remain dangerously outside the law, since libidinal predilections and gender dysmorphism are less easily changed than minds. When it loses its bawdiness, its intimacy with the theater's prostitutional past, and reaches for the cerebral, the avant-garde begins to shed its queerness. It may be that the German cabaret comic, Wilhelm Bendow, with his swishy question-and-answer routines, and the American drag artist Bert

Savoy, with his gay-savvy stream-of-consciousness, were more genuinely avant-garde in their queerness (and more genuinely queer in their vanguardism) than such elaborate confections as Nijinsky's *Jeux* or Cocteau's *Les Mariés de la Tour Eiffel*. When Colette appeared in 1907 at the Moulin Rouge in a sketch called *Le Rêve d'Egypte*, playing a love scene with her lesbian "chum" the Marquise de Belboeuf dressed as a man, she was exhibiting a more authentically queer performance than all the dramatic, operatic, and balletic Salomes of early modernism. Or, to put it in the context of our own spectrum of theatrical innovation, Martha Wilson is queer theater, Robert Wilson is not. ⟶ look these two up.

A Queer Repertory?

The early *kabuki* actors, because of their status as outcasts, served, by their very existence, as provocateurs, irrespective of what they may have played onstage. Similarly, performers in queer theater, whether or not they feel like members of a community, have to take their own experiences as the inspiration for and endorsement of their work; their lives provide the validity and credibility for their art. This is why queer theater is so often "merely" confessional and also why antecedents for queer theater are found more often in the past of performance than in drama of the past. This is why the mere appearance of a homosexual character in a drama of the modernist period is not enough to qualify the play as "queer." The outsider has got to become the insider if the label is to stick.

The institutional transvestism of theater of the past has often been taken as a clue to *Ur*-queerness. What could be queerer than John Lyly's *Gallathea* (pub. 1585) in which two girls, disguised as boys, fall in love with one another; as a reward for their chastity, Venus decides to turn one of them into a male (though which is to undergo the transformation is left moot at the final curtain). Add to this the fact that the girls are played by male children (the boy actors of St. Paul's), and the gender frolics become queer indeed. A modern production might well stress the inherent *bizarrerie* of these situations, but there is no indication that Lyly or his original audience, which included the Queen, saw anything in it but a charming rendering of a mythical debate between carnal love and virginity.

When we turn, however, to the scene between Jupiter and Ganymede that opens Christopher Marlowe's *Tragedy of Dido, Queen of Carthage* (pub. 1594), what we know of Marlowe's sexuality leads us to suspect that he is drawing on personal experience. The doting god and the boy dandled on his knee engage in bantering foreplay too telling to be wholly fictional. This is not the place to engage in discussions of whether a quintessential homosexuality persists throughout human history, but when this scene was played out at the Queer Theater Conference, Ganymede's teasing extortion and Jupiter's compliant promises evoked the laughter of recognition from a largely gay audience, which drew parallels with their own paltering with lovers, pickups, and hustlers. The nexus between Marlowe's life and his literary reworking of it renders this scene queer.

In the same way, we may locate queerness more specifically in plays of the showbooth than in French pornographic drama of the late eighteenth century which is rife with scenes of lesbian love and sodomitic orgies, as in this passage from Nerciat's *The Spirit of Morals in the 18th Century* (1789). The characters, members of the aristocracy, have a certain license to behave more freely than do commoners:

> THE MARQUISE (*kisses Lesbosie, and begins to tickle her charms rather briskly*): How delicious the two of you were, grouped lovingly on the ottoman. I thought I was seeing Psyche in the arms of Cupid, except that you were lovelier than Venus's son's wife. My desires were kindled to excess. Jealous of Victor, I was about to cry out: Stop, audacious Victor! You have too much pleasure: I must share it with you! (*The marquise continues her finger game.*)
>
> MADEMOISELLE DE LESBOSIE (*feeling a sweet and sharp emotion*): But . . . but, madame . . .
>
> THE MARQUISE (*equally affected*): What charming eyes! Ah! you rascal, you . . .
>
> MADEMOISELLE DE LESBOSIE (*letting herself be led to the ottoman*): You're the one who's . . . making me . . . die. (*The marquise, enflamed by this dalliance, abruptly moves so as to place her mouth on the part her finger had just aroused.*) O heavens! What are you after, madame? No, I cannot let . . .
>
> THE MARQUISE (*fighting off this resistance successfully*): Let me at it, you little prude!
>
> MADEMOISELLE DE LESBOSIE (*giving in*): Heavens! . . . what is all this? . . . it's a dream . . . I . . . I'm dying. (*There is a moment of silence, during which the marquise observes with a sort of admiration Mademoiselle de Lesbosie, intoxicated with pleasure, lying inert.*)[8]

This sort of thing has been concocted for the delectation of those who may or may not share the tastes of the characters, but whose introduction to such recondite practices will ultimately affect their erogenous zones. The Enlightenment obsession with instruction and edification informs even such erotica (as it also does the works of that superdidact Sade), but there is a lack of irony and engagement which prevents the clandestine libertinage from being genuinely queer.

The first "homosexuals" on the European stage were viewed from outside, and even when presented sympathetically, were regarded as aberrant. Out of step with the norms of society, they had the option either of suffering as victims (whether of social persecution, personal rejection, unresolved sexuality, or suicidal depression) or of exulting for a short span as villains, manipulating society to avenge their own sense of rejection.[9]

As an example of the former option, we might look at *Faults* (*Fehler*) by Herbert Hirschberg, a problem play of 1906, written to serve the cause of reforming Clause 175 of the Wilhelmine judicial code which imposed prison sentences on male homosexual activity. Yielding to his father's wishes, a young lawyer, Edmund, marries the heiress Elsa, though he knows that in doing so he is injuring her, his own homosexual nature, and his friend Kurt, a physician who truly loves Elsa. Later in the play, a dismissed servant with whom Edmund has had relations blackmails him by sending a letter to Elsa. Believing that there may be grounds for suspicion, she dips into Krafft-Ebing's *Psychopathia Sexualis* (conveniently at hand) and sends for Kurt to explain the situation to her. The Doctor hems and haws, before finally declaring:

> **KURT:** All right then. Edmund, your husband, is one of those unhappy persons denied the ability to love the female sex—denied it by nature. Nevertheless, as a man of noble character, which he is in every fiber of his being, he will be your friend and comrade.
>
> **ELSA** (*having turned away during Kurt's admission, passionately goes back to him*): I will never go on living with this madman!
>
> **KURT:** Edmund is not a madman, Frau Elsa. [. . .] How sorry I am for you! At the time of your marriage, which was prearranged by your fathers, no one paid the slightest heed to your personal natures! [. . .]
>
> **ELSA:** It was the fondest wish of my old father, who had no idea he was pushing me into the arms of a criminal—(*she sobs deeply*) a madman for a husband.
>
> **KURT:** But Edmund was also carrying out the "fondest wish of his father."
>
> **ELSA:** He should have given some thought to his disease.
>
> **KURT:** Disease has nothing to do with it. Edmund is completely normal except for his emotional proclivities.—His only fault is to have got married, and for that he will either be punished or have his union annulled.[10]

Thinking only of the offenses to her, Elsa decides to get a divorce and let the blackmail run its course.

KURT: But then he goes to jail!

ELSA (*coldly*): To the penitentiary, if it were up to me. So far as I'm concerned, he no longer exists!

The dilemma is neatly resolved by Edmund's suicide, a solution which would become endemic in plays whose homosexual heroes were portrayed as victims.

Despite its subject, there is nothing in the least "queer" about this play or in any of those subsequent dramas which regard homosexuality as a problem—from Edmond Bourdet's *La Prisonnière* to Robert Anderson's *Tea and Sympathy* (in fact, in a recent interview Anderson has admitted that the plight of the youth in his play was actually a metaphor for victims of McCarthyism.)[11] *Fehler's* dramatic form is stodgily sub-Ibsenite, a set of drawing-room dialogues debating a social question, and Edmund is invariably seen agonizing over the most recent crisis in his unhappy life. He is never presented in tandem with anyone who shares his tastes or difficulties; the servant he has had sex with is from another class, speaks a heavy Berlin dialect, and is characterized as riffraff from the first.

A somewhat different, yet somehow more empathetic treatment, occurs in Armory-Dauriac's *Le Monsieur aux chrysanthèmes* (1908), a boulevard comedy, which may be the first appearance in drama of the homosexual as cultural arbiter (Bunthorne in Gilbert and Sullivan's *Patience* is avidly heterosexual). Gil Norvège is a *fin de siècle* Truman Capote or Andy Warhol, an iron butterfly whose columns can make or break reputations, and who is wooed by anyone eager for celebrity; his sexual peccadilloes, also vulnerable to blackmail, are usually overlooked, hushed up, or passed off as "eccentricities." The dramatist treats him as a modern-day Tartuffe, dangerous but ludicrous, who resiliently survives scandal.

Norvège is allowed the privilege of stating his credo; in the last act, "heavily pomaded, yellow chrysanthemum in his button-hole," he explains his malaise to his fellow aesthete Lantigny. Smitten with an unresponsive young poet (who is, incidentally, in love with the woman who loves Norvège), he fantasizes about putting the object of his infatuation into fiction.

GIL: He's precisely the type I was dreaming of for the young condottiere in my novel. I'll never find a more perfect model. [. . .]

LANTIGNY: You also thought you saw a hero of the Renaissance in that boy Georges we picked up outside the Opera. And where did that get you? A young lord of Siena, you called him . . . an African postman, I should call him! . . . since he's an expert at blackmail.

GIL: But we're not dealing with a hustler now. [. . .] Can you picture him, this Romagne, dolled up in a golden tunic, neck and arms bare, cruising the streets of Verona on horseback, protected by a gang of his henchmen, drunk with glory, against a background of an enthusiastic crowd pelting him with flowers . . . His face impassive, his eyes aloof, pale with emotion, he has placed beneath his helmet two red roses which bleed on to his temples through his raven locks. And even the men greet him with offers of love, applaud him, aroused, yes, aroused by this apotheosis!

LANTIGNY (*admiringly*): What an artist you are!

GIL: Yes. Those were the epic days in which we could plumb our emotions, poor overbred creatures that we are! Ever since then our era has been trying to impose laws on Beauty and prescribe what gender it's to be. Ah! It's ridiculous, really! As if we weren't to live by our aesthetics, by making our works come to life! . . . That's what Leonardo did and the exquisite Sodoma, that painter who created grace, so infatuated with beauty that it earned him his nickname. I often dream of a heaven where we shall meet those charming creatures again. A heaven that'll be a bit like ancient Greece beneath a blue sky, governed by liberal laws that respect Art . . . And to think that we shall never ever know such a heaven, we who are reviled, persecuted, condemned, we who plod with measured tread in this vale of whores and horrors, unable to slake our thirst or spread our wings without their being torn . . .[12]

The playwright evidently intends us to be amused by this potpourri of Ruskin, Pater, Wilde, and the French symbolists, and is himself amused by the contrast between such high-flown sentiments and the squalid realities of cruising for rough trade. But for the first time in drama, a queer protagonist is allowed to reveal an aesthetic ideal and not simply confess to a psychosis.

Norvège was pieced together from a number of contemporary models in Parisian society: the flamboyant journalist Jean Lorrain, the aesthete Robert de Montesquiou, the pederast Count Adelswärd Fersen, the Rumanian-born actor De Max, and the Danish novelist and man of the theater Herman Bang. But his reference to torn wings allies him more closely to someone Armory had probably never heard of: the Russian poet Mikhail Kuzmin. Kuzmin's novel *Wings* was Norvège's argument posed in earnest, a defense of homosexuality as a loftier, more ideal form of love with noble antecedents in the past; its constant striving upward out of the grime of the industrial age met with a great many obstacles, but could triumph.

In Kuzmin's plays we find the germs of a genuinely queer drama. Renouncing the grim naturalism of the post-Ibsenite theater, he turns to the *commedia dell'arte*, eighteenth-century *opéra comique*, and the medieval mystery play for his models. His plays are short divertissements, taunting and ironic, often set to music of his composing. In *The Dangerous Precaution* (1907), he provides a queer twist to the standard disguise plot: for reasons of security Prince Floridal, son of King Posthumous, is being passed off as the maiden Dorita, but for reasons of state Dorita is disguised in men's clothes. This is Kuzmin's overtly homosexual rewriting of *As You Like It*. Dorita/Floridal is in love with the courtier René, who reciprocates the feelings but assumes he is in love with a girl in boy's clothing. René insists that Dorita confess she is a woman, but Floridal prefers honesty.

RENÉ: You do not love me, you despise me!

FLORIDAL: I didn't say that I didn't love you or that I despise you, I only said that I am not a woman, and I speak in deadly earnest, I swear by your love and mine as well.

RENÉ: Not Dorita, not Dorita!

FLORIDAL: O youth, though your plight makes me cry, I am not Dorita, Floridal am I.

Do women have such ruddy lips
As I do?
Do women have such slender hips
As I do?
Do women cuddle up so snug
As I do?
Do women with such passion hug
As I do?
    I weep with you, René, but what are we to do?
    Though your plight makes me cry,
    I am not Dorita, Floridal am I.
    Do you still disbelieve me, tell me true?[13]

René is baffled to discover that, despite this unwelcome revelation, he still loves Dorita/Floridal, and the play rapidly ends with, to use his image, the cork popping on his fermented grief, as musicians strike up a wild jig. Gender distinctions are obliterated in a Dionysiac finale, and *amor*, even between two men, *vincit omnia*. Kuzmin remains the puppet master pulling the strings of his rather flimsy marionettes; the action remains at the level of a charade, the dialogue badinage.

He gives nothing away about his own convictions, beyond the insouciance of the treatment.

The next stage in the evolution of queer drama is a greater personal investment on the part of the dramatist, the play as confessional or self-revelation. A prime example of this is Klaus Mann's *Anya and Esther* (1923). At seventeen, Thomas Mann's gay son had bemused the family with a revue in which he sang a music-hall song with the chorus:

Perversion's really swell, my boy,
Perversion keeps you well, my boy,
Perversion beats the standard brand,
Perversion makes your willy stand.
Perversion is beyond compare—[14]

whereupon a big metal sign swung down, with "Perversion" written in gaudy letters. This was a prelude to an unsuccessful audition for a cabaret career. Mann then took all his experiences to date and distilled them into this odd expressionist piece, in the process putting himself and his circle onstage.

Anya and Esther, which was staged in Munich and Hamburg in 1923 and later in Vienna, is set in a "convalescent home for fallen children," whose absent-minded director is part pedophile scoutmaster, part Blake's God. A close-knit but spiritually complex relationship among four of the school's charges, Anya, Esther, Kaspar, and Jakob is thrown into confusion by the intrusion of the handsome Erik, a quondam circus and cabaret performer. In contrast with the sensual, worldly Erik, who has been kept by both men and women, the adolescents suddenly strike each other as insipid and artificial. When Esther decides to leave with him, the other three are cast into impotent despair. The play's essential theme is the collision of adolescent fantasies and ideals with the seductive call of the real world.

In the Hamburg production, eighteen-year-old Klaus, his lesbian sister Erika, and their friend Pamela Wedekind, the dramatist's daughter, played the lead roles along with Gustaf Gründgens, who directed the play as well. At this period, the ambitious homosexual actor was one of Klaus's closest friends and was later briefly married to Erika. This public unveiling of the private lives of *Dichterkinder* was violently attacked for its homophilic sentiments, and Klaus was condemned as a "felon against the German people" in one right-wing newspaper.[15]

By today's standards, the play is veiled and ambiguous, as in this speech in which Esther speculates that the sex life she shares with Anya may lead to canonization.

ESTHER: [. . .] I was wondering whether the two of us, you and I, will ever be made saints—saints, yes, by the church, by the Pope himself—the Old Man suggested it, I'm sure he must be a close friend of the Pope's. Then we shall be St. Anya and St. Esther. And we shall stand silver over the doors of peasants' cottages. And old women will pray to us in their hoods and so will skinny blond schoolgirls and the boys too. And gentlemen will listen to our weak voices. And when we die, there will be a great flurry among the angels—they will flap their stiff feathered wings in a festive greeting to their new companions.—And whatever we do will be holy—(*suddenly very quiet*)—even the things we always do with one another. (*Another, almost jubilant outburst.*) Because we'll be saints!

ANYA (*strokes her hair*): Is that really what you want?[16]

For all the Germanic haze of the dialogue, there is no doubt that Anya and Esther have been having a love affair, that Kaspar (Klaus Mann's role) is madly in love with Erik, and that the director regularly seduces his underaged charges. What makes this play a queer forebear, besides its lack of concern for conventional morality (or rather its adolescent joy in flouting convention) is a kind of solipsistic defiance. "These are our lives and our emotions," it seems to be saying to an audience. "You are privileged to be admitted to behold them, but you have no right to judge." This is made especially clear in a dressing room scene: the protagonists have been performing an end-of-term revue for a mass of stolid burghers, but as they come off the stage, they describe how the gorgeous costumes and ingenious routines they had devised with such devotion have met with total incomprehension. To put off confronting this unsympathetic "real life," they have created a surrogate fantasy life too fragile to withstand intrusions from out there.

A Queer Production Style

Such traces of queerness are sometimes easier to spot in published plays than in the unrecorded aspects of performance. In the 1960s, when the New York critical establishment attacked the prevalence of homosexuals in the professional theater, it purported to object to the masking of deviant concerns and sentiments under a guise of heterosexual normality. "Let Blanche DuBois or George and Martha be drag queens," they protested, "rather than passing them off as straight Americans."[17] This was disingenuous for two reasons: first, at the time, portrayals of sexual nonconformists were pretty much confined to the fringe theater and wouldn't have been suffered on a commercial stage, except as comic relief; and second, their protests were themselves camouflaging a more fundamental complaint. What really galled them (as it does the foes of the NEA) was that the theater was an art form dominated by the sexually heterodox, a major arena for the expression of their talents and concerns. In the unvarnished words of the actor John Colicos, "The faggots have taken over."[18] The recent decimation of the theater's personnel by AIDS has driven this point home most brutally.

The paranoia of the critics was driven by a suspicion that the fare they and their readers were regularly ingesting had been somehow tainted by queer subversives. Politically deplorable this may have been, but they were, at bottom, right. However repressed, sublimated, and disguised for public consumption they might be, the accomplishments of Noël Coward, Eva Le Gallienne, Tennessee Williams, Cecil Beaton, Benjamin Britten, Margaret Webster, Jean Cocteau, Franco Zeffirelli *i tutti quanti* were bound to be permeated with their tastes and penchants. It was when these submerged interests bobbed to the surface, as they began to do in the sixties, that the establishment found its prejudices both vindicated and rendered impotent.

One interesting example of establishment resistance to overt queerness, no matter how superb the achievement, was the Glasgow Citizen's Theater, which, throughout the early seventies, was the most exciting repertory company in Great Britain. The Citizen's had had an illustrious history as a showcase for Scottish leftist drama but had fallen on evil days when, in 1970, it was taken over by a triumvirate of gay men who happened to constitute a pleiad of theatrical brilliance. Philip Prowse, the resident designer and a skillful director specializing in the ghastlier Jacobean tragedies, compensated for a limited color sense by a spectacular use of black and silver and stunning silhouettes. Director, playwright, and translator Robert David Macdonald, who had studied with Piscator, began his career in opera and was Rolf Hochhuth's official translator; he brought to his productions a musician's ear and a polyglot's sense of language. Giles Havergal, the managing director, wielded the plausibility that could coax and cajole local councils and schools to support the Citizen's; some of the most successful productions were his brainchildren, particularly a havoc-wreaking *Tamburlaine* that was for a time the company's showpiece.

These three immediately jettisoned the standard roster of classics and drawing room drama along with safe, naturalistic productions. Housed in a former music hall in the Gorbals, one of Europe's nastiest slums, the Citz (as it came to be known) cultivated an audience of students, lower-middle- and working-class people, in addition to the theatrically sophisticated. For a time they did away with the subscription system and offered seats at 50p (approximately one dollar), resulting in a nightly attendance of more than five hundred for such arcana as *Thyestes* and *The Changeling*. "Popular imagery" was what it claimed to offer to its audiences, and Havergal fondly recalled for me the reaction of two local toughs leaving the hypercamp, transvestite production of *Camino Real*. Wondered one to the other, "That's foockin' magical, Jock, that's foockin' magical."

There was no deliberate attempt to establish a queer theater. Although a play occasionally had a gay theme (*Total Eclipse*), it was the sensibility of the makers dictating style and substance that made the difference. The three directors made no bones about satisfying their own tastes and aesthetic convictions in their choices, and these proved to be more challenging and more elegantly presented than their counterparts elsewhere. The repertory in these early days showed no interest in the Greeks, the Golden Ages of France or Spain, Shaw or Ibsen, or modern realism. It was heavy with the Elizabethans and Jacobeans, Brecht and the German Expressionists, such equivocal playwrights as Williams, Orton, Wilde, Cocteau, Genet, and rarities never before seen in English (Balzac's *Vautrin*, Lermontov's *Masquerade*, Karl Kraus's *Last Days of Mankind*). These were outspoken plays of "blood and glitter," strong passions and mouth-filling language, that also packed an intellectual punch. The acting company was polymorphous, energetic, and under thirty, making up in raw vitality and sexual magnetism what it lacked in finesse: many who are England's leading actors today cut their teeth at the Citz. Attractive bodies were often displayed nude or nearly so, and cross-gender casting was common at a time when it could be seen in Britain only in Christmas pantomime (Lindsay Kemp was briefly in the company). Prowse's sets and costumes were marvels of monochrome, mirrors, leather, barbaric jewelry, posing straps, uniforms, bandages, and invariably, whorls of cigarette smoke blurring the action.

The house style extended even to the publicity. The company insignia, a rondel of the Bard in bra and corset, rouged and mascaraed, appeared on buttons, car stickers, programs, and flyers. "Sheila," as Shakespeare was affectionately nicknamed, was also to bedizen the Citz's bus, a garishly painted vehicle that traversed the downtown area until the city fathers indignantly intervened. A series of flashy photographs, showing the company members in various stages of undress laying out lines of cocaine in their dressing room, were used as full-page ads in *Plays and Players* for a year. This was provocation with a vengeance, and perpetuated the critics' distrust of the theater. Because it wore its queerness with open panache and insouciance, it made them nervous. Its intellectual and artistic sophistication, its theatrical *savoir-faire* and its raw appeal to its audiences were, however, recognized and awarded throughout Europe, and eventually even in the United Kingdom. Nowadays every rep British company (not to mention such American wannabe trend-setters as the ART) has adopted for its revivals the leather-coated, close-cropped, chain-smoking look that the Citz pioneered in the early seventies. Back then, it was taken to be decadent self-indulgence; now it is the norm.[19]

Macdonald had a special talent for adaptations, his achievements including *Camille*, a complex conflation of the play, the opera, and the true story of Marie Duplessis, and a Proustian compression called *A Waste of Time*. His versions of Sade never stinted on grotesque violence—Justine is raped with a lighted taper, locked inside a coffin on which the characters picnic, pissed on from a great height, forced to mouth the castrated genitalia of a valet during a parody of the Mass—but they always did justice to Sade's philosophic message. The atrocities were punctuated by reasoned, wickedly witty discourse in which the metaphysics behind the gruesome was expounded. At a time when the English-speaking world took Sade to be a pornographer in a periwig, the Citz recognized and theatricalized him as a sexual outlaw articulating an alternative vision of human fate.

The supervention of a queer sensibility in illumining a classic is best seen, perhaps, in Macdonald's production of *Woyzeck*. Büchner had made his browbeaten protagonist a private soldier, lowest man on the totem pole of proletarian conscription and long-term military servitude. Ill-paid, ill-fed, ill-used, the recruit's lot was, throughout nineteenth-century Europe, a byword for hardship. Anyone was free to abuse him, from his superior officers to the tavern keepers and whores who bilked him of his meager pay. His life was, literally, not his own.

How is one to convey this sense of passive victimization to an audience unfamiliar with these conditions? Macdonald made his Woyzeck a bathhouse attendant, whose oppressors are all the more alarming because they lack the uniforms and bourgeois frockcoats that otherwise invest them with authority. Anonymous, clad only in Turkish towels, they are still empowered to subjugate him and make his life miserable. Prowse's black-tiled steam room, dense with cloudy billows, suggested something hellish; the pool became the pond in which Woyzeck was ultimately drowned. With some adjustments to what is, after all, a fragmentary and inchoate text, the concept worked brilliantly.

Although any director might have conceived of a bathhouse as a metaphor for the world, I think that only a gay man with experience of steam room promiscuity would have understood the leveling process that occurs. Anonymity and nudity create a complicity and Masonic fraternity that excludes only the attendants, clothed servitors of the needs of the clients. The exigent desires of others blot out the needs of the underclass. Queer experience did not impose a distortion on the play, but illumined it by figurative imagery.

In 1979 Prowse and Macdonald were invited to the Phoenix Theater in New York, to restage the latter's play *Chinchilla*. Ostensibly about Diaghilev and the Ballets Russes, the play (like Macdonald's *Webster*, set in a Jacobean playhouse) actually dealt with the internecine relationships at the Citz, and beyond that, with the mechanics of how one creates. Its credo is that art is not necessarily edifying or socially relevant or even humane, but can be inspired by such things as physical lust, perverse desire, hatred, cruelty and jealousy, and serendipitous venality. It can also provoke such responses. Reared on the humanistic principle that art is good for you, the Upper East Side audiences and the reviewers went, as they say, ballistic. Marilyn Stasio of the *N.Y. Post* even proclaimed that this production cast the whole future of the venerated Phoenix into doubt! Of course, they were irked at the production's use of the undraped male form as a decorative element and by the casual acceptance of same-sex liaisons as part of the artistic landscape. But, ultimately, the ire was provoked by such speeches as that of the ersatz Diaghilev, Chinchilla, demanding that the Nijinsky character create a scandal:

Only with me will you survive . . . There are, in the depths of the Brazilian jungle, orchids whose organs of generation are so placed that only one species of bee, whose tongue is equally abnormal, can fertilise them. The bee depends on its survival upon the orchid, and the orchid upon the bee. In consequence, both are extremely rare. The bee is large, black, lumbering and ugly, but the orchid, should it flower, is the most beautiful flower we can imagine. Our meeting has been fortuitous, and we have shown the world something whose rarity cannot be repeated. But beauty is the most difficult thing to survive. If you can survive beauty, you can survive anything.[20]

The notion of a great ugly man obsessing over a lissome youth, having sex with him, and out of this union producing *die ewige Kunst* was too queer an aesthetic for the Manhattan cultural Brahmins to swallow. The idea that promiscuity is necessary to an artist and that preoccupation with form may lead to excess comes from Plato's *Phaedrus* (in a passage read in the play), but it went right by them.

Obiter Dicta

Theater, as I said above, is most truly itself when it is most queer. The more the theater tries to conform with some illusionistic norm of reproducing external reality and with some societal norm of behavioral morality, the less faithful it is to its own nature. When the theater sets itself up as an alternative reality, an improved or distorted or wholly unrecognizable universe, then it is really doing its job. What has, in the past, prevented the theater from being merely a playground for minorities is its long-standing function as a voice of community values. Historically, it has always walked this knife-edge: on the one hand, a socially sanctioned institution with roots in religion and myth, expected to clarify and convey the establishment ethos in a public forum; and, on the other, a haven for outcasts, misfits, and uncomfortable temperaments of all stripes, offering opportunities for self-expression otherwise unavailable. Much of the theater's excitement comes from this dynamic, an oscillating tension between these two roles.

But now that the live theater is no longer the preeminent form of popular entertainment, it has fragmented into a number of diverse fora, speaking to disparate and discrete constituencies. Queer theater has no mandate to address any audience other than the community out of which its creators come; but, if past experience is anything to go by, when these exclusive creations are imaginative and authentic, the world cannot help but be influenced.

Notes

Portions of this essay have appeared in my book *The Changing Room: Sex, Drag, and Theater* (New York: Routledge, 2000).

1. Donald H. Shivley, "Notes on the Word Kabuki," *Orients* 10 (1957):144–46; Benito Ortolani, *The Japanese Theater from Shamanistic Ritual to Contemporary Pluralism* (Leiden: E. J. Brill, 1990), 154–47.

2. Quoted in Shivley, "Notes." Richard Cocks, an Englishman resident in Hirado from 1615 to 1622, used the term exclusively for women players.

3. Dante, *Inferno*, Canto 21, line 139, trans. Charles Singleton (Princeton: Princeton University Press, 1990), 221.

4. Samuel Johnson, "Life of Hughes" (1779), *Lives of the English Poets* (London: Oxford University Press, 1964), I, 451.

5. The exception is *Sakura Hime Azuma Bunsho* (*The Scarlet Princess of Edo*) by Tsurya Namboku IV and others (1817). The plot is triggered by a Buddhist priest and the acolyte he loves escaping the monastery to carry out a suicide pact; the boy dies but the priest is too cowardly to follow him. The rest of a very long and intricate play melodramatically entangles the lives of the priest and the boy, now reincarnated as a princess, with a wily thief. The play is very much a showcase for the three leads, and its place in the modern repertory has a lot to do with opportunities it offers to such a brilliant *onnagata* as Tamasaburo. See James R. Brandon, *Kabuki: Five Classic Plays* (Cambridge, Mass.: Harvard University Press, 1975), 239–349.

6. The best discussion of *fumisterie* in English is in *The Spirit of Montmartre: Cabarets, Humor and the Avant-Garde, 1875–1905,* ed. Phillip Dennis Cate and Mary Shaw (New Brunswick: Rutgers University Press, 1996).

7. Moe Meyer, "Reclaiming the Discourse of Camp," in *The Politics and Poetics of Camp,* ed. Moe Meyer (New York: Routledge, 1994), 1–22.

8. Nerciat (Mérard de Saint-Just), *L'Esprit des moeurs au XVIIIe siécle ou la Petite-Maison, proverbe en deux actes et en prose,* in *Le Théâtre gaillard revu et augmenté 1776–1865* [Brussels: Poulet-Malssis, 1865], II, 113–14. My translation.

9. See Laurence Senelick, "The Homosexual as Villain and Victim in *Fin-de-Siécle* Drama," *Journal of the History of Sexuality* 4,2 (Oct. 1993):201–29.

10. Herbert Hirschberg, *"Fehler," dramatische Studie in 3 Aufzügen* (Strassburg and Leipzig: Josef Singer, 1906), 68–70. My translation.

11. Jackson R. Bryer, ed., *The Playwright's Art: Conversations with Contemporary American Dramatists* (New Brunswick: Rutgers University Press, 1995), 37.

12. Armory (Carle Dauriac), *Le Monsieur aux chrysanthèmes. Pièce en trois actes* (Paris: Librairie Molière, 1908), 110–13. My translation.

13. Mikhail Kuzmin, *Opasnaja predostoroznost. Komedija s peniem v 1 dejstvii* (1907), in *Teatr v cetyrax tomax,* ed. A. Timofeev, V. Markov and Z. Serov (Berkeley: Berkeley Slavic Specialists, 1994), II, 225. My translation.

14. Klaus Mann, *Kind dieser Zeit* (Reinbeck bei Hamburg: Rowohlt, 1983), 170. My translation.

15. *Der Querschnitt* (Berlin), V 12 (Dec. 1925), 1075.

16. Klaus Mann, *Anja und Esther. Ein romantisches Stück in sieben Bildern* (Berlin: Oesterheld, 1925). My translation.

17. E.g., Howard Taubman, "Not What It Seems," *New York Times* (6 Jan. 1961); Stanley Kauffmann, "On the Acceptability of the Homosexual," *New York Times* (6 Feb. 1966).

18. Interview in *Toronto Globe and Mail* (5 June 1976).

19. For a history, see Michael Coveney, *The Citz. 21 Years of the Glasgow Citizens Theatre* (London: Nick Hern Books, 1990); for production photos from the period under discussion, see Laurence Senelick, "Blood and Glitter in Glasgow," *After Dark* (Nov. 1976):54–61.

20. Robert David Macdonald, *Chinchilla, A Play in Two Acts* (Newark: Proscenium Press, 1980), 16–17.

3   "Porno-Tropics"[1]

Some Thoughts on Shakespeare, Colonialism, and Sexuality

Ania Loomba

Reading John Lyly's late-sixteenth-century play *Gallathea* was an uncanny experience for me. It tells the story of two women, Gallathea and Phyllida, whose doting fathers disguise each of them as a boy in order to protect them from being sacrificed to Neptune, whose price for not flooding the Humber River is a beautiful virgin every five years. Both Gallathea and Phyllida are unhappy about having to cross-dress, and when they meet in the forest and fall in love, each thinks the feeling is okay because she knows herself to be a woman. They are occasionally suspicious about the other's gender, but this doesn't detract from their love. Although confused about their identities, they are not confused about their desires. So a substantial part of the play depicts two boys, whom the audience knows to be girls, in love. At the end of the play, Venus agrees to change one of them (neither we nor they know who this will be) into a real boy so that their love can be legitimized. In Lyly's source, Ovid's story of Iphis and Ianthe in *Metamorphoses*, the transition from woman to man is crucial; in *Gallathea* it is downplayed and becomes merely a formal ending. What is important is the constancy of Phyllida and Gallathea's love, which is unchanged through all the mutations of identity. Desire and sexuality are not entirely dependent upon gender.

Years before I read *Gallathea*, I had heard a Rajasthani folk tale about the love of two women called Beeja and Teeja for each other. In this story too, after various travails, the gods had consented to change one of them into a man. Unlike Lyly's story, though, this one did not end poised on the brink of normative heterosexuality—after the transformation, Beeja and Teeja are miserable as a heterosexual couple because they find that their relationship has changed, for it has got to be structured in accordance with prevalent gender hierarchies. They who have known same-sex love now beg the gods to change the "man" back into a woman, and prefer to take their chances with social disapproval.

Another uncanny cross-cultural connection surfaced when I read Natalie Zemon Davis's *The Return of Martin Guerre*, a book that had become important within Renaissance studies when I started working on my doctoral degree. This is the story of Martin Guerre, the sixteenth-century French peasant who reappeared in his native village after a long absence, apparently picking up where he had left off except that now his previously unhappy marriage has become sexually and emotionally more stable. (The book inspired a film by the same name, and many years later, a fuzzy Hollywood "version"—*Sommersby*.)[2] Martin's demand for his share in the family property sparks off his uncle's accusation that he is not Martin but an imposter. Various trials follow, till finally one day, the real Martin returns and the imposter is hanged.

Davis's masterly retelling highlights the enormous appeal of the imposter's flawless impersonation for the judge, Jean de Coras, who finally tried the case and wrote its first influential account *Arrest Memorable*. At a time when the Protestant notion of the primacy of coupledom was in its formative years, the judge is strongly moved by the dilemma of Bertrande, Martin's wife, whose testimony is crucial to the case. Is she a dupe or a willing accomplice? And is her unhappy marriage to a man who has long since disappeared more valid than her more vital involvement with this other? Coras recognizes that "there was something not only profoundly wrong but also profoundly right about the invented marriages of the new Martin and Bertrande de Rols" (1983: 103). So who is the "real" husband? Who is the real Martin? What are the origins of our identity?

While all tales of mistaken identity highlight the question of social and personal existence, the crucial place of sexuality and the wife in Davis's account resonate strongly with another Rajasthani folk tale, whose many retellings include a Hindi short story by the novelist Manu Bhandari and a film by Mani Kaul. "Duvida" (Dilemma) is the story of a ghost who while wandering in the desert sands, encounters a marriage party returning after the ceremonies to the bridegroom's village and falls in love with the young bride. He follows them home, and when soon after, the husband embarks on a trading trip, the ghost fakes his early return, and takes his place at home and at work. When the real husband returns, the bride's testimony is crucial because the ghost is a perfect impersonator. The wife's dilemma mirrors Bertrande's: should she choose the ghost who so passionately loves her and gives her sexual as well as emotional happiness, or the money-minded man with whom she shares nothing but a legal bond? Should she choose a strange, spectral, sexless being who only assumes a specific identity to have access to her over a "normal" man who will otherwise be wrongly punished and humiliated?

I narrate these stories not because the overlaps are startlingly unique, but precisely because they are recurrent. The cultural uncanny is a constant feature of our readings of literature, our watchings of theater and film. However, unlike the examples I have cited, these overlaps, the feelings of transcultural or transhistorical identification are not established only by way of similar tales, but more often by common themes, twists of language and images, characters, or even something more elusive we cannot put our finger on. We especially look for these commonalities in texts that are supposed to be "great" (such as the plays of Shakespeare). As John Dias put it in the Queer Theater Conference's panel discussion on Shakespeare and Sexuality, we search for ways of "finding a way into something that's genius." Traditional literary criticism had a special way of creating such identifications—it was via something called "human nature." We can all find something in Shakespeare's plays that speaks to us because Shakespeare has a special insight into "human nature." And if we don't find these identifications, there is something wrong with us.

Now, such a theory depends of course on particular readings and interpretations of Shakespeare. They are not meant to allow queer readers to identify with, or to dislike, Shakespeare's representations of same-sex love, or black and colonial subjects to identify with or dislike Shakespeare's representations of nonwhite peoples. Thus no one taught us *The Merchant of Venice* so that we could discuss the homoerotic relations between Antonio and Bassanio. For centuries, Shakespearean critics downplayed the color of Othello, the Moor of Venice, so that he represented a universal masculine trait called Jealousy, rather than a person caught up in a complex pattern of racial and gendered relations.

For us, reading Shakespeare in India, the webs of identification or alienation were further complicated by the fact that these plays had been a staple of colonial education for many years. In the colonial situation, if students did not like the Shakespeare they were taught, it reflected adversely on their entire capacities and culture. This attitude of reverence toward the Western canon persisted even after formal independence, so that postcolonial Shakespeare did not look very different from his colonial predecessor. The Shakespeare given to us by our teachers and by Western criticism was deeply patriarchal and conservative—there was little sense of the political and sexual confusion and debates of his time, or indeed of ours. Both were bypassed to construct Shakespeare and a contemporary Indian reader who would meet in a zone of "universal values." Of course many of us reacted by simply getting bored with this imposed canon, or dutifully complying with pedagogic demands knowing that after the examinations these plays need never be read again.

At the same time, I felt that there was a way in which this drama resonated strongly with us, but in ways that had little to do with a universal human culture. Shakespeare and contemporary urban Indians might meet, but in a space marked by turmoil and contestation. These plays were written at a time of strong social, sexual, and cultural transformation which, while far from identical with the transitions India was going through, struck certain familiar chords, and thus aroused some thought and much emotion. To establish the connections we would need to highlight, not suppress, the tensions of both cultures. The uncanny was thus not testimony to transcendental patterns but perhaps to a curious historical juncture whereby the turmoil of Renaissance culture became curiously alive in our present moment.

The early modern debates on gender and women resonated with special force because the early 1980s in India witnessed both an increased violence against women and an urgent and vital women's movement. This period was also marked by the mushrooming of new and exciting work (in the Western academy) on Shakespeare and the early modern period in general, much of it done (not by accident) by queer and/or feminist men and women. This work outlined the ways in which the Renaissance marked the transition into "modern" structures of civil and personal life, including the separation of workplace and home, the enforced restriction of women into domestic spaces, the codification of the patriarchal nuclear family and of heterosexuality, the germs of cultural nationalism and of protocolonialist ideologies. To me, looking for alternative ways of connecting with the so-called "Renaissance," what was instructive and exciting about the period was that ideas about femininity, sexuality, and race were in upheaval at that time, and therefore one could see how they were *constructed* rather than universal and timeless. What was socially sanctioned as "normal" in our times—whether it be attitudes to sexuality or race or class—was not quite so then.

43

As an Indian, reading Shakespeare or Lyly, or indeed a story such as Martin Guerre, a sense of difference between the "then" and the "now" of European culture was especially crucial. Sexuality in Shakespeare's time had not settled into the structures that are considered "normal" today. But in India, one is always fluctuating between different sets of "norms" anyway. Is arranged marriage "normal," and "love marriage" a hugely daring affair, as would be true still for a majority of my students in India? Or is "love marriage" (a term that one hears only in India, since all marriages in the West are supposed to be based on "love") normal, and arranged marriages weird (affairs that happened in the distant past or that take place in distant places), as most students in the United States think? *Much Ado about Nothing* thus speaks very differently to different sets of readers—for students in India, the Hero-Claudio affair may be "normative" in a statistical sense, while American students, who are much more heavily invested in the ideologies of romantic coupledom, find it harder to see how the Beatrice-Benedick relationship is also arranged and structured by patriarchal and heterosexual norms. For middle-class Indians, the "norm" is itself an unstable construct, much as it is in Shakespeare's plays.

This is also the reason why various kinds of "marginal" readings of Shakespeare share something with each other. Feminist, queer, and anticolonial readings are all invested in wrestling Shakespeare away from "his" dominant readings and finding something that speaks to a diversity of readers who are alienated (though not in identical ways) from the Bard as he has been available to them. I should clarify that this does not necessarily mean finding a Shakespeare who is sympathetic to independent women, blacks, or queers—but in every case it does mean highlighting the contestation over sexuality or race in Shakespeare's time and our own. These contestations allow us to locate points of identification. As Alan Sinfield has put it:

It is not that Shakespeare was a sexual radical, therefore. Rather, the early modern organization of sex and gender boundaries was different from ours, and the ordinary currency of that culture is replete with erotic interactions that strike strange chords today. Shakespeare may speak with distinct force to gay men and lesbians, simply because he didn't think he had to sort out sexuality in modern terms. For approximately the same reasons, these plays may stimulate radical ideas about race, nation, gender and class.[3]

But this also means that in some ways marginalized readers—blacks, postcolonials, women, queers—have a special vantage point from which to view the past. Our disjunctures from dominant culture allow us to read the past not just in terms of the present but in terms of its differences from the present. In some ways, this common exclusion from dominant culture, and common investment in alternative ways of seeing and reading literature, forges an important connection between different sorts of marginal positions and histories. I learned hugely from the debates about sexuality and gender at the Queer Theater Conference although these rarely touched the question of race or colonialism. This is not only because various marginal positions question the same dominant order, but because there is a historical linkage, as well as tension, between these different aspects of our being.

Some of these linkages are quite spectacular. During the "Shakespeare and Sexuality" panel discussion, John Dias mentioned the confusion about whether Shakespeare's Dark Lady was a black woman or a gay man. Colonial ideologies in fact have a rich history of overlapping gay and black subjects. Kim Hall perceptively connects the dark ladies of the sonnets with the foreign women in Renaissance travel narratives.[4] In these writings, the foreign women (and men) are repeatedly represented as having excessive or deviant sexuality. Racial and cultural outsiders and faraway places become "a porno-tropics for the European imagination—a fantastic magic lantern of the mind onto which Europe has projected its forbidden sexual desires and fears."[5] Thus non-Europeans, especially women, were constructed as libidinally excessive, and sexually uncontrolled. John Bulwer's *Anthropometamorphoses* suggested that African as well as Indian men had oversized genitals.[6] Francis Bacon's *New Atlantis* claimed that when "an holy Hermit . . . desired to see that the Spirit of Fornication . . . there appeared to him, a foule ugly Ethiope."[7]

More specifically, non-European peoples were imagined as widely indulging in same-sex relationships. Harem stories, in particular, fanned fantasies of lesbianism. In his early seventeenth-century account of Turkey, for example, George Sandys contemplates what happens when women are cloistered with each other, engaged in massaging and pampering their bodies for long hours: "Much unnaturall and filthie lust is said to be committed daily in the remote closets of these darksome [bathhouses]: yea, women with women; a thing incredible, if former times had not given thereunto both detection and punishment."[8] Another traveler to Turkey claims that the men too "are extremely inclined to all sorts of lascivious luxury; and generally addicted, besides all their sensuall and incestuous lusts, unto Sodomy, which they account as a daynty to digest all their other libidinous pleasures." Finally, the alien space itself is described in sexual terms: Constantinople becomes "A Painted Whoore, the maske of deadly sin."[9] Renaissance writings on Islam always emphasize that it encourages licentiousness because it promises "marvelous beautiful women, with their Breastes wantonly swelling" as well as "fair Boyes" in Paradise.[10]

Leo Africanus, a converted Moor whose real name was Al Hassan Ibn Mohammed Al Wezaz Al Fazi (and on whom Shakespeare's *Othello* is sometimes supposed to be modeled), fueled such imaginings with his *A Geographical History of Africa* which was widely translated from Arabic and Italian (including into English in 1600) and became the most "authoritative" account of Africa. Africanus repeatedly attributes "venerie," "lecherie," homosexuality, drugs, and cross-dressing to Africans.[11] Thus, for example, the "Inne-keepers of Fez being all of one Family, called Elecheua, goe apparalled like Women, and shave their Beards, and are so delighted to imitate women, that they will not only counterfeite their speech, but will sometimes also sit downe and spin" (1905: 413). In Tunis they "have here a Compound, called Lhasis, whereof whosoever eateth but one Ounce, falleth a laughing, disporting, and dallying, as if he were halfe drunken, and is by the said confection marvellously provoked into lust" (1905: 498). In Fez there were witches who

have a damnable custome to commit unlawful Venerie among themselves, which I cannot expresse in any modester termes. If faire women come unto them at any time, these abominable Witches will borne in lust towards them, no otherwise then lustie Younkers doe towards young Maides, and will in the Devils behalfe demand a reward, that they may lie with them: and so by this manes it often followeth out, that thinking thereby to fulfill the Devils command they lie with the Witches. Yea, some there are, which being allured with the delight of this abominable vice, will desire the company of these Witches, and faining themselves to be sicke, will either call one of the Witches home to them or will send their husbands for the same purpose. (1905: 435)

The point about such accounts is that they do not exist in isolation simply as stories about "the Other" but serve also to define deviant and normative behavior at home. This very story of the witches of Fez is cited by the French surgeon Ambroise Pare to "verify" his descriptions of female parts which "grow erect like the male rod" enabling the women to "disport themselves . . . with other women" and then to defend the excision of such parts.[12] At the same time, these stories also circulate as desired fantasies that can work both to legitimate the status quo and to subvert it. In George Sandys's *Relation*, the Turkish patriarchy is censored for its barbaric attitudes to women, but at the same time it becomes a model for English life:

If their husbands have been abroad, at his entrance into the house, if any one of their women be sitting on a stool, she riseth up, and boweth herself to her husband, and kisseth his hand, and . . . (standeth) so long as he is in presence . . . If the like order were in England, women would be more dutiful and faithful to their husbands than they are: and especially, if there were the like punishment for whores, there would be less whoredom: for there if a man have a hundred women, if any one of them prostitute herself to any man but her own husband, he hath authority to bind her hands and feet, and cast her into the river, with a stone about her neck and drown her.[13]

These images, fantasies and opinions percolate into the drama of the period, which, it must be remembered, provided the most graphic images of "otherness" for large sections of the populace, many of whom were illiterate and would not have read the travel stories for themselves. In Philip Massinger's *The Renegado* (1621), for example, the images of Turkey are taken straight from Sandys. In that play the beautiful Donusia, niece of the Sultan Amurath, is informed by her English-born eunuch of the superior status enjoyed by Englishwomen; unlike her, they can roam the streets unveiled and consort with men. She is literally a princess but they "live like queens" (I, ii). Donusia finally converts to Christianity and runs away with the Venetian Vitelli to live with him in Italy as his wife. While both Sandys and Massinger use the Turkish attitudes toward their women as exemplifying barbarism, yet their representations may also be seen to function as lessons in female deportment for rebellious Englishwomen.

In Fletcher's *The Knight of Malta*, in Webster's *The White Devil*, in Heywood's *The Fair Maid of the West*, in Daborne's *A Christian Turn'd Turke* and in many other plays, the "other women" are neither modest nor convertible to Christianity but lascivious in the extreme. Non-European men too are represented as excessively "masculine," that is, with uncontrolled sexual appetites, especially for white women. So Shakespeare's Othello and Caliban, while very different from one another—the former being the prototype of the noble, royal outsider, the latter of the savage, uncivilized other—are both accused of thrusting their attentions upon the white heroine. The King of Fez in *The Fair Maid of the West* and his Queen both engage in various tricks to get the white hero and heroine into bed with them.

But conversely, the non-European male is also seen as not quite "masculine" enough. Iago plays upon the latter ideology by repeatedly asking Othello "Are you a man? Have you a soul or sense?" (III, iii, 378). Eastern or African cultures threaten to unman men: hence in many contemporary travelogues and plays, the attraction of these foreign cultures is represented or accompanied by literal or figurative castrations. For example, in Shakespeare's *Antony and Cleopatra*, Antony's desire for the Egyptian queen is described in terms of a loss of manhood. Both he and his soldiers have been "turn'd into women" by Cleopatra, whose court is full of women, magicians, and eunuchs. Of course, sexual relations with women are seen to unman men, and render them effeminate. Such a threat is heightened when the woman is non-European. More generally, alien cultures themselves threaten European masculinity. Those who "turn Turk" (that is, go native and betray European culture and religion) are often represented as being literally castrated. In Heywood's *Fair Maid of the West Part I*, for example, the foolish Gazet, who is dazzled by the promise of Moorish lucre, is taken off to have his jewels cut. Thus travelogues also report that the Janizzaries who were the strongmen of the Turkish court were reportedly not Turkish at all, but castrated European men.

A growing body of critical work has been at pains to establish the differences between modern and early modern perceptions of "homosexuality." Among men, same-sex relations were permitted, encouraged, even glamorized as long as they did not threaten property or patriarchal relations. Sodomy was a crime, but loving male friendships an ideal:

Whatever served to undergird patriarchal authority in early modern England fell within the range of permitted behaviour. In certain circumstances, that might involve sexual relations among men. Indeed, the oxymoronic images of embracing and fisting in Aufidius's welcome to Coriolanus in IV.v. 102–36 would suggest that homoerotic desire served to fuel the patriarchal enterprise: it strengthened the male bonds that kept patriarchy in place. In terms of political utility, the ends of the continuum, I would argue are marked by two figures: the sodomite and the whore. Although one end of the continuum is thus gendered "male" and the other "female," the issue that places the two figures is the same: power. When a man engages in sexual behaviour that somehow compromises [the] patriarchal power structure, he becomes a sodomite. When a woman assumes power over her own body, she becomes a whore.[14]

Thus, the capital punishment prescribed for sodomy was put into place only when issues of class or race or political affiliations were also at stake. Lesbian desire, as Valerie Traub has shown, is another matter altogether, for it is necessarily filtered through existing ideologies about women. Thus, in literary and other writings, it is rendered literally invisible.[15]

Similarly, ideologies of racial difference also work in conjunction with, and through, other social differences. The insider-outsider boundary comes into play in order to protect entrenched sexual and/or economic interests. Early modern

England devoured stories about the cruel Turks with the same zeal with which it attempted to maintain trade and diplomatic ties with them. Othello, Caliban, or Shylock are all crucial to the social order, and yet they also threaten it. Why are some racial outsiders seen as potentially convertible to European Christianity, while others must be violently expelled? The answers lie in the intricate ways in which race, sexuality, gender, class, and other markers of social difference are knotted together to create images of desire, fear, glamor, or power.

And yet, we have only begun to think about how these interactions might have worked in Shakespeare's society or in Shakespeare's times. Kim Hall's book *Things of Darkness* shows how the language of color is central to consolidating ideologies of gender as well as nation. It analyses how a juxtaposition of black and white is repeatedly deployed both in language and material objects (such as jewelry and paintings) to construct normative femininity as well as the idea of Englishness. And as I have tried to suggest, in the early modern period a central aspect of later colonialist discourse was already in place whereby, as Anne McClintock puts it, "colonized peoples were figured as sexual deviants, while gender deviants were figured as racial deviants."[16] It is difficult to think about early modern constructions of racial otherness without confronting images of sexual, particularly female, unruliness.

And yet queerness and race in Renaissance studies have not been theorized or historicized in relation to one another. For example, recent Shakespearean criticism has been especially sophisticated and nuanced in considering the question of cross-dressing on the Renaissance stage and within the plays themselves. The boys who played women's roles allowed complex and ambiguous sexual attractions to circulate through the audience. Critics have connected these ambiguous desires with the strict sumptuary laws that operated in Renaissance England, and which forbade women to dress as men, or the lower classes to don the clothes of the nobility. On the stage, low-born boy actors put on female as well as noble personas, and then transformed themselves back into boys. But very few critics have considered that all the black characters were white men in disguise. How did blacking up refract the play of sexual and class transgressions? What intersections of homoeroticism and cross-cultural disguise are visible in these performances?

Hence, establishing overlaps or analogies between different kinds of social differences, as I have been doing, is clearly not enough. In Shakespeare's plays (as in other texts of the period) different kinds of marginal subjects are pitted against each other: thus Portia, Antonio, and Shylock's interests conflict with one another; Othello is the murderer of a white woman, and Caliban cannot establish any solidarity with Miranda or Ariel. These patterns remind us that although various kinds of marginalities ought to be allied with one another, they are often hostile to one another. At other times, they are unable to translate their good faith into critical practice: thus antiracist movements or thinking have been actively or implicitly misogynist or heterosexist, feminist and queer theory can be racist or simply color-blind. At the Queer Theater Conference, queerness was in some danger of emerging as a transhistorical, culturally unnuanced category, just as queer perspectives are routinely missing from discussions of postcoloniality and race. As Bruce Smith puts it, "Critical movements may begin in polyglossia, but they tend to end in monologia" (1996: 98).

Usually, exclusions are most effectively pointed out by those whose identities cross obvious dividing lines—thus black women were the most articulate critics of racist tendencies within feminism, and so on. But identity politics can close off as many questions are they open. How can we address this problem? Surely it is as important to attend to the specificity of particular histories as it is to work against isolationist tendencies? In a thought-provoking recent essay, Alan Sinfield explores some of these questions by considering the pros and cons of constructing queer identities on an "ethnicity model." On the one hand, he says, this model, "following the precedent of the Black Civil Rights movement, has offered the dominant paradigm for political advancement . . . So we too claim our rights: That is what ethnic groups do."[17] On the other hand, such a model "consolidates our constituency at the expense of limiting it" because the gay identity so envisaged both squeezes diversity within the gay community and lets others off the hook: "by inviting us to perceive ourselves as settled in our sexuality, the ethnicity and rights model releases others from the invitation to re-envision theirs" (1996: 273). Sinfield discusses how an "ethnicity and rights model encourages us to imagine a process whereby, win some/lose some, we all advance gradually towards full democratic citizenship," and how such a pluralist myth works precisely by appealing to the good faith of the dominant culture.

At the same time Sinfield acknowledges that theorists of "race" and "ethnicity" no longer take those terms as self-evident or stable. Blackness, race, ethnic or national identities—all these are now increasingly seen as hybrid, unstable cultural constructs. For Sinfield, this has "obvious resonances for lesbian and gay cultural politics" because "gay culture, certainly, is hybrid; to the point where it is difficult to locate anything that is crucially gay—either at the core of gayness, or having gayness at its core" (1996: 279). But the essay indicates the limits of the idea of hybridity which is currently widely celebrated by theorists of sexuality as well as postcoloniality. (Incidentally, Robert Young rightly reminds us that a hybrid is a cross between two different species and that the term hybridization evokes both the botanical notion of interspecies grafting and the "vocabulary of the Victorian extreme right.")[18] Sinfield indicates the connections between Homi Bhabha's celebration of mimicry in the colonial context and Judith Butler's of cross-dressing: both suggest that mimicry "plays back the dominant manner in a way that discloses the precariousness of its authority" (1996: 282). But as the essay points out, capitalism actually thrives on instability, and dominant cultures are also capable of reappropriating subaltern acts of mimicry. It concludes that an uncritical celebration of hybridity detracts from thinking about identity, subcultures, or resistance in ways which are not aimed at "disturbing nor pleasing the *straightgeist*, but to meeting our own diverse needs" (1996: 287).

I have quoted at some length from this essay partly because its discussion of hybridity overlaps with similar debates within postcolonial theory. There, too, the most tricky issue is whether anticolonial resistance is enabled by emphasizing difference between the colonizers and the colonized, or by recognizing the multiple hybridities that are put into place during the colonial encounter. Many nationalists and anticolonialists seized colonial ideologies of difference and appropriated the notion of a binary opposition between Europe and its others. Liberation, for them, hinged upon the discovery or rehabilitation of their cultural identity which European colonialism had disparaged and wrecked. Stuart Hall identifies this as a search for "a sort of collective 'one true self' . . . which people with a shared history and ancestry hold in common," or, in Fanon's words, a search for "some very beautiful splendid era whose existence rehabilitates us both in regard to ourselves, and in regard to others."[19] Such a search has been essential for anticolonial struggles and postcolonial identities, and yet by endorsing cultural and racial difference, it can feed into resurrecting racist and colonialist binaries. In the words of Anthony Appiah, "the overdetermined course of cultural nationalism in Africa has been to make real the imaginary identities to which Europe has subjected us."[20] According to some critics, "racial categories are meaningless in isolation, its markers of difference always serving the function of identification, drawing borders, operating at the interface in a dangerous and messy confusion of attractions and refusals. We now know vividly that the sheer cultural opposites of Black and White are nothing more than powerful constructs, mind-forged masks in fact."[21] And yet, these "mind-forged masks" shape real lives, and direct all too real forms of oppression and exclusion.

Thus, in postcolonial theory as in queer theory, the debates about authenticity versus creolization are central and unresolved. But although the debates may be similar, and even draw upon one another, they also have a tendency to remain somewhat isolated from one another. Postcolonial theory, for example, both uses and criticizes psychoanalytic theory, but it has not really developed a dialogue with queer critics of that theory. Thus, I found Sinfield's essay refreshing in asking us to think between as well as within different notions of oppression and identity. Perhaps it is only by doing so that we can revisit Shakespearean and early modern notions of race, sexuality, gender, and class in a more organic fashion. Stuart Hall, in the essay quoted above, goes on to suggest that identity is a matter of "becoming" as well as of "being." Thus, colonized peoples cannot simply turn back to the idea of a collective precolonized culture and a past "which is waiting to be found, and which when found, will secure our sense of ourselves into eternity" (1994: 394). Hall is careful not to dismiss such a turning back as romantic nativism, as some other postcolonial critics are apt to do. Although there are no pure and fixed origins to which cultures and peoples can return, "it is no mere phantasm either. It is something—not a mere trick of the imagination. It has its histories—and histories have their real, material and symbolic effects. The past continues to speak to us. But it no longer addresses us as a simple, factual 'past,' since our relation to it . . . is always-already 'after the break'" (1994: 395).

Our relation to Shakespeare is also always-already "after the break." These plays, or the society in which they were first performed, certainly need to be thought of in terms radically different from those outlined by traditional Shakespeareans. But such theatrical and social practices cannot simply be read as offering unlimited space to the play of desires, identities, and ideologies that were subsequently repressed. For queer, postcolonial, and other revisionist readers, going back to Shakespeare to find images, ideas, and issues that speak to us thus involves a process not unlike the one Hall outlines above. We search for identifications as well as ruptures, cognizant always of the complex negotiations that mark our scholarly and cultural transactions. We intuit difference and are astonished by uncanny repetitions; we claim a kinship and a continuity with identities and structures in the past and learn, via our reading and thinking, that such oneness is precisely what is qualified by our understanding of historical processes. The postcolonial critic today who claims the racial other in Shakespeare as her sister, or the queer theorist who studies Renaissance same-sex relations, have both to admit that those histories are not theirs, except insofar as we choose to make them so, and for purposes that we must specify. But in that specification we do more than just keep our intellectual pursuits honest; in fact, in making clear why we do what we do, we make our writings political, and articulate the reasons why we must share projects that seek to learn and unlearn the past.

Notes

1. I owe the term "porno-tropics" to Anne McClintock's *Imperial Leather* (see note 5 below). This essay was written several years ago; since then the intersection of race and sexuality in early modern culture has received more attention than is indicated here.

2. Natalie Zemon Davis, *The Return of Martin Guerre* (Middlesex: Penguin, 1983).

3. Alan Sinfield, "How to Read *The Merchant of Venice* without Being Heterosexist," in *Alternative Shakespeares*, vol. 2, ed. Terence Hawkes (London: Routledge, 1966), 139.

4. Kim Hall, *Things of Darkness, Economies of Race and Gender in Early Modern England* (Ithaca: Cornell University Press, 1995), 64.

5. Anne Mclintock, *Imperial Leather: Race, Gender and Sexuality in the Colonial Context* (New York: Routledge, 1995), 22.

6. John Bulwer, *Anthropometamorphoses: Man Transformed or the Artificiall Changeling Historically Presented* (London, 1653), 404.

7. Peter Fryer, *Staying Power: The History of Black People in Britain* (London: Pluto Press, 1984), 140.

8. George Sandys, *A Relation of a Journey begun An. Dom 1610*, 3d ed. (London, 1627), 69.

9. William Lithgow, "Rare Adventures and Painefull Peregrinations," ed. B. I. Lawrence (London: Jonathan Cape, n.d.), 85, 102.

10. T. Warmistry, *The Baptized Turk, or a Narrative of the Happy Conversion of the Signior Rigep Dandulo* (London, 1658), 145.

11. Leo Africanus, "Navigations, Voyages, and Land-Discoveries, with other Historical Relations of Afrike . . . taken out of John Leo," in Samuel Purchas, ed., *Hakluytus Posthumus* (Glasgow: James Maclehose and Sons, 1905), vol. 5, 307–529.

12. See Patricia Parker, "Fantasies of 'Race' and 'Gender': Africa, *Othello*, and Bringing to Light," in *Women, "Race" and Writing in the Early Modern Period*, ed. Margo Hendricks and Patricia Parker (London: Routledge, 1994), 84–100. Quotation on 84.

13. *The Travels of Foure Englishmen* (1608), 792, in *A Collection of Voyages and Travels*, ed. T. Osborne, 1745.

14. Bruce R. Smith, "L[o]cating the Sexual Subject," in *Alternative Shakespeares*, vol. 2, ed. Terence Hawkes (London: Routledge, 1996), 99.

15. Valerie Traub, "The (In)Significance of 'Lesbian' Desire in Early Modern England," in *Erotic Politics: Desire on the Renaissance Stage*, ed. Susan Zimmerman (New York:

Routledge, 1992), 150–69. See also her "Setting the Stage behind the Seen: Performing Lesbian History," in this volume.

16. Mclintock, *Imperial Leather*, 182.

17. Alan Sinfield, "Diaspora and Hybridity: Queer Identities and the Ethnicity Model," *Textual Practice* 10, 2 (1996): 271–93. Quotation on 271.

18. Robert Young, *Colonial Desire, Hybridity in Theory, Culture and Race* (London: Routledge, 1995), 10.

19. See Stuart Hall, "Cultural Identity and Diaspora," in *Colonial Discourse and Post-Colonial Theory*, ed. P. Williams and L. Chrisman (New York: Columbia University Press, 1994), 392–403.

20. Kwame Anthony Appiah, "Out of Africa: Topologies of Nativism," in *The Bounds of Race, Perspectives on Hegemony and Resistance*, ed. Dominick LaCapra (Ithaca: Cornell University Press, 1991), 150.

21. Terry Collits, "Theorizing Racism," in *De-Scribing Empire, Postcolonialism and Textuality*, ed. Chris Tiffin and Alan Lawson (London: Routledge, 1994).

4 Setting the Stage behind the Seen

Performing Lesbian History

Valerie Traub

. . . Cupid's fiery shaft
[was] Quench'd in the chaste beams of the wat'ry moon, And the imperial
vot'ress passed on,
In maiden meditation, fancy-free.[1]

Several years ago in Nashville, Tennessee, director Barry Edelstein staged a theatrical production of Shakespeare's *Twelfth Night* which comically highlighted the
operatic dimensions of human passion. Although the performance closely followed Shakespeare's script, Olivia and Orsino, Aguecheek and Antonio all expressed their desires in over-the-top vocal performances that were observed, and
wryly commented upon, by an earnest yet mischievous Viola/Cesario. My partner,
at that time a theater critic for a local "alternative" newspaper, commended Tennessee Repertory Theater for its entertaining, witty, superbly acted production.
She also praised the performance for its open exploration of the ways homoerotic
attractions infused the interactions of Olivia and Viola, Orsino and Cesario, Antonio and Sebastian. Having sat through a number of plays in which closeted gay
actors performed homophobic material, having spoken to actors anguished by
their compromises with what some local directors deemed "the audience"—and
aware that Tennessee at the time upheld a sodomy statute which criminalized
consensual same-gender erotic acts—she considered this mainstreaming of homoerotic performance a momentous occasion.[2]

Momentous, indeed. The actress who had played Olivia with such passionate
aplomb wrote a letter to the editor in horrified protest; the possibility of such an

55

interpretation had never entered her mind. She did not play Olivia as "a homo-sexual"; nor did Shakespeare intend her to. Needless to say, her horror did not stem from a social constructivist view that the category of homosexual did not exist that far back in time. Vehemently, she declared she would never consent to play a part contrary to her personal ethics.[3] What about Medea or Salome? my partner wondered in response.

What happens when female-female desire is enacted today on the Shake-spearean stage—in Nashville, New York, Stratford (England or Ontario)? Given that the trope of invisibility has governed discussions of lesbianism prior to 1800, what happens to Shakespeare (that icon of literary genius), to notions of the Re-naissance (that icon of high culture), to actors and audiences in professional, com-munity, and college theaters when women's homoerotic desires are granted a cul-tural presence? Insofar as theatrical and cinematic productions of Shakespearean drama are the primary medium through which most North Americans encounter "the Renaissance," how might directors, dramaturgs, and actors intercede *now* in popular knowledge of what was possible, erotically speaking, *then*?[4]

Contemporary theatrical performance provides a point of departure for this chapter's consideration of how to recognize, interpret, and make manifest the cul-tural presence of lesbianism in the early modern period. Distinctively homoerotic representations of female desire in Shakespearean drama, and in Renaissance drama generally, can emerge from an awareness of the various historical dis-courses of female intimacy—from tribadism to female-female marriages to adoles-cent friendships. In order to set the stage for subsequent analyses, I first provide an overview of the theological, legal, and medical discourses that informed the so-cial practices of female homoeroticism across Europe, and punctuate discussion of these discourses with examples drawn from selected literary texts.

The second half of this essay correlates these discourses, practices, and repre-sentations to a range of affective desires dramatized in one of Shakespeare's most frequently performed plays. My aim is not to provide a reading of *A Midsummer Night's Dream*, but to use its repeated, if tantalizingly brief, allusions to female in-timacies to lift the curtain on occluded practices within early modern culture. Bringing together seemingly disparate phenomena, I argue that not only can his-tory be brought to life through today's performances, but that theatrical compa-nies could broaden their resources by attending to historical discourses of les-bianism. The pun embedded in this essay's title implies that visibility is a function of location: what is positioned *behind the scene* is denied visibility. Such a denial has been the governing condition of early modern lesbianism. If we materialize the theatrical metaphor, however, we can recognize that what goes on behind the scene—the work, for instance, of stagehands, lighting technicians, directors, costumers, financiers—is also what makes the actors' performances possible.

By appropriating this metaphor of constitutive but unacknowledged work, I propose that lesbianism has played a more important role in our cultural heritage than is commonly supposed. I investigate cultural production through that canonical icon, "Shakespeare," because his name and the industry it now represents is a repository of cultural assumptions that I wish to vex and a site of cultural capital that I wish to employ.[5] As recent mainstream films of *Henry V, Richard III, Romeo and Juliet,* and *Titus Andronicus,* as well as films that allude to, cite, adapt, and revamp Shakespearean materials suggest, Shakespearean drama remains, even in a postmodern global economy, a privileged site of cultural production and interpretation. Despite its marginal status vis-à-vis other forms of television and cinema, Shakespearean performance, whether acted live or filmed, screened in an art house, the mall, or on TV, contributes in unique and pervasive ways to contemporary understanding of "high culture," "the arts," "human nature," and, perhaps most important for my purposes, "history." Even as contemporary production values "update" characters, clothes, and plots, making them "relevant" to today's viewers, "Shakespeare" remains one of the few cultural forms from which interpretations of the past are disseminated.

Indeed, the cultural capital of the Shakespeare industry seems in direct proportion to its ability to proffer a fantasy of historical tradition and authority (or to contest it), whether through the means of period costume drama or postmodern pastiche. If, as the editors of *Shakespeare, the Movie* assert (after a spate of Shakespeare films in the 1990s), "just where the film industry will take Shakespeare seems quite up for grabs,"[6] the time seems right to grab what has been "behind" and to bring lesbianism onto center stage—not to enforce a politics of identity, but to destabilize some long-standing theatrical conventions and to activate the queer potential of today's global audience.

Theatrical and cinematic productions have many tools for dramatizing noncanonical interpretations of Shakespeare's plays, from the reinterpretation of character and reassignment of speeches to transpositions of time, place, and costume. But as progressive as the productions of some theatrical companies have been, not all the creative energies that can be brought to bear on Shakespearean performance stem from theatrical practitioners themselves. In this regard, contemporary performance has much to gain from the insights of feminist and queer criticism and theory. Often, however, the aims of feminist textual criticism and performance seem to be at odds. According to theater critic Lorraine Helms, "[p]er-formance, like criticism, may either reproduce or reevaluate the ideology with which a dominant culture invests a play text. But if a production is to challenge the theatrical tradition . . . it must move from critique to revision." The problem with much feminist textual criticism of Shakespeare, Helms argues, is that it takes the form of critique rather than creative reenvisioning. Because the feminism of such criticism, she argues, often is "theatrically inert," "were it taken as the conceptual foundation for performance," it would unwittingly affirm rather than subvert "a misogynist interpretation."[7]

My aim here is to begin to envision ways in which a lesbian analytic might make available to the stage (and cinema) new strategies for performing relations of gender and eroticism. By suggesting that a historical awareness of the range of female desires and bonds in the early modern period could profitably pressure the way female characters are represented and erotic desire thematized, I do not mean to imply that contemporary Shakespearean production has totally avoided dramatizing homoerotic desire. Indeed, in response to contemporary politics—and sometimes in advance of academic theorizing—some theater companies have brought attention to, for instance, Antonio's love for Bassanio and the erotic relation between Salerio and Solanio, as in the New York Public Theater's production of *The Merchant of Venice*, or Orsino's attraction for Cesario, as in a recent Shakespeare Santa Cruz production.[8] Rather than invest certain characters with homoerotic desires in otherwise "straight" productions, other companies have queered the entire play by using male drag—as in Cheek by Jowl's all-male *As You Like It*, Theatre Rhinoceros's all-male *Twelfth Night*, Reginald Jackson's high camp *House of Lear*, and Shakespeare Santa Cruz's *A Midsummer Night's Dream*.[9]

The theatricalization of lesbian desire in Shakespearean drama occurs far less frequently. When it does occur, it tends to depend on cross-gender casting to parody or "modernize" Shakespeare. Cheek by Jowl's 1991 *As You Like It* portrayed Celia in love with Rosalind, but did so through the mediation of an all-male cast.[10] A 1996 Cornerstone Theater Company adaptation of *Twelfth Night*, committed to exploring the debate about "gays in the military," cast the love-sick Malvolio as a woman and set the action at a Southern California naval base.[11] Likewise, cross-gender casting animated Jill Dolan's 1991 University of Wisconsin production of *A Midsummer Night's Dream*, in which the forest was transformed into a gay disco, Oberon was played as a "fashionable, sexy, butch lesbian," and Demetrius, upon waking, discovered he had been transformed into a woman—thus altering both his and Helena's erotic orientations.[12]

Cross-gender casting, parody, and modernization have their attractions, of course, including audience accessibility and appeal, as well as the communal joy of celebrating gay identity. And there are several good reasons for the reliance of companies on male drag: the historically vibrant presence of transvestism in gay male culture;[13] the Renaissance theatrical tradition of using boy actors to play female roles;[14] and the theoretical import of drag as a performative subversion of identity.[15] But the problem with such strategies, when employed to the exclusion of other possibilities, is that they tend to reinforce the all-too-prevalent assumption that issues of erotic diversity are distinctively *modern* concerns. According to Susan Bennett, the attempt to resist or revise the Shakespearean text in theatrical or cinematic performance typically has meant to dehistoricize it.[16] While the use of Shakespeare for the purposes of multiculturalism or gay community building implicates Renaissance drama in queer genders and sexualities, it tends to do so by highlighting metatheatricality at the expense of early modern history. If directors and actors wish to demonstrate the contemporary relevance of Shakespeare's erotic plots, they need not feel limited to the strategy of modernization. Nor, if they wish to resurrect historical traditions, need they limit their approach to cross-dressing and the use of boy actors. To what extent, for instance, do current productions employing drag register the actual tradition of passing women—women who cross-dressed not only for economic advantage and/or freedom from patriarchal marriage, but to act on their erotic desires for other women, to cohabit with, and sometimes, to marry them?

The goal in asking this question is not to forget the difference between stage representations and individual lives nor the absence of actual women from the Renaissance stage, but rather to investigate how theatrical drag registers—or fails to register—a specifically lesbian mode of representation. Such an investigation might ask which performance strategies beyond cross-gender casting and drag might make visible the full range of women's emotional and erotic attachments.[17] We do not need to laminate a lesbian presence *onto* Shakespeare's texts; once we begin to think historically about desires and practices, we can draw homoerotic meanings *out* of them. The point is not to deploy a discourse of authenticity to trump "trendy" postmodernism, nor to populate the Shakespearean stage with women whose desires are intelligible only in the idioms of the present.[18] To invoke—if only to reconceptualize—the title of the groundbreaking anthology, *Queering the Renaissance*: it is less a question of queering the past than of discovering the terms by which the past articulated its *own* queerness.[19]

. . .

VALERIE TRAUB

If erotic desires and practices in the early modern period were not organized by an essential and exclusive division of homo- and heterosexual, how was eroticism organized? To begin with a critical commonplace: most aspects of women's lives were determined by their age, marital status, and position within the patriarchal household. Familial status relations (whether one was husband, wife, or child), along with hierarchies of social rank (whether one was master, mistress, servant, or apprentice) established each person's opportunities and responsibilities. The legitimate social identities available to women—maid, wife, mother, and widow—were tied to marital status. Patriarchal authority and material necessity compelled most women to marry, and while daughters usually had the right to veto the recommendations of their fathers and advisers, in many espousals the hope was that women would come to love after, if not before, marriage. Noblewomen in particular were held accountable to considerable financial and political concerns, including the purity of genealogical lineage, inheritance of fortune and title, and consolidation of huge tracts of land. Daughters of the "middling sort" likewise were expected to make matches that helped the family's fortune by linking guildsmen and potential business partners, while daughters of the working poor may have had the least to lose or gain by the economic connections cemented by marriage.

The dominance of marriage as a social and political institution does not negate the pervasiveness of illegitimate heteroerotic activity, including frequent adultery at the highest levels of society. The fact that England was ruled for almost half a century by a woman whose own legitimacy was contested suggests the extent to which the edicts of patriarchal marriage could be, and were, ignored. Nonetheless, the disproportionate conceptual weight accorded to marriage, combined with a phallic standard of sexuality and the absence of a concept of erotic identity, provided the conceptual and social framework for lesbianism across Europe. Within this framework, the social treatment and semiotics of lesbianism were paradoxical. Authorities in all European societies were concerned about the threat posed by behaviors that crossed gender boundaries and/or the conjugal unit; thus, certain female-female erotic acts were met with harsh denunciation, punishment, and considerable publicity. Other behaviors that seem manifestly lesbian to twentieth-century minds, however, did not cause much social concern, and often were compatible with patriarchal marriage and alliance.

As Isabel Hull notes, the disciplining of illicit erotic acts was, in this time of nascent state formation, primarily a function of the church and community:

The church and the social nexus in which people lived—their family, neighbors, and fellow workers—exerted for a long time a stronger and more effective sexual discipline than the rudimentary state. . . . The church set the basic framework within which the absolutist territorial state later exercised regulation. From the secular standpoint, the church's two most powerful contributions were the great significance it ascribed to sexual (mis)behavior and the paramount position it accorded to marriage as the only locus of accepted sexual expression. Following these principles (among others) the church carefully developed the hierarchy of sexual offenses that absolutist penal codes later adopted from canon law.[20]

Thus, even after secular statutes replaced ecclesiastical law, denunciation of nonreproductive erotic acts as "unnatural" was the universal aim of religious and secular authorities across Europe.[21] Paul's *Letter to the Romans*, in which he speaks of women who give up natural intercourse for unnatural, and of men who reject women and are consumed with passion for men, provided the primary biblical authority for condemning what was called the *crimen contra naturam*.[22] Although sodomy today is most often defined as anal penetration, in the early modern period sodomy functioned as a catch-all category for a range of erotic activities and positions: anal penetration (involving penis, finger, or other instrument, and engaged with men or women), masturbation, bestiality, rape, and child molestation.[23] Female-female eroticism was considered by medieval church fathers as one among a panoply of unnatural acts, included in penitentials and investigated in the confessional.[24] After 1550, legal statutes became more specific about the inclusion of female sodomy. By the sixteenth century in many European states, a woman's conviction for sodomy (whether enacted with women or men) resulted, like that of men, in the penalty of death.

Two essential paradoxes define the legal status of lesbianism throughout the sixteenth and seventeenth centuries: not all sodomy statutes explicitly mention female-female activities; and in those jurisdictions that criminalize female-female acts, prosecution is the exception rather than the norm. England is a prime example of the first paradox: in 1533 an Act of Parliament made buggery (the vernacular term for anal penetration) a secular rather than religious crime, punishable by death; however, this statute, *25 Henry VIII, chapter 6*, did not mention women. In 1644, Sir Edward Coke, a prominent English interpreter of the law, proffered the opinion that if women committed buggery, it was by having sex with an animal.[25] Indeed, despite the fact that by the late seventeenth century vernacular dictionaries would include references to "woman with a woman" under the heading of "Buggerie," in reference to this crime Coke cites only an incident of "a great Lady [who] had committed Buggery with a Baboon, and conceived by it, etc."[26] In Scotland, however, Kirk Session records reveal one case of female sodomy in 1625, charged by the Glasgow Presbytery against two Egilshame parishioners, Elspeth Faulds and Margaret Armour; they were forced to separate from one another upon pain of excommunication.[27]

In colonial North America, sodomy laws likewise differed by locale. A criminal code drawn up by John Cotton in 1636 for the Massachusetts General Court described sodomy as "carnal fellowship of man with man, or woman with woman," but the authoritative Body of Liberties omitted women from the final draft. Other New England colonies, with the exception of Rhode Island, took their cue from the Massachusetts Bay Colony, drafting codes without reference to female-female contact. New Haven included sex between women as a capital offense, its statute of 1656 being the most detailed and comprehensive in the colonies. The two known colonial cases in which women were charged with "unclean" behavior, however, invoked neither sodomy nor the draconian punishments typically associated with it: in 1642, "Elizabeth Johnson was whipped and fined by an Essex County quarterly court for 'unseemly and filthy practices betwixt hir and another maid, attempting To Do that which man and woman Doe,' and in 1648/9, Sara Norman and Mary Hammon of Plymouth Colony were publicly admonished for 'leude behavior each with other upon a bed.'"[28] In Virginia, an official inquiry into the anatomical sex of the cross-dressing Thomas/Thomasine Hall may have been instigated by a rumor that Hall "did ly with a maid . . . called greate Besse," but the case was resolved without resort to capital punishment; Thomas(ine) was forced to adopt a hybrid form of dress and live a life devoid of erotic contact.[29]

Similar patterns of legal prosecution in Europe reveal that, in contrast to the high incidence of prosecution of women for prostitution, adultery, bastardy, and witchcraft, comparatively few women in Europe and colonial North America were prosecuted for sodomy before the eighteenth century.[30] In fact, the official treatment of female-female erotic acts throughout the early modern era was somewhat incoherent, with the paucity of prosecutions at odds with the supposedly horrific nature of the crime. When read in the context of court testimony, the selective enforcement of sodomy laws suggests that the primary concern of authorities was women's appropriation of masculine prerogatives, whether in the form of cross-dressing and passing as a man, the use of instruments of genital penetration (dildos made of leather, wood, or glass), or other challenges to patriarchal authority.

Some statutes specifically mandated harsher punishments for acts involving "material instruments" or devices for penetration.

When women were prosecuted for homoerotic acts, lawyers generally acted in concert with medical authorities, both physicians (exclusively men) and midwives (primarily women). Medical theorists and practitioners became involved in legal cases because, both in medicine and popular lore, women's erotic transgressions typically were read in relation to the dominant discourse of psychophysiology, the humoral theory derived from the classical Roman physician, Galen. According to humoralism, the body is a dynamic, self-regulating process.[31] Each of the four humors (blood, choler, melancholy, phlegm) possesses two primary qualities: blood is hot and moist, choler is hot and dry, melancholy is cold and dry, and phlegm is cold and moist. Each has specific physiological functions: blood warms and moistens the body, choler incites the expulsion of various excrements, melancholy provokes the appetite, and phlegm nourishes the cold and moist organs such as the kidneys and the brain. The related doctrine of the four temperaments (also called complexion theory) diagnoses sanguine, choleric, melancholic, and phlegmatic temperaments as caused by the dominance of one of the humors. Temperament (and thus behavior) is a matter both somatic and psychic.

In humoral theory, physiological sex exists on a continuum: although typically men are hot and dry, some men are too moist; while most women are moist and cold, some women are too hot. Such variation in the humors explains the presence of manly women (dry and cold) and womanly men (moist and hot). Indeed, because medically (and theologically) women are considered imperfect versions of men, women occasionally—so it was said—turn into men. The spontaneous eruption of a penis from sudden motion or increased body heat is a logical extension of the belief that women's genital anatomy is merely an inverted (and imperfect) version of men's. Since nature always strives for perfection, virilization rather than effeminization is nature's preferred course.[32] Throughout the sixteenth and seventeenth centuries, instances of miraculous sex change were narrated among villagers and used as evidence of the devil's ability to use natural causes to work his evil.

Whereas such cases of sex transformation pepper the literature on witchcraft and marvels, physicians and anatomists began to voice skepticism as anatomical investigation challenged the traditional homology of male and female reproductive organs. Over the course of the seventeenth century, medical writers increasingly denied the possibility of metamorphosis, arguing that such phenomena were attributable either to hermaphroditism or to unusual genital anatomy. In the latter case, the problematic "member" that made a woman look (and act) like a man was either a prolapsed vagina or, more commonly, an enlarged clitoris. In the latter case, such women were likely tribades, women who gained erotic satisfaction from rubbing against or penetrating other women's genitals with their "female yards." Helkiah Crooke, author of the English vernacular anatomy, *Microcosmographia, A Description of the Body of Man* (1615), for instance, summarized reports of sex transformation from the classical age forward for the purpose of arguing against its probability. He termed all such stories "monstrous and some not credible": persons alleged to have changed sex are either hermaphrodites or women who are "so hot by nature that their *Clitoris* hangeth foorth in the fashion of a mans member."[33] During the late seventeenth century, English medical popularizer Nicholas Culpeper was inclined to agree; but he hedged his bets, taking cover under the traditional adage that the size of the genitals correlates with the capacity for desire:

Some are of opinion, and I could almost afford to side with them, that such kind of creatures they call hermaphrodites, *which they say bear the genitals both of men and women, are nothing else but such women in whom the* clitoris *hangs out externally, and so resembles the form of the yard, leave the truth or falsehood of it to be judged by such who have seen them anatomised: however, this is agreeable both to reason and authority, that the bigger the clitoris is in women, the more lustful they are.*[34]

Culpeper's maxim, which correlates quantity of lust with size of genitals, exposes a powerful incoherence within the humoral dispensation. According to Galenic theory (and biblical doctrine), women, weaker and more inconstant than men, are more subject to lust. However, if women's lust becomes excessive, they perversely and paradoxically threaten to become like men. Female insatiability generally is linked not to the genitals, but to a weak will and susceptibility to temptation; if, however, a woman's body evinces bigger (more manlike) sexual equipment, she is less likely than men to be able to control it.

I want to stress here the tight associations forged between sex transformation, hermaphroditism, tribadism, and sodomy in most European legal and medical practices. These associations derive from conflicting medical models of the causality of hermaphroditism as well as the pervasive tendency to read the tribade in terms of her bodily morphology. Early moderns always tended to view sex, gender, and eroticism in terms of one another; thus, the boundary was continually blurred between hermaphroditism (which we tend to consider an anatomical category) and tribadism (which we tend to consider a behavioral category). The line proves to be a fine one in the chronicle of the count Froben Christop von Zimmern, who reports the following case:

There was also at that time a poor serving-girl at Mösskirch, who served here and there, and she was called Greta. . . . She did not take any man or young apprentice, nor would she stand at the bench with any such [that is, work with them as husband and wife and sell his goods], but loved the young daughters, went after them and bought them pedlars' goods, and she also used all bearing and manners, as if she had a masculine affect. She was often considered to be a hermaphrodite or androgyne, but this did not prove to be the case, for she was investigated by cunning, and was seen to be a true, proper woman. To note: she was said to be born under an inverted, unnatural constellation. But amongst the learned and well-read one finds that this sort of thing is often encountered among the Greeks and Romans, although this is to be ascribed rather to the evil customs of those corrupted nations, plagued by sins, than to the course of the heavens or stars.[35]

Because of her erotic behavior, Greta is considered by many to be a hermaphrodite; nonetheless, she is revealed as "a true, proper woman" after being "investigated by cunning." Such investigations into the truth of bodily morphology were serious, and sometimes highly public, occasions. Three separate medical commissions examined the case of Marie le Marcis, who in 1601 defended herself against charges of sodomy with her female lover, Jeane, on the grounds that she was a man. Pursued all the way to the Parlement of Rouen, this case of a chambermaid instigated a heated medicolegal debate between Jacques Duval, a provincial physician, and Jean Riolan, professor of anatomy and botany at the University of Paris.

Their published disquisitions hinge on the ideological conflict between the Galenic-Hippocratic belief that hermaphrodites represent an intermediate sex (Duval's position), and the Aristotelian denial of true hermaphroditism and insistence that so-called hermaphrodites simply possess doubled or redundant genitalia (Riolan's position).[36] Whereas the Aristotelian model of reproductive anatomy tended to dominate, a mid-sixteenth-century resurgence of interest in Hippocratic theories redirected attention to the erotic possibilities posed by the hermaphrodite's gender ambiguity.[37] Within France, legal proceedings to determine the hermaphrodite's dominant sex increasingly focused on the possibility of sexual fraud and malfeasance; thus they depended more on the external testimony of medical experts than on the hermaphrodite's self-description or articulation of desires.

The difference between being judged a hermaphrodite or a tribade, then, was as crucial as it was uncertain. A further contribution to the confusion was the status of clothing as a signifier of identity. Discourses about hermaphrodites,

65

tribades, female sodomites, and spontaneous transsexuals were also discourses about cross-dressing. During this period of unprecedented geographical exploration, warfare, and colonization, many women took advantage of the rise in social status that a change in clothing could bring about. Under the cover of male dress, women's migration to urban centers, service as a soldier or shipmate, and immigration to the New World afforded them new opportunities for social advancement. Popular street ballads, broadsheets, and prose narratives extolled the exploits of female soldiers and sailors who accomplished heroic deeds while successfully passing as men—especially if they did so in order to accompany husbands or male lovers into battle.[38]

However, despite avid interest in tales of passing women, in many continental countries cross-dressing (legally considered a form of fraud) was a serious, even a capital, offense.[39] Although English sumptuary legislation regulated status boundaries rather than gender, and it is probably the case that very few women actually cross-dressed, the anxiety that cross-dressing would become a viable fashion was still evident: during the height of the pamphlet controversy about the nature of women in the early years of the seventeenth century, King James of England and Scotland instructed clergymen to preach against women wearing masculine accoutrements such as doublets and swords.

Much of the social anxiety expressed about women's transvestism had more to do with concerns about their lewdness with men than with homoerotic transgressions. Most female cross-dressers whose tales are recorded profess to have adopted masculine identities in order to pursue adventure, economic gain, or the men who had abandoned them. However, some of them were motivated by their own commitment to "female masculinity" and/or their attachments to other women.[40] Exposure was sometimes the result of a sexual liaison, as in an account published in *The Gentleman's Journal: Or the Monthly Miscellany* (April 1692), which speaks approvingly of an English soldier who

served two years in the French Army in Piedmont as a volunteer, and was entertained for her merit by the Governor of Pignerol in the quality of his Gentlemen of the Horse; at last playing with another of her sex, she was discover'd; and the Governor having thought fit to inform the King his master of this, he hath sent him word that he would be glad to see the lady; which hath occasion'd her coming to Genoa, in order to embark for France: Nature has bestow'd no less beauty on her than courage; and her age is not above 26. The French envoy hath orders to cause her to be waited on to Marseille, and to furnish her with all necessaries.[41]

Other accounts from England, France, Germany, and the Netherlands document female cross-dressers marrying women, and often attest to the wife's sexual satisfaction, as well as to her knowledge (whether before or after marriage) of her "husband's" sex. The three "autobiographies" of Catalina de Erauso, a cross-dressing Basque conquistador, as well as a play written about her, recount her amorous flirtations with Spanish ladies in the New World.[42]

More prosaically, a London Consistory Court document details the annulment of a marriage contracted between Arabella Hunt and her "female husband," Amy Poulter (a.k.a. James Howard).[43] In her suit for annulment, apparently brought after six months of cohabitation, Hunt maintained that, when they married in 1680, Poulter had been legally married to a husband still living, that she alternated dressing as a woman and a man, and that she was "of a double gender." Although Poulter freely admitted to the first two charges, and asserted that she had married Hunt on a lark, she flatly denied being a hermaphrodite—a denial supported by the five midwives who subsequently examined her. Because she was deemed "a perfect woman in all her parts"—that is, complete and without defect—she was not held liable for bigamy (two women could not contract a valid marriage) and neither she nor Hunt were charged with a crime. In fact, the Court determined them free to remarry—as long as the husband was a man. Neither, however, did.[44]

These documents and narratives of female masculinity, tribadism, hermaphroditism, and sex transformation tell us little about the subjective experience of women's erotic desires and practices. In *Hunt vs. Poulter*, for instance, the ecclesiastical court was concerned with the legal status of their marriage, not their personal motivations. These texts do tell us, however, about some of the conditions under which women's erotic activities with other women were construed as a social problem. Such a construal, it is important to note, was not inevitable. Female-female eroticism was not universally or uniformly scandalous, or even criminal.[45] An informal allegation lodged against Susannah Bell, for instance, occurs only in the context of a proceeding against her previous husband, Ralph Hollingsworth, who was sued by his later wife, Maria Seely, in 1694 for bigamy. In his defense documented in the London Consistory Court, Hollingsworth describes Susannah: "now as to Susannah Bell: she knowing her infirmity ought not to have married; her infirmity is such that no man can lie with her, and because it so she has ways with women as well, as with her old companions men, which is not fit to be named but most rank whorish they are."[46] Whatever "infirmity" Susannah had (a small vaginal opening? an enlarged clitoris?) that prompted her to have "ways with women," she was not prosecuted for her behavior; her bigamist husband was.

It usually took some extraordinary circumstance to motivate a community to involve local officials or for such officials to embark on a legal proceeding. As Hull remarks of criminal prosecution in general: "The prosecution of sexual crimes was at the mercy of the local populace: they provided the original information for indictment, the testimony at the trial, and the audience for public punishments. If the parties to a dispute arising from sexual behavior could solve the problem among themselves, then the authorities might never hear of it."[47] It appears that female-female intimacy did not, on its own, generally occasion sufficient concern to warrant the involvement of authorities. Several court cases were initiated, not because of community outrage, but because one of the women sought a legal annulment, generally after several months, or even years, of cohabitation. Those women who *were* accused of sodomy, tribadism, or hermaphroditism seem to have gained local notoriety prior to their prosecution, whether through flagrant cross-dressing, prostitution, vagrancy, or dissenting religious beliefs. Often they were strangers, wayfarers from other locales. Among those unfortunate women, it generally was the woman who cross-dressed or used penetrative devices who received harsher punishment than her ostensibly more "feminine" partner—a system of punishment that both derived from and enforced a prevalent assumption that illicit female liaisons were governed by a logic of gender imitation.

To recognize the contingencies of prosecution is not to deny the lethal energies exercised against women who came to the attention of authorities, but rather to insist that the history of lesbianism is not one of unrelieved oppression. Homophobia itself is a historically specific and variable phenomenon, deployed intermittently and under certain social conditions.[48] Many female-female couples may have lived unremarked by their neighbors and therefore unmolested by the law. With regard to a sodomy trial of 1477, for instance, Helmut Puff maintains that the "female husband" Katherina Hetzeldorfer had "shared at least part of her secret with individual members of Speyer's urban community."[49] The cohabitation of female couples may have been spoken about as different or strange, but may not have been a particular community concern. Such couples may have been subject to good-natured or ill-favored gossip, or to community harassment short of legal action. Even when subjected to official scrutiny, however, women were not censured uniformly. Whereas Elpeth Faulds and Margaret Armour were excommunicated by the Glasgow Presbytery, the London Consistory Court acted with indifference to the marital cross-dressing of Amy Poulter/James Howard.

Several female transvestites in sixteenth-century France and Spain were executed, while Catalina de Erauso was awarded a military pension for her colonial services by Philip IV and special permission from Pope Urban XIII to continue dressing as a man.

Such conceptual and material contradictions suggest that there is no one history of lesbianism in early modern Europe and the Americas. Rather, there are multiple histories, each of them dependent upon complex and sometimes competing ideologies of gender, social status, and authority—not to mention the different personalities involved. Variations in local standards of morality and tolerance of diversity, contending medical cultures and contradictory "truths" about anatomy and physiology, and the evolving contests between church and state all had an impact on the construction and treatment of early modern lesbianism. Traversed by different discourses and subject to a variety of cultural investments, women interested in other women pursued erotic adventure, pleasure, and satisfaction by seeking modes of accommodation within the patriarchal landscape they inhabited.

Few women were directly affected by allegations of transvestism, tribadism, hermaphroditism, or sex transformation. Another discourse, however, had a direct if equivocal impact on the bodies of all early modern women. The ideology of chastity, an element of Catholic doctrine that continued in secular form after the Reformation, provided the sine qua non of women's social status. As the humanist educator Juan Luis Vives put it, "chastity is the principal virtue of a woman, and counterpeiseth with all the rest. If she have that, no man will look for any other; and if she lack that, no man will regard other."[50] Despite doubts among anatomists about the hymen's existence and its reliability as a sign of virginity, the intact hymen popularly was considered the guarantor of female virtue.[51] Yet, because the discourse of chastity figured the threat of phallic penetration as the only socially intelligible form of erotic congress—as the only erotic practice that *mattered*—a range of other erotic behaviors, technically chaste, might be pursued by adolescents and adult women. Adolescent Russian and Italian girls, for instance, regularly played mock wedding games, physically enacting the erotic positions and actions of husband and wife; because none of them possessed a penis or wielded a dildo, their erotic play was considered a harmless preparation for adult marital roles.[52]

The contradictory social functions of chastity dovetailed with the material conditions of the early modern English household. As Lena Cowen Orlin makes clear, most house chambers, including bedchambers, were "communal and multipurpose," while beds themselves (relatively expensive household furniture) were located "in nearly every conceivable space—halls, parlors, stair landings, outbuildings, and kitchens, as well as bedchambers." Orlin's larger point—that boundaries between the private and public had not yet settled into their modern binary configuration—is supported by surviving floor plans and household inventories, all of which suggest "that privacy was not an object of the architecture of the period."[53] Nor was it the object of individuals, for, as Hull notes, "no one expected 'privacy' in the modern sense, where solitude is simultaneously a sign that the sexual act is nobody's business, that it is not social. Early modern Europeans assumed just the reverse; transparency was therefore not just the product of limited spatial resources (few separate bedrooms), it was positively desirable."[54] The architectural constraints on privacy and social expectations of communal life, congruent as they were with the ideology of chastity, insured that throughout Europe and across social rank, adolescent girls as well as married and unmarried adult women regularly shared beds with kinswomen, female friends, and servants. What Margaret Hunt says of laboring singlewomen in the eighteenth century is true for the earlier period:

Girls from poor and middling families generally began working very young. . . . At some point between about age ten and fifteen many of them were put out to service or (less often) apprenticeships. . . . The standard assumption was that they would save their money . . . so as to be able to marry some time in their mid- to late twenties. During this lengthy period, often fifteen or more years, they habitually slept in the same bed with a succession of other girls or women, other female servants if there were any, the daughters of other women of the household, or not uncommonly, the mistress of the house herself. . . . Many female servants would have experienced the sleeping arrangements of half a dozen households before they turned thirty, and that during a period when they were lonely, often deprived of affection, and, at least part of the time, at a high libidinal pitch. The potential this system offered for risk-free, same-sex erotic activity was very great.[55]

With sharing beds a usual practice in households across the social spectrum, bodily intimacy conserved heat, fostered companionship, and enabled erotic contact.[56] We should not forget that the miraculous female-to-male sex transformation at Reimes reported to Paré supposedly occurred while the woman "played somewhat wantonly with a maid which lay in the same bed with him"—an activity that warrants no comment from Paré.[57]

The invitation to a woman to lie with her mistress or a noblewoman was considered a privileged sign of favor.[58] In a letter written in 1605 by Lady Anne Clifford to her mother, Anne apologizes for her inability to go "to Oxford, according to your Ladyship's desire with my Lady Arbella [Stuart], and to have slept in her chamber, which she much desired, for I am the more bound to her than can be, but my Lord would not have me go with the Court thither."[59] The sharing of beds with female intimates seems to have been an expected, yet nonetheless highly emotive, occurrence in Lady Anne's life. In her diary she records that, in punishment for having ridden a horse alone with a man, her mother instructed that she should sleep alone in her room. This, Lady Anne writes, "I could not endure, but my Cozen Frances got the Key of my Chamber and lay with me which was the first time I loved hir so verie well."[60] "Loved hir so verie well"—Anne's affection for her kinswoman Lady Frances Bourchier, with whom she slept on other occasions, is expressed in the ambiguous, yet overlapping, terms of aristocratic kinship and passionate friendship.[61]

Further down the social scale—indeed, outside the household proper—the bedding down of two indigent women is briefly noted by Thomas Harman who, in his epistle dedication to the Countess of Shrewsbury in his *Caveat or Warening for Commen Cursetors*, describes the funeral of a gentleman:

at his buryall there was such a number of beggers, besides poore housholders dwelling there abouts, that unneath [with difficulty] they mighte lye or stande aboute the House: then was there prepared for them a great and a large barne, and a great fat ox sod out in Furmenty [wheat boiled in milk] for them, with bread and drinke aboundantly to furnesh out the premises; and every person had two pence, for such was the dole. When Night approched, the pore housholders repaired home to their houses: the other wayfaring bold beggers remained alnight in the barne; and the same barne being serched with light in the night by this old man (and then yonge), with others, they tolde seven score persons of men, every of them having his woman, except it were two wemen that lay alone to gether for some especyall cause. Thus hauing their makes to make mery withall, the buriall was turned to bousing and belly chere, morning to myrth, fasting to feasting, prayer to pastyme and pressing of papes, and lamenting to Lechery.[62]

In his analysis of Harman's censure of these "wayfaring bold beggars," Daryl Palmer points out that for Harman, "When plebeians take hold of hospitality, they overturn all, reversing every positive value . . . in an alliterative welter of 'pastime and pressing.' Even sexual preference submits to revision."[63] Of interest here is that whereas Harman condemns the beggars in general, no special condemnation is reserved for the two women. Whatever the "especial cause" for them to "lay alone to gether," it evidently is not one that much troubles Harman.

Further archival research into local social conditions and controversies no doubt will nuance this synopsis, and enable more specific studies of temporal changes as well as comparative analyses of national, religious, political, and community differences. Wills, household itineraries, correspondence, and funeral monuments all need to be scrutinized with an eye on people's outlook on the ways women lived and loved. But even with the expectation that our knowledge base will change as such materials come to light, we know enough now to inform our reading, as well as future performances, of Shakespeare's plays.

The homoeroticism entailed in Shakespearean cross-dressing has already been analyzed by several critics, myself included; indeed, interest in theatrical transvestism—whether that of the boy actor playing female roles or that of the cross-dressed heroine—offered literary critics an initial point of access to the textualization of homoerotic desire. Let us consider briefly one cross-dressing play that has figured centrally in critical discussion of Shakespearean gender and sexuality. In *Twelfth Night*, when Viola/Cesario confronts the implications of a love token sent to her by Olivia, she denounces her own masculine costume, describes disguise as a wickedness and herself as a "poor monster" (2.2.34). As many commentators have recognized, in condemning herself as a monster, Cesario employs the vernacular term for hermaphrodite,[64] while also indicating the "poor" nature of her sexual equipment. No critic, however, has pursued the erotic rather than gender implications of this association by taking up the historical point that hermaphrodites often were accused of being tribades and forced to undergo a medical examination. Similarly, Cesario's oft-cited bawdy joke just prior to being forced into a duel with Sir Andrew—"A little thing would make me tell them how much I lack of a man" (3.4.302–3)—has been interpreted as a comically abject double entendre that resounds against women's anatomy. Critics have neglected to notice that these repeated invocations of anatomical "lack" implicitly invite the audience to perform imaginatively the kind of scopic investigation a woman accused of tribadism might face. Cesario's allusion to the absence of a penis wittily avows the feminine nature of her body, but it also begs the question: why is this avowal necessary?

In contemporary criticism Cesario's self-indictment implicitly has served as a summation of early modern attitudes toward female homoeroticism: any woman desirous of another woman could only be viewed as monstrous. Yet this orthodox position is precisely what much of the action of the play contests. The meaning of femininity has been called into question not only by Cesario's masculine costume—which, despite the audience's awareness of the ruse, is convincing enough to fool the other characters—but also by her obvious delight in playing the erotic part of the man. Both the enjoyment with which she stands in for Orsino in wooing Olivia and the extent to which she elicits Olivia's desire carry a potent homoerotic charge. As a surrogate for the Duke, Cesario speaks some of the most beautiful love lyrics in the play. In response to Olivia's question about how she would love her, Cesario vows that she would

> Make me a willow cabin at your gate,
> And call upon my soul within the house;
> Write loyal cantons of contemned love
> And sing them loud even in the dead of night;
> Halloo your name to the reverberate hills,
> And make the babbling gossip of the air
> Cry out "Olivia!" O, you should not rest
> Between the elements of air and earth
> But you should pity me! (1.5.263–71)

It is as object of another woman's desire that Cesario finds her own erotic voice. Olivia's response to this wooing—"You might do much" (272)—marks the moment when the mournful lady gives her heart to the woman she takes for a man.[65] The erotic tension between Cesario and Olivia (and the pleasure the audience takes in this tension) does much to explain why Cesario does not forsake her masculine costume when the confusions her impersonation have wrought threaten her with violence. What is more, the emphasis at the play's conclusion on finding Cesario's "women's weeds" (5.1.270) so as to reconfirm her female gender, gestures toward common legal practice regarding confirmed hermaphrodites.

Recognition of the eroticism entailed in moments that call attention to her gender bending allows us better to understand Cesario's desire for Orsino, not in terms of her character's capitulation to romantic love (by which standards it is palpably incomprehensible, as many commentators admit), but in terms of the structural force of the courtship plot. Because marriage and service are presented as the only legitimate social currencies in this drama, the drive toward marriage (and out of service) overpowers the erotic play—and the erotic wit—that is at the heart of *Twelfth Night*'s theatrical magic.[66] The erotic friction between Olivia and Cesario, which intensifies until Cesario is threatened with bodily harm, is resolved structurally rather than characterologically with the substitution of Sebastian for Cesario. In the course of the play's action, Shakespeare teases his audience with a culturally available, if implicit, association between cross-dressers, hermaphrodites, and tribades; then, through the force of the marriage plot, the audience's attention ultimately is directed away from the specter of such erotic possibilities. Contemporary directors of *Twelfth Night* thus have a choice: they can dramatize the associations between Cesario's transgressions of gender and eroticism, or they can minimize such connections in a production shorn of the queerness of history.[67]

Let us next consider at greater length *A Midsummer Night's Dream*, one of Shakespeare's most popular,[68] and ostensibly one of his most heterosexual, plays.[69] Unlike *Twelfth Night, As You Like It, The Merchant of Venice,* and *The Two Gentlemen of Verona*, no cross-dressing female character authorizes a homoerotic reading of this play. Rather, in its story of the Athenian lovers, *A Midsummer Night's Dream* depicts a close female friendship disrupted by jealousy and competition for men. But just as the gender politics in this play are fractured and inconsistent, presenting, as Louis Montrose has argued, early modern "precepts of domestic authority" as a matter of contestation and dispute, so too the erotic politics of this play convey a variety of affections and desires that must be rejected or elided for the courtship plot to conclude in patriarchal marriage.[70] If these alternative desires do not interrupt the structural movement toward the blessing of the bride bed in the final act (indeed, one could argue that they provide part of the foundation for that movement), they nonetheless register, *behind the seen*, a range of female affiliations. Rather than offer a reading of *A Midsummer Night's Dream*, in what follows I employ the play heuristically, using its representational traces of female intimacy to speculate further about possible sites of homoerotic desire.

Both the possibility and structural elision of female intimacy are intimated early in the play when Hermia begins to unfold to Helena her plan to elope with Lysander: "in the wood where often you and I / Upon faint primrose beds were wont to lie, / Emptying our bosoms of their counsel sweet, / There my Lysander and myself shall meet" (1.1.214–17). The place where, day after day, these close friends chatted, relaxed, sought and offered advice, has now become the place of heterosexual assignation, as girlhood affections are displaced by the social imperatives of patriarchal marriage. But rather than simply reiterate the structural exigencies of the conventional courtship plot, and thereby reassert without question the force of dramatic and ideological orthodoxy, let us focus for a moment on the significance of the primrose *bed*. Although the phrase refers to flowers rather than a piece of furniture, it nonetheless is significant that beds are thematized elsewhere in Renaissance literature as an ambiguous site of hetero- and homoerotic contact, especially in the genre of romance. For instance, in Book Four of Edmund Spenser's *The Faerie Queene*, the cross-dressed amazon Britomart interacts so amorously with the lady Amoret that Dorothy Stephens writes, "Britomart dallies more with Amoret than she ever does with [the male knight] Artegall, and it is tempting to say that at this stage of the game, she mostly feigns [as a man] in order to flirt [with a woman]. By keeping her helmet on, Britomart can afford to raise the dialogue to a higher erotic pitch, engaging in a closer intimacy than would otherwise be allowable."[71] At the same time, Britomart's removal of her helmet is swiftly followed by an "innocent" invitation to Amoret's bed:

And eke fayre Amoret now freed from feare,
More franke affection did to her afford,
And to her bed, which she was wont forbeare,
Now freely drew, and found right safe assurance theare.
Where all that night they of their loues did treat,
And hard adventures twixt themselues alone,
That each the other gan with passion great,
And griefull pittie priuately bemoane.[72]

As Stephens notes, this passage is highly if ambiguously erotic, for what, precisely, is the "right safe assurance" found between these women who "now freed from fear, More frank affection" show one another? How precisely "of their loues did [they] treat," and which "hard adventures twixt themselues alone" did they "gan with passion great"? The pronouns provide no sure anchoring of who is doing what to whom.

Just as Spenser maintains the chastity of this feminine sleep-over while exploiting its erotic ambiguity, so Sir Philip Sidney mingles eroticism with chaste intimacy in the *New Arcadia* (written for his sister, Mary Sidney, the Countess of Pembroke, and her circle). Lying in bed together, the sisters Pamela and Philoclea "impoverished their clothes to enrich their bed which for that night might well scorn the shrine of Venus: and there, cherishing one another with dear though chaste embracements, with sweet though cold kisses, it might seem that love was come to play him there without dart, or that, weary of his own fires, he was there to refresh himself between their sweetbreathing lips."[73] As Stephen Orgel remarks about this passage: "I do not think it can be argued that such a scene would not have been considered overtly sexual in 1590: Sidney's insistence that the embracements were chaste, the kisses cold, are surely there to contradict the inevitable assumption that they were, respectively, libidinous and hot."[74]

By the early seventeenth century in England, the pleasures of the shared bed are common enough currency to be explicitly debated in Thomas Dekker's stage play, *Satiromastix: Or The Untrussing of the Humorous Poet* (1602).[75] A gentlewoman asks her "bedfellow" why people bring "sweet herbes and flowers" to weddings; the second gentlewoman responds: "One reason is, because tis—ô a most sweet thing to lye with a man." The first gentlewoman replies, "I thinke tis a ô more more more more more sweet to lye with a woman"—a remark that incites the bawdy reply, "I warrant all men are of thy minde" (1.1.16–21). In Richard Brome's play, *The Antipodes* (1640), a similar reference to maids lying in bed becomes the means for emphasizing a married woman's ignorance and, not incidentally, an occasion for homoerotic bawdiness.[76] Martha Joyless, suffering from a melancholy straight out of Robert Burton, is upset that her marriage has never been consummated: "He ne'er put child, nor anything toward it yet / To me to making" (1.4.41–42). At the same time, she expresses ignorance about the actual means of making children:

> For were I now to die, I cannot guess
> What a man does in child-getting. *I remember*
> *A wanton maid once lay with me, and kiss'd*
> *And clipp'd and clapp'd me strangely, and then wish'd*
> *That I had been a man to have got her with child.*
> What must I then ha' done, or (good now, tell me)
> What has your husband done to you?

Barbara, her interlocutor, says in an aside, "Was ever / Such a poor piece of innocence three years married!" She then asks directly: "Does not your husband use to lie with you?" Martha's answer is full of earnest ignorance:

> Yes, he does use to lie with me, but he does not
> Lie with me to use me as he should, I fear;
> Nor do I know to teach him. Will you tell me?
> *I'll lie with you and practise, if you please.*
> *Pray take me for a night or two,* or take
> My husband and instruct him but one night.
> Our country folks will say you London wives
> Do not lie every night with your own husbands. (1.4.54–70, emphases mine)

The focus throughout is on Martha's "simplicity" which leads her into unintentional puns (75); not only is she willing to expose her ignorance of sexual matters, but she is so eager for instruction that she would place her husband in Barbara's bed. But her lack of knowledge about the mechanics of intercourse is curiously accommodating to her memory of a "wanton maid" who kissed, clipped, and clapped her. Indeed, this experience is depicted as Martha's only source of erotic knowledge, including the knowledge that women cannot impregnate one another. That "clipping and clapping" are glossed by the editors first as "embraced and patted," then amended with the suggestion that clapped "may imply something more firmly administered; 'slap and tickle' is a recent equivalent," suggests that the maid's wantonness defies gendered expectations of activity and passivity. Her behavior, which takes the form of aggressive, even forceful erotic play along with the desire to be penetrated, provides a mirror to Martha's own ecumenical position regarding whether it be she or her husband to receive erotic instruction from Barbara.

In his analysis of the passage from *Satiromastix*, Mario DiGangi stresses how a "woman's desire for a woman can be more safely represented within the confines of a conditional statement that suggests her 'proper' desire for a man"—a description broadly applicable to the situations of the romance heroines discussed above. He reads the second gentlewoman's bawdy repartee as serving "to erase or subsume female homoeroticism by shifting the terrain away from any consideration of a female desiring subject towards the heteroerotic desire felt by 'all men.'"[77]

This recognition of the move toward ideological containment is an accurate appraisal, from which any further analysis of the representation of homoeroticism must devolve. But the critical focus on the power of restraint also evacuates the agency of the characters and thus reproduces the containment it seeks to expose. While I agree that attempts to minimize and trivialize are a regular feature of representations of female erotic intimacy, I am not convinced that this feature actually accomplishes what it sets out to do; in the very act of articulating alternatives, a fault line in the dominant ideology is exposed. The ideology of chastity depends on the belief that, although women may share beds, caresses, and kisses, such phenomena do not "count" as sex. Yet what "counts" is precisely what is thematized in both these plays, and however they may attempt to mitigate a homoerotic response (in either the dramatic character or the audience/reader) their efforts at containment are insecure.

In *The Antipodes*, part of what is at stake in this private talk among women is knowledge about eroticism, including female-female sex. In *Satiromastix*, efforts to control behavior are undermined by the rhetoric of amplitude employed by the first gentlewoman. Her insistence that it is "more more more more sweet to lye with a woman" not only poses a challenge to the second woman's initial characterization of what is "most sweet," but does so through a quantifying idiom that appropriates and destabilizes the conventional patriarchal surety that phallic male (hetero)sexuality is the *more*, compared to the woman's *less*. In both cases, the overt bawdiness suggests a cultural awareness of the presence, as well as the ambiguous epistemological status, of female-female eroticism.

In each of these instances, the trope of the household (or primrose) bed suggests that specific physical spaces provided women access to bodily intimacy away from the scrutiny of fathers and husbands. As recent work on place and space informs us, one's physical location within a specific locale or geography informs the subjectivity constructed therein; space is not just a backdrop for the subject, it helps to constitute the subject and her desires.[78] Approaching the history of lesbianism through spatial terms allows us to see the potential for female-female intimacy that existed alongside the oft-noted trope of the female *hortus conclusus* or "the body enclosed."[79] For whereas the dominant ideology maintained that the closed door of the household contributed to a closed body and closed mouth,[80] certain enclosures *within* the patriarchal household—the bed, the bedchamber— might have been productive of female affectivity, where bodies and mouths sought and found their own pleasures. Thus, although we would err in conceptualizing early modern beds and bedchambers as private, they nevertheless seem to have functioned as a space *between* visibilities: their very "transparency," to invoke Hull, seems to have sanctioned an erotic architecture eccentric to patriarchal mandates. The *hortus conclusus*, in other words, may have functioned occasionally as a *locus amoenus*.

Certain enclosures located *outside* the household may also have permitted some women a space of independence and intimacy. One such locus was the convent. As "brides of Christ," nuns were relieved of many of the duties of patriarchal marriage, including reproductive labor. They experienced considerable opportunities for political, emotional, and erotic independence within a female community of work and support that, while geographically and politically marginal, nonetheless figured importantly even in a post-Reformation culture. The ambivalent relation of female monastic life to patriarchal culture has been explored by a generation of feminists; and although it is not my intent to claim the cloister as a de facto lesbian space, I do want to insist on its potential as a site for erotic contact.[81]

Martin Luther set the tone of much anti-Catholic polemic when he characterized Catholic monks as whores of the devil, the Pope as an arch whore, and the
Church as the whore's anus. Given Luther's association of popery with sodomitical vice, it is hardly surprising that anti-Catholic polemic alleged that nuns performed all manner of "unnatural vice." Although most frequently nuns were accused of fornication with monks and priests, the litany of debauchery was obses-
sively inclusive. In *Actes of the Englishe Votaryes*, for instance, the radical Puritan
John Bale presents the nun as one among others who, with their "prodygyouse
lustes of uncleanesse . . . leavying the naturall use of women . . . have brent in their
owne lustes one to an other, . . . man wyth man . . . monke with monke, nonne
with nonne, fryre with fryre & prest with prest." In Bale's diatribe, chastity itself
is "a fylthy Sodome," for the church of Rome is a "preposterus *amor*, a love out of
order or a love agaynst kynde."[82] In this logic, same-sex transgressions are fostered
by the innate hypocrisy of Catholics and the deprivations of sex-segregation: celibate, and therefore burning in lust, the wily nun is imagined to satisfy her lust either with other hypocrites like herself or, particularly egregious, with unsuspect-
ing novitiates.

Other literary texts continue to exploit the connection between women's eroticism, gender separatism, and heresy up through the religious upheavals of the
seventeenth century. These associations provide a central trope, for instance, for
Andrew Marvell's "Upon Appleton House," which figures the nun's "slippery
tongue" as the agent of a religious and erotic apostasy, a kind of "spiritual cun-
nilingus,"[83] even as the nuns themselves bespeak their homoerotic desire in terms
of chaste insignificance:

Each Night among us to your side
Appoint a fresh and Virgin Bride;
Whom if our Lord at midnight find,
Yet Neither should be left behind.
Where you may lye as chast in Bed,
As Pearls together billeted.
All Night embracing Arm in Arm,
Like Chrystal pure with Cotton warm.[84]

By the time Shakespeare began writing plays, English monasteries and con-
vents had been dissolved by royal decree, and English Catholics had become a persecuted minority; hence, convent life was unattainable to any except the most
elite of Catholic daughters, who were sent to the continent, particularly northern

France, for education by their recusant families.[85] Nonetheless, the nunnery appears frequently in Shakespeare's plays, usually as a metaphor for the bawdy (Hamlet's imperious command to Ophelia to "get thee to a nunnery" puns on the double meaning of nunnery as convent and brothel) or as an indication of perverse female willfulness (Isabella's determination to enter the novitiate in *Measure for Measure*). Women's religious vocation consistently is viewed by male characters as a fate worse than death, as when, in *A Midsummer Night's Dream*, Duke Theseus pronounces this edict on what will befall Hermia if she refuses to wed Demetrius:

> Either to die the death, or to abjure
> Forever the society of men.
> Therefore, fair Hermia, question your desires,
> Know of your youth, examine well your blood,
> Whether, if you yield not to your father's choice,
> You can endure the livery of a nun,
> For aye to be in shady cloister mew'd,
> To live a barren sister all your life,
> Chanting faint hymns to the cold fruitless moon.
> Thrice blessed they that master so their blood
> To undergo such maiden pilgrimage;
> But earthlier happy is the rose distill'd,
> Than that which withering on the virgin thorn
> Grows, lives, and dies in single blessedness. (1.1.65–78)

Despite Theseus's post-Reformation vision of a withered, barren virginity, the threat of abjuring "forever the society of men" and "enduring the livery of a nun" may not have been the correlative to death that he and scores of critics have made it out to be.[86] Hermia's appropriation of Theseus's rhetoric in her answer, "So will I grow, so live, so die, my lord" (1.1.79), resourcefully affirms the possibility of growth and life within a religious sisterhood. I am not suggesting that Hermia is represented as *wanting* to enter the novitiate; this character wants to marry Lysander. Yet it is important to recognize that, faced with what Theseus figures as a kind of death, Shakespeare permits Hermia to imagine a kind of life. And monastic life, for thousands of actual women across Europe, undoubtedly meant that their most generative and sustaining bonds were found in the company of other women.

That Hermia has been the recipient of intense female affection is clear from Helena's reminiscence about their friendship:

We, Hermia, like two artificial gods,
Have with our needles created both one flower,
Both on one sampler, sitting on one cushion,
Both warbling of one song, both in one key,
As if our hands, our sides, voices, and minds
Had been incorporate. (3.2.203–8)

As Sylvia Gimenez observes, *A Midsummer Night's Dream* associates female intimacies with all-female spaces that in various ways elude patriarchal control: in addition to the "primrose bed" and what Gimenez calls Helena and Hermia's adolescent "sewing circle," Hippolyta is queen of Amazonia; Titania and her votaress gossip on the Indian shore; Lysander's widowed aunt lives seven leagues from Athens; and an unnamed vestal virgin wings her way across the sky, away from Cupid's arrow.[87]

The mythical Amazons provided the prototype of female autonomy in this period. Their alleged military prowess, practice of male infanticide, and instrumental use of men for reproduction were considered the height of female insubordination; accordingly, Amazons often were viewed as embodying a dangerous and unnatural political self-sufficiency. According to Louis Montrose, "Amazonian mythology seems symbolically to embody and to control a collective anxiety about the power of the female not only to dominate or reject the male but to create and destroy him."[88] Both Montrose and Kathryn Schwarz imply that legends about Amazons at the margins of the known world are a repository of male castration anxiety: "Amazon myth plays out the fear that the object of desire, the body looked at or, in the case of the Amazon quest, looked *for*, may itself possess sexual agency: that all women might be sexually voracious, given half a chance."[89] Given this emphasis on the Amazons' agency and hostility to men (not to mention the European predisposition to view foreign women as unnatural in their sexual tastes), it seems worthwhile to ask whether Amazons ever were associated with same-gender desire. In general, Amazons seem not to have been interpreted routinely as erotic separatists. According to Schwarz, "the Amazons of English Renaissance texts are aggressively implicated in social structures; in narrative after narrative they are not lesbian separatists or ritualized descendants of goddesses but mothers, lovers, and in some cases wives."[90] In her more recent work, Schwarz modifies this account to note the presence of "a powerful and explicit amazonian discourse of desire between women." The catch, however, "is that one of the women is a man."[91] Yet, one masque performed in 1618 at the country house of

Sir Thomas Beaumont suggests that the move from female separatism to erotic separatism was neither far-fetched nor dependent necessarily on transvestism. Performed as a country-house entertainment celebrating the wedding of Lady Frances Devereux and Sir William Seymour, the Cole-Orton masque figures six female masquers representing the traditional feminine virtues.[92] With their masculine counterparts mysteriously imprisoned by Juno and Iris, the women masquers descend onstage while a song encourages them to enact "the precedencie of female virtue":

> Rejoice, all woman kinde,
> Juno haes her will of Jove.
> Each of you that list to prove,
> shall easie conquest finde.
> Be not, o be not blind,
> But know your strength & your own Vertues see
> which in everie Several grace
> of the mind, or of the face,
> Gives women right to have Prioritie. (334:26–34)

The extraordinary suggestion that women not only deserve equality with men but possess more virtue, leads to the following song:

> Brave Amazonian Dames
> Made no count of Mankind but
> for a fitt to be at the Rutt.
> Free fier gives the brightest flames;
> Menns overawing tames
> And Pedantlike our active Spirits smother.
> Learne, Virgins, to live free;
> Alass, would it might bee,
> woemen could live & lie with one another! (334:35–43)

Penned during the apex of the pamphlet controversy over women's roles and explicitly staging social and amorous conflict between men and women, the Cole-Orton masque expresses in this song the fantasy of women living apart from men, taking one another as sexual partners, and making no account of men except for erotic pleasure (with a possible bawdy pun on "count" as cunt). The heavily conditional nature of the two final lines, however, attempts to undercut precisely this fantasy by reinscribing the conventional topos of impossibility; and, indeed, this portion of the masque concludes with a dance celebrating the equality and harmony of masculine and feminine virtues, figured through the trope of male-female coupling:

> Mix then and together goe,
> This be hers, and that be thine;
> All jarrs end by coupling so,
> 'Tis not long to Valentine. (335:30–33)

In this instance at least, mythological Amazons provided the masque audience with a titillating vision of a world in which women "could live & lie with one another," while also reasserting the impossibility of such a world.

Hippolyta, of course, has been wooed by Theseus's sword, her love won by the injuries done to her (1.1.16–17). If her martial courtship renders Hippolyta's female separatism and possible erotic connections a thing of the past (a view reiterated by another Hippolyta in Shakespeare and Fletcher's *The Two Noble Kinsmen*), the faerie queen Titania carries the implications of her female intimacies into her marital present. In a speech both seductive and troubling, Titania describes her relationship with the mother of the "Indian boy," who is the ostensible cause of the conflict between her and Oberon:

> The fairy land buys not the child of me.
> His mother was a vot'ress of my order,
> And in the spiced Indian air, by night,
> Full often hath she gossiped by my side,
> And sat with me on Neptune's yellow sands,
> Marking th' embarked traders on the flood,
> When we have laughed to see the sails conceive
> And grow big-bellied with the wanton wind;
> Which she with pretty and with swimming gait
> Following—her womb then rich with my young squire—
> Would imitate, and sail upon the land
> To fetch me trifles, and return again,
> As from a voyage, rich with merchandise.
> But she, being mortal, of that boy did die.
> And for her sake do I rear up her boy;
> And for her sake I will not part with him. (2.1.122–37)

This friendship, which has survived marriage, the bearing of children, and death, remains so compelling that Titania risks the wrath of Oberon by refusing to relinquish the child. That the "lovely boy" was "stolen" from his father, an "Indian king" (2.1.22), evidently at Titania's behest, makes clear that what is at stake in this domestic quarrel is Titania's assertion of female affection and autonomy over the authority of both father figures. Titania is psychologically threatening precisely to the degree that she upsets the homosocial "traffic in women" formally negotiated by Egeus and Theseus in the opening scene, and implicitly played out by Demetrius and Lysander in the forest.[93] By inverting the gendered relations of the homosocial triangle, Titania not only "effeminizes" the boy but usurps patriarchal power, fracturing Oberon's pretension to control. The child is the manifest link of a prior affection between women that is associated with their shared fecundity and maternal largesse. With the repetition of the line, "And for her sake," and her later reiteration that she will not part with the boy, "Not for thy fairy kingdom" (2.1.144), Titania insists on the primacy and loyalty of female bonds. Her affront motivates Oberon's attempt to incapacitate Titania's body, to humiliate her erotically, to capture the boy, and secure him for martial, exclusively masculine, purposes.

Titania's bond with her votaress fails to occasion full admiration, however, for the pleasure she takes in her beloved friend is articulated through a mercantile rhetoric implicated in the colonization of both Old World and New. The Indian boy, after all, has been "stol'n" from his homeland and his father. As Margo Hendricks notes in her reading of Titania's speech: "Titania evokes not only the exotic presence of the Indian woman's native land but also the power of the 'traders' to invade and domesticate India and, aided by the 'wanton wind,' return to Europe 'rich with merchandise.' In Shakespeare's 'poetic geography,' India becomes the commodified space of a racialized feminine eroticism."[94] It is the votaress who serves Titania's fancies, who fetches her trifles; and it is the faerie queen who steals the most fetishized piece of "merchandise" in the play, the dramatic structure of which depends upon a series of psychic and material exchanges (for example, Lysander for Helena in Hermia's affection; Helena for Hermia in Lysander's attraction; Demetrius for Lysander in Helena's attraction; Lysander for Demetrius in Egeus' approval, and so on). Furthermore, the ease with which Titania stands in for the dead loved one, acting as a surrogate mother to the boy, enacts a dubious form of identification and substitution. At the exoticized Indian shore, in the "spiced Indian night air," racial differences, erotic possibilities, and gender identifications intersect in an ambivalent coding of bodies and bonds. If the reputed affection shared between Titania and her votaress complicates the relation between colonized and colonizer, their colonial dynamic equally problematizes their inti-macy, even as it offers an alternative to the patriarchal structures of Oberon's faerie kingdom.

Perhaps the most provocative figure of female erotic autonomy and resistance to patriarchal affiliation in *A Midsummer Night's Dream* is the one about whom we know the least. As Oberon hatches his plan to humiliate Titania, he describes to Puck "a fair vestal throned by the west," whom Cupid attempted to pierce with his arrow. But "Cupid's fiery shaft / [was] Quench'd in the chaste beams of the wat'ry moon, / And the imperial vot'ress passed on, / In maiden meditation, fancy-free" (2.1.161–64). With her story narrated by Oberon as part of the prehis-tory of the dramatic action, this "imperial vot'ress" is an absent presence, never appearing onstage—she literally exists *behind the seen*. Yet it is she who enables all the subsequent action: her escape leads to the "wounding" of the "little western flower" whose magic nectar becomes the faerie potion Puck uses to wreak havoc among Titania and the Athenian lovers. The fact that the vestal virgin remains unpenetrated by Cupid's "fiery shaft" releases into the world a principle of un-controlled libido. Her pharmaceutical ghostly presence disturbs the closure of the courtship plot, for not only do the lovers fall in and out of love based on the po-tion, but Demetrius is never freed from the effects of the drug.[95] That this figure of maidenly integrity and self-sufficiency is connected in scholars' minds to an-other "imperial vot'ress," Queen Elizabeth, provides a point of entry into the chaste erotics of Elizabeth's court.[96]

At the same time, this figure might have evoked more immediate associations. That a virgin might pass on, "in maiden meditation, fancy-free," was not all that unusual in Shakespeare's time. Although patriarchal ideology mandated the trans-fer of daughters directly from the governance of a father to the protection of a hus-band, and in practice marriage was the usual experience of most European women, demographic and legal research reveals that almost 20 percent of adult women in northwestern Europe never married. While reasons for this high rate of lifelong singleness are complex, and proportions varied across region, locale, and time, there were more singlewomen in northern than southern Europe, they were connected more often to poor than elite households, and their proportions grew over the sixteenth and seventeenth centuries.[97] Particularly in urban centers, sin-glewomen often worked outside the home, usually in domestic service or appren-ticeship and sometimes in all-female guilds. Many such women lived in their fathers' or brothers' households; others lived together, often under the auspices of charitable communities (*Beguinages*, widows' hospices, houses for reformed prostitutes, or hospitals for poor and immigrant women). In fact, at any given time, most adult women in England were not married (they were either widowed or never married); in addition, most widows did not remarry. Probably half of all singlewomen headed households or lived alone, and there were more of them doing so than singlemen.[98] In London for much of the seventeenth century, around 15 percent of households were headed by women; the proportion in rural areas hovered around 20 percent.[99] At any moment in time, the number of singlewomen could be significantly higher, if one includes widows and adult women who may have married later. Studies of two English communities at both ends of the early modern period demonstrate the high number of singlewomen: in Coventry in 1523, singlewomen made up at least 38 percent of the adult female population, while in Southampton in 1696, they comprised 35 percent.[100]

A funeral monument located in Westminster Abbey erected near the end of our period testifies to the existence of unmarried women living together in terms that suggest the intensity of their friendships, while also underscoring the compatibility of female intimacies to the early modern household. The monument of Mary Kendall, commissioned by her cousin, Captain Charles Kendall, is located in the chapel of St. John the Baptist.[101] On her tomb, an effigy of Mary Kendall is shown kneeling in prayer. Under her figure, the inscription reads:

This Monument was Erected by Capt. CHARLES KENDALL.

Mrs MARY KENDALL,

Daughter of Thomas Kendall Esqr,	*These admirable Qualitys,*
And of Mrs Mary Hallet, his Wife,	*In which She was eqall'd by Few of her Sex*
Of Killigarth, in Cornwall,	*Surpass'd by None,*
Was born at Westm^r. Nov. 8. 1677.	*Render'd Her every way worthy*
And dy'd at Epsome, March 4. 17^{09/10}.	*Of that close Union & Friendship,*
Having reach'd the full Term	*In which She liv'd, with*
Of her blessed Saviours Life:	*The Lady CATHARINE JONES;*
And study'd to imitate	*And, in testimony of which, She desir'd,*
His spotless Example.	*That even their Ashes, after Death,*
She had great Virtues,	*Might not be divided:*
And as great a desire of Concealing them:	*And therefore, order'd her Selfe*
Was of a Severe Life,	*Here to be interr'd,*
But of an Easy Conversation;	*Where, She knew, that Excellent Lady*
Courteous to All, yet strictly Sincere;	*Design'd one day, to rest,*
Humble, without Meanness;	*Near the Grave of her Belov'd*
Beneficent, without Ostentation;	*And Religious Mother,*
Devout, without Superstition.	*ELIZABETH Countess of RANELAGH.[102]*

Although Mary Kendall may have been married at one time—it is unclear if "Mrs." is merely a title of respect—no mention is made of her husband; rather, her "close Union & Friendship" with Lady Catharine Jones is presented as the defining relationship of her life, one which she hoped to continue after death. At the same time—and this is crucial for our understanding of the meaning accorded to female intimacies in this period—the ties celebrated here are firmly embedded within larger social arrangements. The burial register for Westminster Abbey records not only Mary Kendall's burial on March 13, 1709–10, but also that of Lady Catharine Jones (April 23, 1740) and, as the tomb inscription would lead us to expect, other members of her Ladyship's immediate family: her mother, the Countess of Ranelagh (August 3, 1695); her father, the Right Hon. Richard Jones, Viscount and Earl of Ranelagh (January 10, 1711–12); her sister, Elizabeth the Countess Dowager of Kildare (April 22, 1758). All of them were interred in the small secluded chapel of St. John the Baptist, outside the choir screen on the north side of the high altar.[103]

The monument extolling the relationship of Mary Kendall to Lady Catharine Jones is located, in other words, in what appears to be a family mausoleum of the Earl of Ranelagh. This, plus the fact that Mary Kendall's tomb was erected by Captain Kendall, Mary Kendall's residuary legatee (the son of a merchant, but a gentleman by virtue of his commission), suggests that more is at stake in the material presence of this monument than loving bonds between women. On the one hand, the rhetoric of the inscription, composed as it was by Captain Kendall, publicly marks the link of his family to the family of the Earl of Ranelagh; the "close Union & Friendship" lauded here is not only between two women, but between two families. On the other hand, the creation of a family mausoleum in a church was a practice that, through the payment of burial fees designated for the support of the poor, reenacted in death the social bonds that a household (ideally) was supposed to have had with the society around it. The embeddedness of Mary Kendall's tomb in a network of such obligations does not thereby lessen the import of her love for Lady Catharine, but it does tell us that such love was located, in death as in life, within the household of the Earl of Ranelagh. In this respect, Mary Kendall is lying in death in the same bed with Lady Catharine Jones as she might have in life: within the Earl's household.

Such monuments, of course, are highly ritualized public expressions. While memorializing private grief, they also perform and attempt to construct additional social obligations; their elegiac purpose guarantees that they express ideals which may or may not correlate with actual reality. Nonetheless, these funerary performances prompt me to look more closely at Lysander's description of his widowed aunt in *A Midsummer Night's Dream*:

> I have a widow aunt, a dowager
> Of great revenue, and she hath no child.
> From Athens is her house remote seven leagues;
> And she respects me as her only son.
> There, gentle Hermia, may I marry thee,
> And to that place the sharp Athenian law
> Cannot pursue us. (1.1.157–63)

As is made clear by her "great revenue" and her physical distance from Athens, Lysander's anonymous, childless, and householding aunt exists beyond the dominant structures of patriarchal alliance and marital reproduction. Given the oft-noted correlations between erotic desire and spatial geography in *A Midsummer Night's Dream* (Athens versus the green world), the widow's "remote[ness]" from the "sharp Athenian law" affiliates her less with the patriarchal order (from which she is now widowed) than with the other spaces of female intimacy I have mapped. We can no more speculate about the widow's erotic behavior than we can about Mrs. Kendall's, but the description of neither woman affirms heterosexuality. Without adducing a gay version of "How many children had Lady Macbeth?" we need to remember that the term "widow" signifies a woman's status vis-à-vis patriarchal marriage. It indicates absolutely nothing about eroticism practiced within her household after she becomes its head—its presence, its absence, or its relation to men, its relation to women.

Shakespeare's characters and images in *Twelfth Night* and *A Midsummer Night's Dream* allow us to glimpse the presence of adult singlewomen, including an unmarried heiress, a widow, and nuns, living relatively unencumbered by direct masculine rule. Reading and watching these plays, we can witness the erotic complications occasioned by a female transvestite who elicits and enjoys the desires of another woman. We can hear the pained longings expressed by one character over the loss of her intimate friend, even as they both seek marriage. These understandings, I maintain, were available as well to members of Shakespeare's audience. That audience, as recent theater history has made clear, included significant numbers of women. Queen Elizabeth so delighted in plays that she overruled attempts by City of London authorities to quell disorder by closing the public theaters, countering their civic concerns with the monarchical rejoinder that players needed to rehearse for command performances at court. The Jacobean Queen Anne "was the prime mover behind the great series of masques that were the most distinctive feature of Jacobean Court entertainment,"[104] initiating the practice of the queen and her ladies silently dancing in masques.[105] Charles I's queen, Henrietta Maria, likewise "took command of the royal theatricals, commissioning plays themselves, and where necessary overruling the dramatic censor; she and her ladies not only danced during the masques, but spoke during pastorals, thus incurring the notorious wrath of the Puritan polemicist William Prynne."[106] Such courtly occasions were not uniformly decorous. Costume designs for masques by Inigo Jones, for instance, depict women with bare breasts,[107] and while we do not know if these costumes were used in performance, we do know that during a masque and pastoral of Queen Henrietta Maria, it was "the masculine dress of some of the ladies which raised the eyebrows."[108]

It was not only noblewomen who had access to theatrical entertainments, including plays from the public repertoire performed at court. Merchant wives, apple wives, and fishwives also attended stageplays in the public amphitheaters and, after 1599, in the private theaters in even greater numbers.[109] Prostitutes were such a notable presence in the public theaters that women who attended unaccompanied by husbands, brothers, or fathers risked sexual harassment and moral censure; yet some women defied these constraints on their behavior and, by the 1630s, groups of ladies and citizen wives arranged to view performances unescorted.

Taking into account the historical factors involved in the production and consumption of Renaissance drama, we can see the broad contours of a renaissance of lesbianism operating *behind the seen* of Shakespeare's creation of plot, character, location, and theme. Figures of female desire, affiliation, and affection, while not the center of dramatic action, are part and parcel of even his most heterosexually driven dramatic practice. As Montrose remarks about the gender politics of *A Midsummer Night's Dream*:

It is obvious that theatrical productions and critical readings originating from beyond the cultural time and place of the text's own origin may work against the grain to achieve radically heterodox meanings and effects. But it may also be the case that the appropriative potential of such subsequent acts of interpretation is enabled by Elizabethan cultural variations and contradictions *that have been sedimented in the text of the play at its originary moment of production.*[110]

As we redefine the conditions of lesbian visibility, then, we might strive to enact in Shakespearean productions neither a realist reification of identity categories (for example, Helena announces herself as a self-identified lesbian) nor a post-modern parody of them (the only available mode of homoeroticism is drag), but the staging of the contingency and historicity of such categories. Imagine, for a moment, a production of *A Midsummer Night's Dream* in which Titania's complex and implicitly colonialist affections for her votaress are not minimized but explicitly motivate her resistance to Oberon; in which Helena's anger over Hermia's betrayal is not an object of hilarity or ridicule but an impassioned expression of longing and heartbreak; in which the convent, the widow's house, the Indian shore, Titania's bower, and Amazonia exist as viable (imaginative and material) female spaces. Imagine a production that brings onstage the female affections rendered retrospective by the text, that gives temporary life to Titania's beloved votaress (perhaps even enacting *her* side of the relationship), and that shows us Helena and Hermia exchanging intimacies on their primrose bed, or sitting on one cushion, stitching one sampler. Imagine a production overseen, in other words, by the silent vestal virgin winging on, "in maiden meditation, fancy-free."

Notes

1. William Shakespeare, *A Midsummer Night's Dream* (2.1.161–64). All Shakespeare quotations are taken from *The Complete Works*, ed. David Bevington, 3d ed. (Glenview, Ill.: Scott, Foresman and Company, 1980).
2. Brenda Marshall, Review of *Twelfth Night, The Nashville Scene*, October 28, 1992.
3. Nan Gurley, Letter to the Editor, *The Nashville Scene*, November 4, 1992.
4. In addition to the exchange in *The Nashville Scene*, my thinking about the terms of lesbian performance in Shakespeare was stimulated by two invitations: that of Barbara Bowen to take part in a panel discussion at the New York Queer Theater Conference in April 1995, and that of Margo Hendricks to present a paper at "Behind the Seen: Text, Translation, Performance, a Weekend with Shakespeare," in conjunction with the 1996 Shakespeare Santa Cruz Festival. I thank Barbara and Margo for those opportunities.
5. For the cultural capital of "Shakespeare," see Marjorie Garber in "Shakespeare as Fetish," *Shakespeare Quarterly* 41:2 (1990):242–50.
6. Lynda E. Boose and Richard Burt, eds., *Shakespeare, the Movie: Popularizing the Plays on Film, TV, and Video* (London: Routledge, 1997), 2–3.
7. Lorraine Helms, "Acts of Resistance: The Feminist Player," in Dympna C. Callaghan, Lorraine Helms, and Jyotsna Singh, *The Weyward Sisters: Shakespeare and Feminist Politics* (London: Blackwell Press, 1994), 102–56; citation on 131–32.
8. The Public Theater, New York (1995); Shakespeare Santa Cruz (1996).

9. For a brief critique of the 1991 Shakespeare Santa Cruz production, see Margo Hendricks, "'Obscured by Dreams': Race, Empire and Shakespeare's *A Midsummer Night's Dream*," *Shakespeare Quarterly* 47:1 (1996):37–60.

10. In *The Wilde Century* (New York: Columbia University Press, 1994), Alan Sinfield notes how this performance's "dissident effect depended on the audience having some knowledge or intuition of how it was intended to work": "I found myself uncertain, from moment to moment, whether I was watching a boy, a girl, a girl playing a boy, or a boy playing a girl playing a boy. . . . However, some of my friends were initially disappointed because they'd been expecting to whoop it up in a gay version; once they got the idea, they were delighted" (1994: 201). In a personal communication, Sinfield adds that the Cheek by Jowl presentation of Celia was "a big revelation": "she is plainly in love with Rosalind. While Rosalind frolics around with her various beaux, Celia stands to one side looking anxious, upset, yearning."

11. Cornerstone Theater Company, "Twelfth Night, or As You Were," performed at the Sixth World Shakespeare Congress, April 10–21,1996, reviewed in the *Los Angeles Times*, April 12, 1996, on F1, F24, F25.

12. Jill Dolan, *Presence and Desire: Essays on Gender, Sexuality, Performance* (Ann Arbor: University of Michigan Press, 1993), 155–56.

13. For a classic statement on gay male drag, see Esther Newton, *Mother Camp: Female Impersonators in America* (Englewood Cliffs, N.J.: Prentice-Hall, 1972).

14. On the tradition of using boy actors, see Stephen Orgel, *Impersonations: The Performance of Gender in Shakespeare's England* (Cambridge: Cambridge University Press, 1996).

15. See Judith Butler, *Gender Trouble: Feminism and the Subversion of Identity* (New York: Routledge, 1989).

16. Susan Bennett, *Performing Nostalgia: Shifting Shakespeare and the Contemporary Past* (London: Routledge, 1996).

17. According to Bruce Smith, in "I, You, He, She, and We: On the Sexual Politics of Shakespeare's Sonnets," in *Shakespeare's Sonnets: Critical Essays*, ed. James Schiffer (New York: Garland, 1999), 411–29, Celia was played as the disappointed lover of Rosalind in Lawrence Boswell's 1997 Shakespeare Theater of Washington production of *As You Like It*, 411. In addition, Gay Gibson Cima describes the transformation of the friendship of Portia and Nerissa to that of lovers in "Strategies for Subverting the Canon," in *Upstaging Big Daddy: Directing Theater as If Gender and Race Matter*, ed. Ellen Donkin and Susan Clement (Ann Arbor: University of Michigan Press, 1993), 91–105.

18. This would seem to be precisely the point of Carl Miller's blithe dismissal of historical difference in *Stages of Desire: Gay Theatre's Hidden History* (London: Cassell, 1996), whose token chapter on female characters in Renaissance drama, entitled "Lesbian Double Cherries," puns its way through the plays of Lyly, Shakespeare, Fletcher, and Heywood.

19. Jonathan Goldberg, ed., *Queering the Renaissance* (Raleigh: Duke University Press, 1994).

20. Isabel Hull, *Sexuality, State, and Civil Society in Germany, 1700–1815* (Ithaca: Cornell University Press, 1996), 9. Although focused on a Reformation-conservative society, Hull's description of the dominance of patriarchal marriage is an accurate portrayal of early modern English culture.

21. The differences between Catholic and Protestant views on sexuality in general are aptly summarized by Hull, who takes issue with James Brundage's assertion that "the post-Tridentine Roman Catholic attitude toward sex [was] more negative than that of Protestants, to the extent that it continued to associate sex with impurity and the generally sinful condition of humanity" (James Brundage, *Law, Sex, and Christian Society in Medieval Europe* [Chicago: University of Chicago Press, 1987]), an assessment that she terms "accurate, but incomplete" (1996: 23).

22. In *Love between Women: Early Christian Responses to Homoeroticism* (Chicago: University of Chicago Press, 1996), Bernadette Brooten provides a lengthy exegesis of *Romans 1:26–27*. On the invention of sodomy as a category within medieval theological discourse, see Mark Jordan, *The Invention of Sodomy in Christian Theology* (Chicago: University of Chicago Press, 1997).

23. For an early overview of European sodomy laws and their effects on women, see Louis Crompton, "The Myth of Lesbian Impunity: Capital Laws from 1270 to 1791," in *The Gay Past*, ed. Salvatore J. Licata and Robert P. Petersen (New York: Harrington Park Press, 1985), 11–25. See also Lillian Faderman, *Surpassing the Love of Men: Romantic Friendship and Love between Women from the Renaissance to the Present* (New York: Morrow, 1981); and Judith Brown, *Immodest Acts: The Life of a Lesbian Nun in Renaissance Italy* (Oxford: Oxford University Press, 1986). On English sodomy statutes and prosecutions of men, see Gregory W. Bredbeck, *Sodomy and Interpretation: Marlowe to Milton* (Ithaca: Cornell University Press, 1991); Bruce R. Smith, *Homosexual Desire in Shakespeare's England* (Chicago: University of Chicago Press, 1991); Jonathan Goldberg, *Sodometries: Renaissance Texts, Modern Sexualities* (Stanford: Stanford University Press, 1992); and Alan Bray, *Homosexuality in Renaissance England* (London: Gay Men's Press, 1982).

24. According to Karma Lochrie, "Presumptive Sodomy and Its Exclusions," *Textual Practice* 13, no. 2 (summer 1999):295–310, both Albert the Great and John Chrysostom refer to woman-woman sins against nature. Although Brundage minimizes the import of references to lesbianism in medieval canon law, he includes in his notes references to theological and penitential texts that condemn same-gender female acts. See Brundage, *Law, Sex, and Christian Society in Medieval Europe*. See also Allan Frantzen's reading of Anglo-Saxon penitential manuals in *Before the Closet: Same-Sex Love from Beowulf to Angels in America* (Chicago: University of Chicago Press, 1998), 138–83.

25. Sir Edward Coke, *Third Part of the Institutes of the Lawes of England* (London: 1644). It would appear that Coke's reference to female bestiality is authorized by medical writing. In *Microcosmographia, A Description of the Body of Man* (London: 1615), Helkiah Crooke observes that

Vesalius hath observed that the prostate glandules are notoriously large & ful in Monkies; and indeed they are of al creatures the most lascivious, as we do not only read in authors, but have also seene by the great Baboons which were heere to be seene among us; for they would in a maner offer violence even to a woman. It is therefore a very wicked and inhumane thing for Gentlewomen to cherish them in their bosoms yea in their beds, as I have seene some doe with mine owne eies. (1615: 209)

26. The only broadside that appears in the Bodleian Library Catalogue of Ballads to refer to female sodomy likewise offers an account of a woman executed for committing buggery with a dog: "A looking-glass for wanton Women by the Example and Expiation of *Mary Higgs*, who was executed on Wednesday, 18th of July 1637, for committing the odious sin of Buggery, with her Dog, who was hanged on a Tree the same day," set to the tune of "In Summer time" (printed between 1672 and 1696).

27. Cited in Elspeth King, *The Hidden History of Glasgow's Women* (Edinburgh: Mainstream Publishing Co., 1993), 31. I am indebted to Lynda Boose for this reference.

28. See Richard Godbeer, "'The Cry of Sodom': Discourse, Intercourse, and Desire in Colonial New England," *William and Mary Quarterly* 3d ser., 52:2 (1995):259–86, citation on 268; Mary Beth Norton, *Founding Mothers and Fathers: Gendered Power and the Forming of American Society* (New York: Knopf, 1996), 347–57; and Roger Thompson, "Attitudes towards Homosexuality in the Seventeenth-Century New England Colonies," *Journal of American Studies* 23 (1989):27–40.

29. Kathleen Brown, "'Changed . . . into the Fashion of Man': The Politics of Sexual Difference in a Seventeenth-Century Anglo-American Settlement," *Journal of the History of Sexuality* 6:2 (1995):171–93; Mary Beth Norton, "Communal Definitions of Gendered Identity in Seventeenth-Century English America," in *Through a Glass Darkly: Reflections of Personal Identity in Early America*, ed. Ronald Hoffman, Mechal Sobel, and Fredrika Teute (Chapel Hill: University of North Carolina Press, 1997), 40–66.

30. Few men were prosecuted under sodomy statutes as well; I would argue, however, that the reasons for the paucity of prosecutions differ along gender lines.

31. Early modern English views on the humoral body—as well as recent scholarship on the body—are synthesized by Anthony Fletcher, *Gender, Sex, and Subordination in England, 1500–1800* (New Haven: Yale University Press, 1999), 30–82. Nancy Sirasi provides a helpful overview of medical theory and practice in *Medieval and Early Renaissance Medicine: An Introduction to Knowledge and Practice* (Chicago: University of Chicago Press, 1990). Interpretations of early modern literature in terms of humoral theory are provided by Michael Schoenfeldt, *Bodies and Selves in Early Modern England: Physiology and Inwardness in Spenser, Shakespeare, Herbert, and Milton* (Cambridge: Cambridge University Press, 1999); and Gail Kern Paster, *The Body Embarrassed: Drama and the Disciplines of Shame in Early Modern England* (Ithaca: Cornell University Press, 1991). The historical contingency of the early modern medical paradigm is beautifully summarized by Steven Mullaney in his review of Paster's book in *Shakespeare Quarterly* 48:2 (1997):242–46. Paster, he writes,

convey[s] in graphic and concrete terms just how alien the humoral body is to our modern sensibilities, accustomed as we are to a more disembodied psychologizing about affective experience and to an entirely different set of assumptions about the body itself. We think of ourselves as self-contained units (and our sense of individuality and even individual autonomy derive from such assumptions), relatively opaque to the gaze of doctors and friends (unless opened up by scalpel or encounter group), and maintained by a circulatory system that is itself understood as closed and self-contained. The humoral body, by contrast, was "a semipermeable, irrigated container in which humors moved" (8) and metamorphosed, one into the other, whose constituent and multiple fluids were not only in dynamic balance (or imbalance) but were also "all reducible to blood . . . [and] entirely fungible. . . . [O]pen and fungible in its internal workings, the humoral body was also porous and thus able to be influenced by the immediate environment" (9). The everyday functioning of internal organs was "tumultuous and dramatic" even in health, and, as Paster astutely notes, this aspect of humoral physiology "ascribes to the workings of the internal organs an aspect of agency, purposiveness, and plenitude to which the subject's own will is often decidedly irrelevant" (10). In the modern age our feelings are intensely personal, signs of our individuality and indeed of our very selves; in the early modern period, "one's" feelings had a life all their own. (1997: 243)

32. My contention in *Desire and Anxiety: Circulations of Sexuality in Shakespearean Drama* (New York: Routledge, 1992) that early modern masculinity was vexed by a fear of effeminization has been challenged by Debora Shuger, "Excerpts from a Panel Discussion," in *Renaissance Discourses of Desire*, ed. Claude Summers and Ted-Larry Pebworth (Columbia, Mo.: University of Missouri Press, 1993), 271–72; and Lorna Hutson, "On Not Being Deceived: Rhetoric and the Body in *Twelfth Night*," *Texas Studies in Literature* *and Language* 38:2 (1996):140–74. Shuger takes me to task for importing a psychoanalytic narrative onto early modern persons, and for presupposing that "erotic desire" (the longing for union with the beloved) is sexual desire (genital arousal)," while Hutson is concerned with my extrapolation of evidence from medical texts.

Although a full response lies beyond the scope of this essay, I will say that the insistence of medical writers that bodies can *only* metamorphose in one direction (from female to male) and not the other evinces a defensiveness unaccounted for by their theories. Noting this points to a fundamental difference in methodology: Hutson and Shuger take medical writers at their word; I examine their rhetoric, repetitions, and elisions. But, even if one limits oneself to reading only the surface of the text, the belief that "nature always strives for perfection" is contradicted explicitly by at least one popular medical writer, Juan Huarte, who, in explaining the properties of heat and cold, articulates the possibility that while the fetus is still in the womb, "if when nature hath finished to forme a man in all perfection, she would convert him into a woman, there needeth nought els to be done, save only to turne his instruments of generation inwards. . . . nature hath sundrie times made a male with his genetories outward, and cold growing on, they have turned inward, and it became female. This is knowen after she is borne, for she retaineth a mannish fashion, as well in her words, as in all her motions and workings." See Juan Huarte, *The Examination of Mens Wits* (1594), trans. Richard Carew, ed. Carmen Rogers (Gainesville, Fla.: Scholars' Facsimiles and Reprints, 1959), 269–70. I thank Michael Schoenfeldt for calling Huarte's text to my attention.

33. Helkiah Crooke, *Microcosmographia, A Description of the Body of Man* (London, 1615), 250.

34. Nicholas Culpeper, *A Directory for Midwives (Culpeper's Midwife Enlarged)* (London, 1684), 22–23. Culpeper's *Directory for Midwives* of 1651 was enlarged in 1671, and appeared in seventeen editions under various names, and in varied size, from quartos to duodecimos, until 1777. This passage does not appear in the first edition. As an apothecary, Culpeper was not experienced in midwifery.

35. Lyndal Roper, *The Holy Household: Women and Morals in Reformation Augsburg* (Oxford: Oxford University Press, 1989), 257.

36. The case of Marie le Marcis, originally recorded by French physician Jacques Duval in *On Hermaphrodites, Childbirth, and the Medical Treatment of Mothers and Children* (Rouen, 1603), has elicited a fair amount of recent analysis. See Katherine Park, "The Rediscovery of the Clitoris," in *The Body in Parts: Fantasies of Corporeality in Early Modern Europe*, ed. Carla Mazzio and David Hillman (New York: Routledge, 1997), 171–93; Katherine Park and Lorraine Daston, "The Hermaphrodite and the Orders of Nature," *GLQ: A Journal of Lesbian and Gay Studies* 1, no. 4 (1995):419–38; Thomas Laqueur,

Making Sex: Body and Gender from the Greeks to the Present (Cambridge: Harvard University Press, 1990), 136–38; Stephen Greenblatt, "Fiction and Friction," in *Reconstructing Individualism: Autonomy, Individuality and the Self in Western Thought,* ed. Thomas C. Heller, Morton Sosna, David E. Wellbery, Arnold I. Davidson, Ann Swidler, Ian Walt (Stanford: Stanford University Press, 1986), 30–52; and Patricia Parker, "Gender Ideology, Gender Change: The Case of Marie Germain," *Critical Inquiry* 19:2 (1993):337–64.

37. At this point, I leave aside Aristotle and Hippocrates, and primarily depend on the model of physiology that tended to dominate English medical practice, Galen's physiology of the four humors. The Galenic view of reproductive anatomy did not go uncontested; rather, it is in part such contestation that gives rise to conflicting interpretations of female-female eroticism.

38. On the emergence of the female warrior ballads around 1600 and their rise in popularity over the course of the seventeenth century, see Dianne Dugaw, *Warrior Women and Popular Balladry, 1650–1850* (Cambridge: Cambridge University Press, 1989).

39. Vern L. Bullough and Bonnie Bullough, *Crossdressing, Sex, and Gender* (Philadelphia: University of Pennsylvania Press, 1993).

40. I appropriate this term from Judith Halberstam's *Female Masculinity*, a study of the range of women's masculine gender performances since the nineteenth century (Durham: Duke University Press, 1997).

41. Excerpted in *Women's Worlds in Seventeenth-Century England: A Sourcebook*, ed. Patricia Crawford and Laura Gowing (London: Routledge, 2000), 151.

42. Catalina de Erauso, *Lieutenant Nun: Memoir of a Basque Transvestite in the New World*, trans. Michele Stepto and Gabriel Stepto (Boston: Beacon Press, 1996).

43. Patricia Crawford and Sara Mendelson, "Sexual Identities in Early Modern England: The Marriage of Two Women in 1680," *Gender and History* 7:3 (1995):362–77.

44. In *Women in Early Modern England 1550–1720*, ed. Sara Mendelson and Patricia Crawford (Oxford: Clarendon Press, 1998), Mendelson and Crawford speculate that Arabella Hunt, who went on to become a celebrated lutenist and soprano at the royal court, may have been the "Mistress Hunt" who appeared in John Crowne's court masque *Calisto* and also speculate that the *Hunt v. Poulter* case inspired Aphra Behn's dialogue in *The False Count* (1682), when an elderly husband says of his wife's relationship with her sister and maid: "I have known as much danger hid under a Petticoat, as a pair of Breeches. I have heard of two Women that married each other—oh abominable, as if there were so prodigious a scarcity of Christian Mans Flesh" (1998: 248–49).

45. Helmut Puff notes that in the late medieval period "northern European powers were more active than Mediterranean societies in penalizing 'female sodomy.'" Puff, "Female Sodomy: The Trial of Katherina Hetseldorfer (1477)," *Journal of Medieval and Re-

naissance Studies 30:1 (2000):41–61. Isabel Hull stresses that after the Reformation both Catholic and Protestant states enacted similar moral legislation and engaged in similar secular efforts at general sexual regulation. Hull, *Sexuality, State, and Civil Society in Germany*, 24.

46. Crawford and Gowing, *Women's Worlds in Seventeenth-Century England*, 149.

47. Hull, *Sexuality, State, and Civil Society in Germany*, 51.

48. Scholarly recourse to a transhistorical homophobia, which psychologizes the appeal of gay oppression, and to theories of gay genocide, which unifies all such oppression under a systematic intentionality, thus are not useful analytical tools.

49. Puff, "Female Sodomy," 44.

50. Juan Luis Vives, *A Very Fruitful and Pleasant Book Called The Instruction of Christian Woman* (1523), trans. Richard Hyrde (London, c. 1529); rpt. in Joan Larsen Klein, *Daughters, Wives, and Widows: Writing by Men about Women and Marriage in England, 1500–1640* (Urbana: University of Illinois Press, 1992), 97–122; citation on 108.

51. Sixteenth- and seventeenth-century anatomists and midwives argue about the presence or absence of the hymen and its reliability as a signifier of virginity. Most anatomists agree that the hymen is not found in all virgins and that it can be broken through a variety of means other than sexual intercourse. In *The Workes*, Ambrose Paré argues against the existence of the hymen (Paré, trans. Thomas Johnson, *The Workes of That Famous Chirugian Ambrose Parey, Translated out of Latine and Compared with the French* [London, 1634], 938). Gabriele Falloppia thought he proved its existence in his *Observationes anatomicae* (Venice: 1561). Crooke views the hymen as a sure sign of virginity. Even when writers uphold the hymen as a sign of virginity, most recognize that this membrane might be broken by means other than phallic penetration, as evinced in Thomas Bartholin's list of eight ways in which the hymen may be harmed, including "If Virgins break it through wantonness with their fingers, or some other Instrument," *Anatomy; Made from the Precepts of His Father* (London, 1665), 73. As this reference to an instrument indicates, the controversy about the hymen was associated with female masturbation and tribadism. In *A Directory for Midwives*, Culpeper occupies the middle ground:

In Virgins these Caruncles or Knobs are joyned together with a thin and sinewy skin or Membrane, interlaced with many small Veins, which hath a hole in the midst, through which the Menstrual blood passeth, about the bigness of ones little finger, in such as are grown up; this is that noted skin which is called Hymen, and is a certain note of Virginity where ever it is found, for the first act of Copulation breaks it. I confess much controversie hath been amonst Anatomists concerning this; some holding there is no such thing at all; others, that it is, but it is very rare; the truth is, most Virgins have it, some hold all; I must suspend my judgement till more years bring me more experience; yet this is certain, it may be broken without copulation, as it may be gnawn asunder by defluxion of sharp humors, especially in young Virgins because it is thinnest in them, as also by unskilful applying Pessaries, to provoke the Terms and how many ways else God knows. (1684: 23–24)

Nonetheless, Culpeper's translation of Johannes Veslingus's Latin *The Anatomy of the Body of Man* (London: 1653), says: "Such Virgins as keep themselves from playing the wantons with themselves, from the use of *Venus* and other external injuries, have a fleshy skin that covers the passage, guarded with *Caruncles*, which Ancients called *Hymen*. . . . this is but in few, and many Midwives tear it away for an unprofitable excrement" (1684: 29–30). In *The Midwives Book, Or the Whole Art of Midwifry Discovered* (London, 1671), Jane Sharp disputes that the hymen is not found in all maids: "doubtless that is false, else it could have been no proof of Virginity to the *Israelites*"; she then repeats Culpeper's judgment that it can nonetheless be broken before copulation (1671: 48).

52. On Russia, see Eve Levin, *Sex and Society in the World of the Orthodox Slavs, 900–1700* (Ithaca: Cornell University Press, 1989), 204.

53. Lena Cowen Orlin, *Private Matters and Public Culture in Post-Reformation England* (Ithaca: Cornell University Press, 1994), 185.

54. Hull, *Sexuality, State, and Civil Society in Germany*, 44.

55. Margaret Hunt, "The Sapphic Strain: English Lesbians in the Long Eighteenth Century," in *Singlewomen in the European Past, 1250–1800*, ed. Judith M. Bennett and Amy M. Froide (Philadelphia: University of Pennsylvania Press, 1999), 270–96, citation on 281.

56. In *Women's Worlds in Seventeenth-Century England*, Crawford and Gowing include a nineteenth-century redrawing of a woodcut from the *Roxburghe Ballads* that depicts two women embracing in bed together (2000: 150).

57. "[W]antonly" is inserted into the seventeenth-century translation of Paré; the French is more neutral.

58. In aristocratic courts, the gentlewomen of the Bedchamber, who closely attended the queen's needs, were the most highly esteemed of her attendants. See Pam Wright, "A Change in Direction: The Ramifications of a Female Household, 1558–1603," in *The English Court: From the Wars of the Roses to the Civil War*, ed. David Starkey (London: Longman, 1987), 147–72.

59. George Williamson, *Lady Anne Clifford: Her Life, Letters, and Work* (Kendal, England: Titus Wilson & Son, 1922), 76.

60. Williamson, *Lady Anne Clifford*, 69. I thank Karen Newman for bringing this entry in Anne Clifford's diary to my attention.

61. In *Desiring Women Writing: English Renaissance Examples* (Stanford: Stanford University Press, 1997), Jonathan Goldberg briefly discusses this diary entry, remarking in a footnote, "This is not the first time they slept together—an earlier incident is reported on p. 23—but it is apparently the first time they had sex" (1997: 39 and 200, note 27).

62. Thomas Harman, *Caveat or Warening for Common Cursetors vulgarly called Vagabones*, in *Awdley's Fraternitye of Vacabondes, Harman's Caveat, Haben's Sermon, &c.* (London, 1567), ed. Edward Viles and F. J. Furnivall, Early English Text Society, Extra Series No. 9 (London: Oxford University Press, 1898; rpt. Millwood, N.Y.: Kraus Reprint Co., 1975), 17–91, esp. 22–23.

63. Daryl Palmer, *Hospitable Performances: Dramatic Genre and Cultural Performances in Early Modern England* (West Lafayette, Ind.: Purdue University Press, 1992), 112.

64. Philip Stubbes, for instance, called cross-dressed women, "Hermaphroditi, that is, Monsters of bothe kindes, halfe women, halfe men," in *The Anatomy of Abuses* (London: 1583), F5v.

65. For a more extended treatment of the homoeroticism in this scene and the play see my chapter, "The Homoerotics of Shakespearean Comedy" in *Desire and Anxiety*.

66. I agree with Stephen Greenblatt's general observation in "Fiction and Friction" that erotic friction in *Twelfth Night* is analogous to verbal wit and that "Dallying with words is the principal Shakespearean representation of erotic heat" (1986: 90)—a contention perhaps even more apropos of *Much Ado about Nothing*.

67. It hardly seems coincidental that the Shakespeare play most often used to fuel lesbian plots in contemporary pornography is *Twelfth Night*. See Richard Burt, "Baroque Down: The Trauma of Censorship in Psychoanalysis and Queer Film Re-Visions of Shakespeare and Marlowe," in *Shakespeare in the New Europe*, ed. Michael Hattaway, Boika Sokolova, and Derek Roper (Sheffield: Sheffield Academic Press, 1994), 328–50. In "The Love That Dare Not Speak Shakespeare's Name: New Shakesqueer Cinema," in *Unspeakable ShaXXXspeares: Queer Theory and American Kiddie Culture* (New York: St. Martin's Press, 1998), 29–75, Burt argues for a queer rather than a gay Shakespeare. See also Laurie Osborne, *The Trick of Singularity: Twelfth Night and the Performance Editions* (Iowa City: University of Iowa Press, 1996).

68. One indication of the popularity of *A Midsummer Night's Dream* is the number of productions worldwide, as listed in the 1996 World Shakespeare Bibliography (*Shakespeare Quarterly* 48:5), 696–709. There are eighty-seven entries of the play, compared to twenty-nine, for instance, for such other popular plays as *The Merchant of Venice* and thirty-five for *As You Like It*. In his "Shakespeare in Production" edition of the play,

Trevor Griffiths notes that *A Midsummer Night's Dream* is "now safely ensconced as one of the three Shakespeare plays to be studied in schools as part of the English National Curriculum" (Cambridge: Cambridge University Press, 1996), 1.

69. For an influential reading of the heterosexual teleology of *A Midsummer Night's Dream*, see C. L. Barber, *Shakespeare's Festive Comedy: A Study of Dramatic Form and Its Relation to Social Custom* (Cleveland: Meridian, 1959). In the Arden edition of the play, Harold Brooks summarizes the dominant critical opinion: "love and marriage is the [play's] central theme: love aspiring to and consummated in marriage, or to a harmonious partnership within it." Harold Brooks, *The Arden Shakespeare* (London: Methuen, 1979), cxxx. As Louis Montrose remarks, "[s]uch romantically inclined idealizations of married love tend to downplay the authoritarian and misogynistic aspects" of the play. Louis Montrose, *The Purpose of Playing: Shakespeare and the Cultural Politics of the Elizabethan Theatre* (Chicago: University of Chicago Press, 1996), 110. Montrose's influential comments on the play, initially published as *"A Midsummer Night's Dream* and the Shaping Fantasies of Elizabethan Culture: Gender, Power, Form," in *Rewriting the Renaissance: The Discourses of Sexual Difference in Early Modern Europe*, ed. Maureen Quilligan, Margaret Ferguson, and Nancy Vickers (Chicago: University of Chicago Press, 1986), 65–87, and "'Shaping Fantasies': Figurations of Gender and Power in Elizabethan Culture," *Representations* 1 (1983):61–94, have been elaborated and nuanced in his book (all subsequent citations refer to the book). Recent editors, responding in part to Montrose's influence, increasingly have acknowledged the coercive aspects of the play; see, for instance, *The Norton Shakespeare (Based on the Oxford Edition)*, ed. Stephen Greenblatt, Walter Cohen, Jean Howard, and Katherine Eisamen Maus (New York: W. W. Norton, 1997).

70. Montrose, *The Purpose of Playing*, 117.

71. Dorothy Stephens, "Into Other Arms: Amoret's Evasion," in *The Limits of Eroticism in Post-Petrarchan Narrative: Conditional Pleasure from Spenser to Marvell* (Cambridge: Cambridge University Press, 1998), 37.

72. *Edmund Spenser: The Faerie Queene* (1590–1609), ed. Thomas P. Roche, Jr. (New Haven: Yale University Press, 1978), 568–69 (Book 4, Canto 1, Stanzas 15–16).

73. Sir Philip Sidney, *The Countess of Pembroke's Arcadia* (1593), ed. Maurice Evans (Harmondsworth, England: Penguin, 1977), 245. In this context, it is interesting to note that in the *Old Arcadia*, Philoclea compares her fervent desire for the cross-dressed Cleophila (Pyrocles) to just such sisterly love:

Thus did Cleophila wade betwixt small hopes and huge despairs, whilst in the mean time the sweet Philoclea found strange unwonted motions in herself. And yet the poor soul could nei-

ther discern what it was, nor whither the vehemency of it tended. She found a burning affection towards Cleophila; an unquiet desire to be with her; and yet she found that the very presence kindled the desire. And examining in herself the same desire, yet could she not know to what the desire inclined. Sometimes she would compare the love she bare to Cleophila with the natural goodwill she bare to her sister; but she perceived it had another kind of working. Sometimes she would wish Cleophila had been a man, and her brother; and yet in truth, it was no brotherly love she desired of her.

In "What? How? Female-Female Desire in Sidney's *New Arcadia*," *Criticism* 39:4 (1997):463–49, Richard A. Levin perceptively focuses on the homoerotics of the passage in which Philoclea comes to recognize her love for Zelmane (the cross-dressed Pyrocles), arguing that "No passage in early modern English literature is nearly as full and explicit dealing with a woman's sexual desire for a woman and the possibility of sexual activity between them" (1997: 464). Although I disagree with some of his conclusions, I appreciate Levin's insistence on the homoeroticism of this representation as well as his generosity in sharing his work before publication. More recently, Kathryn Schwarz has analyzed the extent to which *The Arcadia* expresses through its use of transvestite Amazonian disguise the "conviction that desire between women is an erotic irrelevance and the fear that it is a sexual fall." *Tough Love: Amazon Encounters in the English Renaissance* (Durham and London: Duke University Press, 2000), 200.

74. Stephen Orgel, "Gendering the Crown," in *Subject and Object in Renaissance Culture*, ed. Margreta de Grazia, Maureen Quilligan, and Peter Stallybrass (Cambridge: Cambridge University Press, 1996), 133–65, esp. 162.

75. Thomas Dekker, *Satiromastix: Or the Untrussing of the Humorous Poet* (London, 1602).

76. Richard Brome, *The Antipodes*, ed. Ann Haaker (Lincoln: University of Nebraska Press, 1966).

77. Mario DiGangi, *The Homoerotics of Early Modern Drama* (Cambridge: Cambridge University Press, 1997), 96. DiGangi is similarly focused on containment in his reading of William Goddard's *A Satirical Dialogue* (Low Countries, 1615):

Alas, alas, what pleasure and delight
Takes one mayde with an other in the night?
But smale god knowes it, for my owne part I
Ne're tooke anie with whom I e're did lie.
For love, noe revells in that bedd doth keepe
Where one girle, by an others side doth sleepe.
For trulye (sisters) there is none that can
Give maydes delight in bedd, but a young man. (sig. civ.)

DiGangi argues, "By having the sister insist so strenuously on the futility of female-female sex, Goddard raises the possibility of just such 'pleasure and delight,' especially for the younger, less experienced, sisters. Yet any speculation about the 'revells' girls keep in bed might well be dispelled by the youngest sister's pornographic account of the man of her dreams . . . [which] seems to prove that only a young man is equipped to give sexual delight to a maid" (1997: 97–98).

78. Henri Lefebvre, *The Production of Space*, trans. Donald Nicholson-Smith (Oxford: Blackwell, 1991); Doreen Massey, *Space, Place and Gender* (Minneapolis: University of Minnesota Press, 1994); David Bell and Gill Valentine, ed., *Mapping Desire: Geographies of Sexualities* (London and New York: Routledge, 1995).

79. Peter Stallybrass, "Patriarchal Territories: The Body Enclosed," in *Rewriting the Renaissance: The Discourses of Sexual Difference in Early Modern Europe*, ed. Margaret Ferguson, Maureen Quilligan, and Nancy Vickers (Chicago: University of Chicago Press, 1986), 123–42.

80. It must be noted that this was ideology, not reality. Mendelson and Crawford argue that during daylight hours, "women treated their dwellings as fluid and open expanses, from which they surveyed the passing scene and emerged at will. They also freely resorted to each other's houses, making use of neighbours' dwellings much like a series of linked female spaces." In this respect, the "male ideal of encloistered femininity was irrelevant to most women's behavior." *Women in Early Modern England*, 206 and 210.

81. See Ann Matter, "My Sister, My Spouse: Woman-Identified Women in Medieval Christianity," *Journal of Feminist Studies in Religion* 2:2 (1986):81–93.

82. John Bale, *The Actes of the Englishe Votaryes, Comprehending their Unchaste Practyses and Examples of All Ages* (London, 1546).

83. The term is Emma Donoghue's, who discusses Marvell's poem in *Passions between Women* (New York: HarperCollins, 1995), 225.

84. James Holstun was the first to examine the homoerotics of "Upon Appleton House," in "'Will You Rent Our Ancient Love Asunder?': Lesbian Elegy in Donne, Marvell, and Milton," *English Literary History* 54:4 (1987):835–67; a more thorough examination is provided by Kate Chedgzoy, "For *Virgin Buildings* Oft Brought Forth: Fantasies of Convent Sexuality," in *Female Communities 1600–1800: Literary Visions and Cultural Realities*, ed. Rebecca D'Monté and Nicole Pohl (London: Macmillan, 2000). I thank the author for sharing her essay with me before publication. See also Dorothy Stephens, "Caught in the Act at Nun Appleton," in *The Limits of Eroticism in Post-Petrarchan Narrative*, 178–209, esp. 179–80.

85. Frances E. Dolan examines anti-Catholic sentiment and emphasizes the systems of support Catholicism provided women in *Whores of Babylon: Catholicism, Gender, and*

Seventeenth-Century Print Culture (Ithaca: Cornell University Press, 1999). In "A Refuge from Men: The Idea of a Protestant Nunnery," *Past and Present* 117 (1987):107–30, Bridget Hill examines the appeal of the idea of a nunnery in post-Reformation England. Arguing that the "idea of a 'Protestant nunnery' goes through something of a renaissance in the late seventeenth and early eighteenth centuries" (1987: 117), Hill suggests that the rise in numbers of singlewomen and concerns about the inadequacy of female education created conditions for the emergence of small communities of "celibate" women engaged in religious retirement, learning, and the pursuit of good works as well as various proposals for such communities.

86. As Montrose notes, Theseus "represents the life of a vestal as a punishment, and it is one that fits the nature of Hermia's crime. . . . [E]ach of these men claims a kind of property in her. . . . Yet Hermia dares to suggest that she has a claim to property in herself. *"The Purpose of Playing,"* 127.

87. Sylvia Gimenez, "The Vestal's Progress: Is Escaping the Bride-Bed Merely *A Midsummer Night's Dream*?" unpublished paper.

88. Montrose, *"A Midsummer Night's Dream* and the Shaping Fantasies of Elizabethan Culture," 71.

89. Kathryn Schwarz, "Missing the Breast," in *The Body in Parts*, ed. Mazzio and Hillman, 158.

90. Schwarz, "Missing the Breast," 158.

91. Schwarz, *Tough Love*, 177.

92. The Cole-Orton masque, performed on Candlemas Night (February 2) in 1618 at Coleorton Hall, Leicestershire, was published by Rudolf Brotanek, *Die Englischen Maskenspiele* (Vienna: Wilhelm *Braumüller*, 1902), 328–37. It is briefly discussed by David Norbrook in *Poetry and Politics in the English Renaissance* (London: Routledge and Kegan Paul, 1984), 250–51, and "The Reformation of the Masque," in *The Court Masque*, ed. David Lindley (Manchester, University of Manchester Press, 1984), 94–110. Douglas Bruster briefly discusses the Amazonian passage in "Female-Female Eroticism and the Early Modern Stage," *Renaissance Drama* 24 (1993), 1–31. More extensive historical treatment of the masque, including debate about its authorship, is given by Karen Middaugh, "'Virtues Sphear': Court vs. Country in the 1618 Masque at Coleorton," in *Subjects on the World's Stage: Essays on British Literature of the Middle Ages and the Renaissance*, ed. David Allen and Robert White (Newark: University of Delaware Press, 1995), 280–94; and Philip Finkelpearl, "The Fairies' Farewell: *The Masque at Coleorton* (1618)," *Review of English Studies* 46:183 (August 1995):333–51, and Philip Finkelpearl, "The Authorship of the Anonymous 'Coleorton Masque' of 1618," *Notes and Queries* 238:2 (June 1993):224–26.

93. The phrase "traffic in women" was first coined by Emma Goldman in her critique of marriage as prostitution, and gained critical prominence through the work of Gayle Rubin, in "The Traffic in Women: Notes on the 'Political Economy' of Sex," in *Toward an Anthropology of Women*, ed. Rayna Reiter (New York: Monthly Review Press, 1975), 157–210.

94. Margo Hendricks, "Obscured by Dreams: Race, Empire, and Shakespeare's *A Midsummer Night's Dream*," *Shakespeare Quarterly* 47:1 (1996):37–60; citation on 53.

95. I am grateful to P. A. Skantze for bringing this to my attention.

96. In the University of Chicago (4th) edition of *The Complete Works of Shakespeare*, David Bevington glosses this as "a complimentary allusion to Queen Elizabeth as a votaress of Diana and probably refers to an actual entertainment in her honor at Elvetham in 1591" (New York: Harper Collins, 1992), an opinion repeated in the Norton Oxford edition. In the New Cambridge edition, R. A. Foakes (Cambridge: Cambridge University Press, 1984) remarks that this image "has often been interpreted as a compliment to Queen Elizabeth; it seems probable that Shakespeare had the queen in mind," and Stanley Wells in the Penguin edition likewise remarks that the vestal virgin is "usually assumed to refer to Queen Elizabeth" (London: Penguin, 1967). In the Oxford edition, Peter Holland glosses this speech as "Usually taken as an allusion to Queen Elizabeth," although he also cites objections to this view (Oxford: Clarendon Press, 1994), 163. Montrose's intervention in this identification of what others see as a topical allusion stresses the extent to which Queen Elizabeth presents "an integral element of the play's dramaturgy and ideology. . . . Shakespeare's ostensible royal compliment may be seen as a complex mediation of the charismatic royal presence that pervaded late Elizabethan culture and as an appropriation of the cult of the Virgin Queen. . . . Shakespeare's play text splits the triune Elizabethan cult image between the fair vestal, who is an unattainable *virgin*, and the Fairy Queen, who is represented as both an intractable *wife* and a domineering *mother*. Oberon uses one against the other in order to reassert masculine prerogatives." Montrose, *The Purpose of Playing*, 176.

97. Judith M. Bennett and Amy M. Froide, "A Singular Past," in *Singlewomen in the European Past, 1250–1800*, ed. Judith M. Bennett and Amy M. Froide (Philadelphia: University of Pennsylvania Press), 1–37.

98. Amy Louise Erickson, *Women and Property in Early Modern England* (London: Routledge, 1993). Erickson's examination of probate documents also reveals that in the making of wills, women had a decided "preference for female legatees"—a preference that Erickson interprets not only as women's recognition of their shared economic vulnerability, but their "close ties of female friendship" (1993: 221–22).

99. Hunt, "The Sapphic Strain," 287.

100. On English communities, see Amy M. Froide, "Marital Status as a Category of Difference: Singlewomen and Widows in Early Modern England," in *Singlewomen in the European Past*, 236–69.

101. Throughout this discussion, I am indebted to the careful research and generosity of Alan Bray, whose forthcoming book *The Friend* (Chicago: University of Chicago Press) examines such same-sex monuments in more detail.

102. Jean Wilson, "'Two Names of Friendship, But One Starre': Memorials to Single-Sex Couples in the Early Modern Period," *Church Monuments: Journal of the Church Monuments Society* 10 (1995):70–83, citation on 83, note 39.

103. Joseph Chester, *The Marriage, Baptismal, and Burial Registers of the Collegiate Church or Abbey of St. Peter, Westminster* (London: Harleian Society, Vol. 10, 1876).

104. Graham Parry, *The Golden Age Restor'd: The Culture of the Stuart Court, 1603–42* (Manchester: Manchester University Press, 1981), 40.

105. David Bergeron, "Women as Patrons of English Renaissance Drama," in *Patronage in the Renaissance*, ed. Guy F. Lytle and Stephen Orgel (Princeton: Princeton University Press, 1981), 274–90.

106. Stephen Orgel, "The Royal Theatre and the King," in *Patronage in the Renaissance*, 261–72, esp. 267. In 1633, the Puritan barrister William Prynne was prosecuted for treason for attacking the royal theatricals in *Histriomastix* in terms that suggested that any woman who performed was a "notorious whore." See David Norbrook, "The Reformation of the Masque," in *The Court Masque*, ed. David Lindley (Manchester: Manchester University Press, 1984), 94–110.

107. Stephen Orgel and Roy Strong, *Inigo Jones: The Theater of the Stuart Court*, 2 vols. (London: Sothebey Parke Bernet and Berkeley: University of California Press, 1972).

108. G. E. Bentley, *The Jacobean and Caroline Stage*, vol. 4 (Oxford: Clarendon Press, 1956), 549. Bentley's comment refers to an unnamed and now lost pastoral and masque, performed to a small audience at court in 1625–26, in which the queen, who was the principal actress, and her ladies took speaking parts. According to a letter from Henry Manners to Sir George Manners, "I heare not much honor of the Queene's maske, for, if they were not all, soome were in men's apparell."

109. Andrew Gurr, *Playgoing in Shakespeare's London* (Cambridge: Cambridge University Press, 1987); Richard Levin, "Women in the Renaissance Theatre Audience," *Shakespeare Quarterly* 40:2 (1989):165–74; and Ann Thompson, "Women/'Women' and the Stage," in *Women and Literature in Britain, 1500–1700*, ed. Helen Wilcox (Cambridge: Cambridge University Press, 1996), 100–116.

110. Montrose, *The Purpose of Playing*, 144, emphasis mine.

The Erotics of Friendship in Restoration Theater

George E. Haggerty

The erotics of male friendship are rarely more vividly represented than in the heroic tragedies of Restoration and early eighteenth-century England. In almost every tragedy by Dryden, Lee, Banks, or Otway, a complicated dynamic of male relations is central to the plot and instrumental to dramatic resolution. Before "she-tragedy" swept the Restoration stage, much of the dramatic interest in tragedy revolved around relations between men.[1]

At the Queer Theater Conference, a questioner challenged a reconsideration of the theater of earlier periods from a queer perspective. He claimed that to do so was simply to force gay or lesbian readings on earlier works. In the discussion that follows, I am not insisting that male-male relations are always sodomitical or that eroticized friendships signify anything that we would understand as gay relations. I do think, though, that these relations need to be examined in light of what we know about the history of friendship, about Restoration theater, about the actors involved, and about the dramatic language that they use. This is cultural criticism to the extent that it tries to look at what is central to this culture and explain how we can begin to understand not by claiming an identity between what we think and do and what the characters in these plays think and do, but rather by seeing the difference and puzzling over the significance of that difference.

The erotics of the Restoration theater have been largely discussed in terms of actresses, their relations with members of the Court audience, and the air of prostitution with which the entire theatrical apparatus was suffused. Critics such as Paula Backscheider, Kristina Straub, and Elin Diamond have been especially convincing in their examination of the theatrics of prostitution and the possibilities of female transgression, both in terms of cross-dressing and female-female desire.[2] Recent discussions of heroic drama, such as those by Joseph Roach, have begun to address the "orientalist" qualities of plays like *Aureng-Zebe* and *The Indian Emperor* and to explain the role such plays could serve in the theatrics of global expansion.[3] No one has adequately explained the presence in all these plays of eroticized male-male affection, central enough both to dramatic plot and to the self-projection of a culture in search of ways to construct a global authority. Nor has the Restoration theater itself been considered as a site of male-male desire. Although we have a great deal of information about the theaters, managers, and players, no one has brought to it the careful consideration of male sexual practice that scholars of earlier periods have brought, say, to Shakespeare's theater. If I attempt here to make a claim about the quality of male-male affection in a number of plays, I hope to be able to extend this discussion to the theater itself, because only in the workings of what Diamond calls the "theater apparatus" can the full content of these suggestive scenes be explored.

Harold Weber begins to establish such a context in his discussion of *Sodom*, the infamous play about a world of male-male sexual activity set in a court that mimics that of Charles II. Weber explores the "dangerous political implications" of the play and hints at the sexual atmosphere of the theater itself.[4] Weber says that the play "generates an unusual literary world of homosexual machismo in which male virility grounds and proves itself on the male body."[5] *Sodom*, of course, proves nothing about audience expectation or the ethos of the theater itself, but it does suggest that issues of male-male desire were as available in the Restoration as they were in the court of Elizabeth I.[6] Kristina Straub makes the point even more forcefully. In "Actors and Homophobia," she argues that "[f]rom the late seventeenth to the late eighteenth century, the image of actors as represented in the British popular press is that of sexual suspects, men who are in some way outside the boundaries of culturally dominant definitions of masculinity."[7] She shows, further, the ways in which "'men . . . are unmanned on the Stage,'" and why an actor could not be "a full-fledged member of the aristocratic, homosocial culture based on the exchange and ownership of women."[8] The plays I am considering would seem to protest such an assessment, at least to the extent that they hold up male friendship as an ideal. Their conservative, Tory agenda seems to demand that the friendship model function soundly. It has a clear political as well as an erotic valence.

In Dryden's *All for Love* (1677), for instance, among the series of Romans that are to convince Antony to give up his Egyptian diversion and return to the straight path of virtue—including his general Ventidius, who lures Antony with his troops, and his wife Octavia, who lures him with his children—is the momentarily incongruous figure of Dolabella, his friend. Dolabella is described as one "whom Caesar [Octavius] loves beyond the love of women," and he uses this lovability to seduce the wavering hero from the pleasures of Alexandria. Antony becomes wistful when Dolabella's name is mentioned in this context:

> He loved me too:
> I was his soul, he lived not but in me.
> We were so closed within each other's breasts,
> The rivets were not found that joined us first.
> That does not reach us yet: we were so mixed
> As meeting streams, both to ourselves were lost;
> We were one mass; we could not give or take
> But from the same, for he was I, I he. (3.90–96)[9]

Antony's hymn of praise, straining at language as it does and stretching to "reach" the expression of their love, encodes in almost blatant terms an affection that is more than "platonic." "The rivets were not found"; "We were so mixed / As meeting streams"; "We were one mass": male-male desire is at work in passages such as this, even if they function culturally in other ways as well. All these images stress physicality, fluidity, and bodily identification in a way that belies any simple "friendship" interpretation, and even if the attempts to dissolve the distinction between the two individuals here could be read as metaphorical, the tenor of these tropes amounts to more than spiritualized affection. Moreover, this is not the poetry of frustrated desire: it recounts a love that is more than lack, an other that could be experienced as the self, a marriage of body and soul without impediments, an attempt at expressing an identity. "[F]or he was I, I he": this expression shimmers with the possibility of a different kind of subjectivity, physically as well as spiritually different, from what was being articulated, already in the late seventeenth century, as isolation and tragic separateness. This outburst of male love, moreover, is not a quiet aside that takes place on the margins of the literary; it is instead one of the definitive speeches of one of the most popular tragedies of the period. This sexualized male relation, in other words, helps to define the heroic.

The discussion of sexual relations between men in the later years of the seventeenth century has been almost exclusively concerned with the question of libertinism. The open sexual bravado of the libertine stance, as well as the ease with which male and female love objects can be interchanged, have made figures like Rochester and others immediately accessible to historians of sexuality. The libertine has in fact offered the terms that define the very battle over "homosexuality" in the Restoration period.[10] Rather than challenge the substance of these discussions directly, I would like to suggest that the heroic spectacle of male friendship resists the explanatory power of the libertine model and offers a different understanding of male-male desire in early modern culture.

In this context, it is helpful to look at an earlier play that made eroticized male relations its central subject. If Marlowe's *Edward II* is in many ways the early modern original for heroic tragedy, then it also problematizes the heroic model by both sexualizing its central friendship with unapologetic male-male desire and then politicizing it by showing how erotic friendship can pose a threat to the cultural status quo. In that play, the king repeatedly defies aristocratic control in speeches to his beloved Gaveston:

> Now let the treacherous *Mortimers* conspire,
> And that high minded earle of Lancaster:
> I haue my wish, in that I ioy thy sight,
> And sooner shall the sea orewhelme my land,
> Than beare the ship that shall transport thee hence:
> I heere create thee Lord high Chamberlaine,
> Cheefe Secretarie to the state and me,
> Earle of Cornwall, king and lord of Man. (ll. 149–56)

Developing arguments made by Alan Bray, Jonathan Goldberg argues that although "sexual relations could go unnoticed in the period precisely because they were not 'sodomitical' social transgressions[;] [t]he sexual relations cannot go unnoticed in *Edward II*, and the radical move in the play lies in having the Mortimers contend that although Gaveston has not remained in his proper place, there is nothing improper in his sexual relationship with the king."[11] Goldberg argues that Edward establishes a "sodomitical" regime when he refuses paternal law and order for the sake of the indulgences of friendship. In Foucault's terms, as Goldberg reminds us, "*sodomy* is the word for everything illicit, all that lies outside the system of alliance that juridically guarantees marriage and inheritance, the prerogatives of blood, as the linchpin of social order and the maintenance of class distinctions."[12]

Later heroic tragedy, although by no means "sodomitical" in this political sense, does address the sexuality of power, or rather the ways in which authority is expressed in terms of physical desire; and like its most important early modern predecessor, *All for Love* sees male-male desire as a potential attribute of royal authority and a prop to kingly prerogative. When Dolabella actually walks onstage in *All for Love*, the raptures that he and Antony express are vividly suggestive:

> **ANTONY:** 'Tis he himself, by holy friendship!
> *Runs to embrace him*
> Art thou returned at last, my better half?
> Come, give me all myself!—Let me not live,
> If the young bridegroom, longing for his night,
> Was ever half so fond.
> **DOLABELLA:** I must be silent, for my soul is busy
> About a nobler work: she's new come home,
> Like a long-absent man, and wanders o'er
> Each room, a stranger to her own, to look
> If all be safe. (3.119–27)

This imagery of the wedding night and of mutual physical exploration gives substance to the erotic suggestions of the earlier speech, but it also subtly feminizes Dolabella, whose soul is female and whose relation to Antony's young bridegroom can be nothing other than the young bride. (Later, Dolabella admits that "nature has cast me in so soft a mold / That but to hear a story feigned, for pleasure, / Of some fond lover's death moistens my eyes, / And robs me of my manhood" [4.12–15].)

"Feminization" is of course a crude way of describing what happens to Dolabella, relying as it does on a rigid gender binary that the play defies. Dolabella is not female; he is a different kind of male. Like a prototype of the "man of feeling," that is, Dolabella is soft, tearful, and somehow not the man, say, that the soldier Ventidius is. Yet this redefinition of masculinity in the object of Antony's affections does nothing to diminish the power of the heroic stance; rather, it increases it. What is so surprising in this context is that the power of Dolabella's attractions for Antony seems to be understood by all characters concerned, not least of all by Dolabella and Antony themselves. This situation contrasts with that in *Edward II*, in which an unsuitable favorite is being pampered at the expense of the realm. Rather, Dolabella is introduced in an attempt to wrench Antony's attentions away from Cleopatra and back to their "proper" subject, his position in the Roman empire.

According to Bray, however, this form of male intimacy—eroticized friendship that functions to maintain legal authority and hegemonic control—is impossible to distinguish from those which are labeled sodomitical throughout the early modern period. As Goldberg says, "friendship and sodomy are always in danger of (mis)recognition since what both depend upon physically—sexually—cannot be distinguished."[13] Dryden insists that friendship is erotic and that such "(mis)recognition" is a fundamental feature of Roman, that is Western, culture. Dryden sexualizes this relationship as a way of increasing its dramatic power, and he hints at a physical intimacy as a way of suggesting the erotics of the male-identified Roman world. This is not to say that Antony and Dolabella are sodomitical partners, but rather that Dryden wants to make it clear that their love has a decidedly erotic power. Indeed, for Antony power and erotic power are synonymous, and that is why Dolabella not only succeeds where Ventidious and Octavia fail, succeeds that is, in getting a rise, as it were, out of the fallen hero; but he also involves Antony in the three-way conflict that brings about the tragic denouement of the play.

Dolabella exerts a seductive power that is second only to that of Cleopatra in the play, and in many ways it is he, rather than Antony's wife Octavia, who represents Cleopatra's greatest threat. As her eunuch Alexas tells her: "he's handsome, valiant, young / And looks as he were laid for nature's bait" (4.80–81):

The least kind word or glance
You give this youth will kindle him with love;
Then, like a burning vessel set adrift,
You'll send him down amain before the wind
To fire the heart of jealous Antony. (4.84–88)

Cleopatra understands Dolabella's burning desire and the danger that it holds both for her and Antony. She invokes it with a resigned and already defeated heart ("I must attempt it / But oh, with what regret!" [4.99–100]). That she cannot finally betray Antony in this way places her above Dolabella in the heroic scheme of the play. Dolabella's erotic intensity gives a heroic quality to his friendship with Antony, but it also makes him a victim to the irresistible charms of Cleopatra. The play does not condemn Cleopatra for her role in seducing Antony from his heroic duty, nor does it shy away from the presentation of the erotic friendship that might seduce him back into the Roman fold. Dolabella's erotic love for Antony is the clearest challenge to Cleopatra, that is; and in the heroic scheme of the play, both have a claim to Antony's affection. If Dolabella offers the last hope for Antony, he does so by eroticizing duty, which elsewhere in the play has been stiffly military or dully domestic. At the same time, Dolabella's erotic youth renders that hope as unstable as erotic attraction itself. When he falls for Cleopatra, the tragic denouement is assured.[14]

Antony's love for Dolabella is heroic by definition. It places him beyond any simple moralistic reading of masculine desire and celebrates aristocratic privilege at the same time that it documents its collapse as a cultural possibility. Dolabella cannot save Antony, of course, and his own desire for Cleopatra makes this ideal of friendship seem particularly fragile and debilitating. Antony becomes the victim of his desires, the "shadow" that his opening speech had predicted. ("Lie there, thou shadow of an emperor. / The place thou pressest on thy mother earth / Is all thy empire now" [1.216–18]). Bray makes the point that earlier in the century both physical intimacy and emotional commitment were a part of the friendship convention, and he notes that "elaborate reflections . . . on the nature of one man's desire for another" are by no means unusual.[15] Antony and Dolabella represent an ideal of friendship that includes the physical as part of what gives their friendship its peculiar cultural force.

Dryden's interest in this topic was surely political as well as personal, and if he tries to make his friendships erotic, he does so in full awareness of the way male-male eroticism can be used politically. Obviously, he thought that the depiction of male love was worth the risk of public censure, and he saw this love as ennobling rather than demeaning. Does that mean that the love is not sodomitical? Must it? The celebration of male love in his play, and others of the period, makes it impossible to generalize about how male-male desire was perceived and how it was protected.

In *Sexual Suspects*, Kristina Straub claims that "[g]iven the ambiguous sexual legacy of seventeenth-century English players as surrogate women or 'sodomites,' discourse about actors' sexuality in the eighteenth century constitutes a site of visible, hegemonic struggle over how masculine sexuality and gender are to be defined. The ostensibly clear lines of gay and straight that organize our present, homophobic culture can be seen in the process of becoming 'natural' assumptions about male identity."[16] I agree, but I also think that a play like *All for Love* shows how far restoration culture is from naturalizing a gay-straight dichotomy. When

Antony and Dolabella profess their love for one another in that play, the hope of the Roman world depends on the intensity of this bond. Such love is the foundation upon which male sexuality is "constructed," I would argue, and the politics of male-male desire in these plays are as crucial to the emerging hegemony as are details of global conquest or female subjugation. Men must love men in a homosocial configuration in order for culture to function smoothly. That means that men must find in one another an erotic attraction in order to compete, as *All for Love* dramatizes, with the debilitating force of female desire. The female must be commodified as an object of exchange and not mistaken as a competing subject, Dryden seems to say. Of course, such love is not always free from the debilitating effects of erotic intensity, as other plays make clear. But even when male-male desire is problematic, it exists in a different register from male-female bonds. If *Sodom* makes this misogynistic point grotesquely clear, heroic tragedy gives it a philosophical rationale.

One playwright who challenges this conservative agenda, at least in his earlier plays, is Nathaniel Lee. Lee's *The Rival Queens* (1677), which presents Alexander at the moment of his fall, can serve as an example of a different portrayal of erotic friendship. In this play, two jealous wives, Roxana and Statira, are fighting for Alexander's attention, and a number of ill-wishers, Cassander among them, are conspiring to bring him down. Central to the action too, however, is the conflict between the young men Hephestion, Alexander's "favorite," and Lysimachus, his rival for the hand of Statira's sister Parisatis. Their duel begins the play, and when it becomes clear that Parisatis is in love with Lysimachus, Alexander's insistence that she be given instead to his favorite is one of the suggestions that his control of power is giving way to emotional irrationality. His preference for the young Hephestion threatens the social order. Alexander places the young man in positions of power over others with more experience, and showers him with his affections in scenes such as this:

Enter Alexander. All kneel but Clytus
HEPHESTION: O son of Jupiter, live forever.
ALEXANDER: Rise all, and thou, my second self, my love,
O my Hephestion, raise thee from the earth
Up to my breast, and hide thee in my heart.
Art thou grown cold? Why hang thine arms at distance?
Hug me, or else, by heaven, thou lov'st me not.
HEPHESTION: Not love, my lord? Break not the heart you framed

And molded up to such an excellence,

Then stamped on it your own immortal image.

Not love the king? Such is not woman's love,

So fond a friendship, such a sacred flame

As I must doubt to find in breasts above. (2.96–108)[17]

This sounds much like Antony's devotion to Dolabella, but as the scene continues it becomes clear that Hephestion functions more like Cleopatra in this play than he does like Dolabella.[18] Alexander's devotion to him and his to Alexander, that is, quickly asserts itself as one of the play's problems. And as in Marlowe's play, the terms of the hero's downfall have to do with the quality of what he is willing to sacrifice for this "sodomitical" affection. In discussing *Edward II*, Goldberg claims that:

One switching point for the proper intimacy between men to be called sodomy rather than friendship was . . . precisely the transgression of social hierarchies that friendship maintained, those transgressions of the kind for which Gaveston is accused when he usurps the privileges that the peers believe belong only to them.[19]

The Rival Queens examines such transgression in terms that Marlowe's play and Castlehaven's trial both suggest:

ALEXANDER: I'll tell thee, friend, and mark it, all ye princes,

Though never mortal man arrived to such

A height as I, yet would forfeit all,

Cast all my purples and my conquered crowns,

And die to save this darling of my soul.

Give me thy hand, share all my scepters while

I live; and when the hour of fate is come,

I leave thee what thou meritest more than I, the world. (2.116–23)

This violation of social hierarchy marks Alexander's love as sodomitical as clearly as any keyhole testimony of physical penetration would. One might ask what a scene like this is doing in the play, when not one but two wives (Statira and Roxana) are fighting over Alexander, and when the politics of the court are complex enough to make the added complication of this particular love seem unnecessary. But perhaps that is just the point. Unlike the hero of *All for Love*, Alexander the Great had a reputation for loving his young officers, and that reputation is being depicted here, loosely and according to the conventions of Restoration tragedy, of course. Nathaniel Lee's attraction to this story needs no further explanation, for it fits the contours of heroic tragedy in its subject and its outline. His main source for the details of the plot was La Calprenéde's vast seventeenth-century romance, *Cassandra*, which was fully translated into English in 1661 (second edition 1676).[20]

Sir Charles Cotterell's translation of *Cassandra* is a source of much overheated male affection as well as of the characters and action of the play. Indeed, the translation celebrates heroic friendship in even more explicit terms than the play does. In an early but representative scene, for instance, Artaxerxes greets Oroodates (Orontes) as follows:

[H]e threw himself into Oroondates *armes, and hugg'd him between his with so much vehemence, that my Master found he truely and ardently loved him.* My dear *Orontes (said he, kissing him a thousand times)* is it possible that it is your self; and that I really see you, and embrace you? Good Gods, if it be a dream, grant that it may last eternally; *and interrupting these words with infinite expressions of kindness, he would not have given them over of a long time.*[21]

Scenes such as this, as typical of French romance as they are difficult to explain, seem to cross and recross the boundaries between male friendship and the eroticization of male bonds so often as to make any such distinction meaningless. In any case, if Lee had looked here for material that would heighten the aura of the erotic in and around the male relations in his play, he would surely have found it. Not only is Hephestion always mentioned as Alexander's "second self," he is also the subject of the most sustained male rivalry and one of the most bitterly expressed elegiac laments of the romance.[22]

Much of Lee's action in this play, however, finds its sources in English historical drama, from Shakespeare to the Jacobean playwrights. This tradition, of course, can be traced back to the work of Christopher Marlowe, and Lee's interest in the heroic implications of male-male desire, here and in his other great plays as well, suggests that he may have had Marlowe as an important literary model.[23] Lee's own reputation for sexual license, so difficult to separate from other lurid tales that circulate around the question of his madness, adds a Marlovian analogy that is very tempting to accept.[24] Lee's drunkenness and his temper are perhaps not the only features of his personality that he shared with Marlowe. And like Marlowe, he works very hard to make the male love that he depicts in his play a political rather than a personal outrage. Alexander's love for Hephestion leads him to make a number of irrational decisions and becomes to a certain extent his "flaw"—he always gives in to erotic emotion when clear thinking would win the day—but at the same time, in scenes such as that quoted above, it is presented as rich, honorable, and defiant. It is celebrated in language that seems to be straining to express something about emotion that is inexpressible. "My second self"; "Hide thee in my heart"; "such a sacred flame"; "this darling of my soul": the language here, and in the passage from *All for Love* as well, seems to be searching for ways to express male-male desire that does not simply replicate the terms of male-female poetry of passion or the libertine hierarchy of activity-passivity ("Whether the *Boy* fuck'd you, or I the *Boy*").[25] Cassander does remark that Alexander's "flesh" is "as soft / And penetrable as a girl's" (1.1.263–64), but this penetrability is precisely what qualifies him for the play's heroic interest. Indeed, his love for Hephestion is repeatedly contrasted to "woman's love," which the play presents as more violent and less powerful than the relations among men. The women in this play are given to spectacle, and in their scenes, which become the model for tragic conflict, tend toward the histrionic. Such scenes implicitly (and misogynistically) pathologize female desire and allow it to consume itself. Masculine desire becomes an alternative center of value here. When Lysimachus tries to change Alexander's mind about his favorite, Alexander replies, "I here command you nourish no design / To prejudice my person in the man / I love, and will prefer to all the world" (2.232–34).

The emphasis in these speeches is on education and formation; on a quality of affection that is full of light and life; on an open public declaration of a passion that functions in the world. Sexual desire between men and women is seen as dishonest, scheming, and debilitating. But the love that Alexander and Hephestion share is powerful, public, and intimidating. Other characters in the play argue that because of Alexander's love for Hephestion, his fate is doomed—the play began with his rival's claims—but they never argue that these expressions of male desire disqualify Alexander for the heroic stance. In fact, they help to define what is meant by heroism in this play.

Paula Backscheider argues that "[in] the early Restoration, when the theater was identified so closely with the court and when the theater openly accepted its function as a site of distribution and interpretation of news, the theater was a hegemonic apparatus that was being used to influence a critical public in order to legitimate an ideology."[26] In Lee's hands, however, the theater always threatens to subvert its putative ideological aims. No Restoration playwright was more threatening to the establishment than Lee. Lee condemned the excesses of the Restoration court and brooded on human motivation in extreme states. One critic says that "moral depravity, melancholy, and madness [are] the sources of conflict in all his plays."[27] More to the point, it would seem, is Lee's willingness to tease friendship with its sodomitical possibilities, expanding the ideal of friendship that Dryden's heroic plays articulate with the obvious suggestion that male-male desire, male bonding, is always already erotically determined and that the consequences for culture are inevitably profound.

The word "bonding" leads to the obvious suggestion that what we are witnessing here is simply a homosocial tie, as Sedgwick would call it, that assures the smooth running of a patriarchal system. In this argument, we might say that the language expresses nothing more than honest male affection. The articulations of male-male desire in *The Rival Queens* (and Lee's other more overtly political plays as well) defy this reading. They make a political point that is moralistic in intent, to be sure. But they also give center stage, as it were, to a kind of male-male desire that challenges social convention. His case is a complicated one. Marlowe may have defended sodomy "not as idealized friendship or some spiritual relationship or as some self-integrative principle of identity," but as *"the proper thing to do."*[28] But Lee seems more than conventionally fascinated with Alexander's failure to control his own libidinal energy, and the political implications of irrational desire, elsewhere ritualistically contained within a love versus duty construction, in Lee's hands become a complex cultural critique. Erotic friendship solidifies cultural control at the same time that it begins the process by which culture must confront its own unreason. Lee's own later mental breakdown may have found its source in the kinds of inherent contradiction that this stance implies. In any case, the friendship he idealizes here is in part responsible for the downfall of his deeply passive hero. But Lee makes no apology for this. In his unusually popular play, the erotics of male affection defy the cultural accommodation that "tragedy" would seem to imply. For Lee, that is, heroic friendship had meaning beyond the limits of tragic form.

In Restoration theater, spectacle and politics are so intimately related as to be indistinguishable.[29] Roach argues, for instance, that the Augustan theater functions "as an instrument, closely analogous to contemporary optical instruments, especially suited to the magnification of behavior. Used within a system of observation and implicit classification," he says, "such an instrument disseminates . . . powerful constructions of social and cultural difference."[30] The behavior that Roach discusses is that of an expanding empire: defining such figures as the "Noble Savage," the conquistador, and the priest all function in a play like *The Indian Emperor* to establish an ocular relation between the English audience and its

dramatized "other." I would argue that male-male desire functions in such a theatrical milieu as the lens through which this bizarre otherness is viewed. Heroic
male friendship underwrites the entire theatrical enterprise, as it were, and the effect is to inscribe male-male desire into the cultural status quo.

The theater apparatus does not just objectify the actress for a male audience, as
Elin Diamond so brilliantly argues, but it works to establish the erotic identity of
the entire culture. Following Brecht, Diamond argues that certain "gestic" moments in performance can make "visible the contradictory interactions of text,
theater apparatus, and contemporary social struggle."[31] If Diamond explains how
the actress could be a figure of both admiration (for her craft) and calumny (for
her sexual activity), then how similar is the representation of the friend/sodomite.
A gestic moment of male-male love could bring together the forces of theatrical
representation in order to make the sodomite visible to a culture that both celebrates heroic friendship and sees male-male love as monstrous. Restoration theater's spectacular elements—its elaborate sets and scenery, its costumes and lighting, the possibility of "discovered" scenes, everything that Diamond describes as
a "new scopic epistemology"—could also be used to expose the cultural function
of the scenes of male-male affection I have been describing.

If I might return for a minute to Rochester, I would suggest that his *Valentinian*,
a revision of a play by John Fletcher, offers the scene with which to place these
other examples of male-male affection. Late in the play, after Valentinian has with
the help of his eunuch Lycius raped Lucina, the wife of his general Maximus, and
after she has died in shame and self-contempt, the scene opens with "Valentinian
and the Eunuch *discover'd on a Couch.*" Such a discovery suggests that we are moving to the heart of the play's meaning, just as Angellica's similar position in *The
Rover* exposes the theatrical fetishization of the actress in Aphra Behn's play. Here,
however, a different erotic obsession is exposed:

> EMP[EROR]. Oh let me press these balmy Lips all day,
> And bathe my Love-scorch'd Soul in thy moist Kisses.
> Now by my Joys thou art all sweet and soft,
> And thou shalt be the Altar of my Love,
> Upon thy beauties hourly will I offer,
> And pour out Pleasure and blest Sacrifice. (V.v)[32]

Everything about this scene is "wrong": nothing in the play prepares an audience
for this last-act embrace; this is not exactly the kind of friendship that I have described in Dryden and Lee, although it does share certain features with those

friendships; and the play is by Rochester, already well-known as a libertine ad-
venturer. Still, this moment has a gestic power that is impossible to resist. Valentinian's pledge of eternal love is clearly the most homoerotic expression in
Restoration tragedy. Lycius's status as a eunuch should not disguise the fact that
he is an attractive young man who offers the Emperor rich and lusty kisses in response to his own. This scenic moment seems to me to offer a great deal: all the
admiration for the friend and all the horror at the sodomite are here combined in
a single moment of dramatic intensity. The very contradictions of Restoration culture brought forward by this "discovery" scene, and more than a single emperor's
sexual interests are being represented. Here at last is a moment that suggests that
male friendship is more than platonic and that male-male love is more than
sodomitical.

The theater itself encourages such a reading. *Valentinian* belongs to the same
period as *All for Love* and *The Rival Queens*. *The London Stage* tells us that the intended cast for the production, which was in fact postponed until 1684, included
Charles Hart as the Emperor and Thomas Clarke as Lycius. Hart was of course one
of the central actors of the King's Company, and he introduced roles as wide-rang-
ing as Horner in *The Country Wife* and the "mad" partner of Nell Gwynn in James
Howard's *All Mistaken, or The Mad Couple* (1667), as well as every other important
part that the King's Company presented. Interestingly, when he introduced the
parts of Antony and Alexander in 1677, his young male partner was Thomas
Clarke.[33] Montague Summers long ago noted the "uranian" features of the
Restoration stage, and he lists Clarke among several actors whom he cites as "homosexual."[34] While Summers's volume displays all the dangers of ahistorical research into the history of sexuality, it does strike a chord that the plays themselves
echo. If Clarke, and other actors such as Kynaston (whom Robert D. Hume and
Judith Milhouse think would have made a better Dolabella than Clarke—"Dolla-
bella is the sort of role in which Edward Kynaston specialized") and Mountfort
(whom Summers says was the subject of several scandals and who did play Lycias
when he was nineteen) were involved in sexual intrigues of various kinds, then
the kinds of scenes I have been discussing would have a valence far different from
that in which "homosexuality" is seen as a breach of decorum.[35] *Valentinian* exposes the erotics of male friendship in unmistakable terms, at the same time that
it suggests that the language of heroic love is steeped in physical affection. The
discovery scene in the last act of the play articulates in the clearest theatrical
terms available that erotic affection between men is at the center of this homosocial culture.

Heroic friendship exposes this tragedy of male love. The prop of kingly prerogative, the excess of physical devotion, the false promise of sexual identity, failure, madness, death; male love is maligned as a curse in the very culture that uses it as its most basic structural principle. If heroic friendship is not platonic, is it necessarily sodomitical? Is there a male love that can be spoken here, a male love that neither defies the dictates of culture nor denies the fact of desire? Something like this is at the center of these plays, and at the center of the culture that would rather euphemize male love as friendship and malign male-male desire as sodomitical. Male love transforms friendship with the urgency of desire, celebrates the physical as having a kind of spiritual power, reaches for a language of its own, claims its place in a hierarchy of value. Male love, in other words, is really a lot like love.

Notes

I have published a different version of this essay in the journal *GLQ*. It is reprinted here by permission of Columbia University Press. I am grateful to Alisa Solomon and Framji Minwalla, the organizers of the Queer Theater Conference and the editors of this collection, for giving me the opportunity to present these ideas. I would also like to thank Jennifer Brody, Joseph Childers, Katherine Kinney, and Traise Yamamoto for offering me suggestions on an earlier version of this piece.

1. The most interesting recent critic of Restoration heroic drama is Joseph Roach; see, for instance, his "The Artificial Eye: Augustan Theater and the Empire of the Visible," in *The Performance of Power: Theatrical Discourse and Politics*, ed. Sue-Ellen Case and Janelle Reinelt (Iowa City: University of Iowa Press, 1991), 131–45. Still among the most useful studies of Restoration drama is that by Laura Brown, *English Dramatic Form, 1660–1760: An Essay in Generic Form* (New Haven: Yale University Press, 1981); see also Robert D. Hume, *The Development of English Drama in the Late Seventeenth Century* (Oxford: Clarendon Press, 1976); John Loftis, *Restoration Drama: Modern Essays in Criticism* (New York: Oxford University Press, 1966); Eric Rothstein, *Restoration Tragedy: Form and the Process of Change* (Madison: University of Wisconsin Press, 1967); Eugene M. Waith, *Ideas of Greatness: Heroic Drama in England* (London: Routledge, 1971).
2. See Paula R. Backscheider, *Spectacular Politics: Theatrical Power and Mass Culture in Early Modern England* (Baltimore: Johns Hopkins University Press, 1993); Elin Diamond, "Gestus and Signature in Aphra Behn's *The Rover*," *ELH* 56 (1989):519–41; and Kristina Straub, *Sexual Suspects: Eighteenth-Century Players and Sexual Ideology* (Princeton: Prince-

ton University Press, 1992). Although Straub is primarily interested in a later period, her comments have particular valence for Restoration theatrical experience as well.

3. See Roach, "The Artificial Eye."

4. Harold Weber, "Carolean Sexuality and the Restoration Stage: Reconstructing the Royal Phallus in Sodom," in *Cultural Readings of Restoration and Eighteenth-Century English Theater*, ed. J. Douglas Canfield and Deborah C. Payne (Athens, Ga.: University of Georgia Press, 1995), 73.

5. Weber, "Carolean Sexuality," 75.

6. For a discussion of the sexual circumstances of the Elizabethan theater, see Stephen Orgel, *Impersonations: The Performance of Gender in Shakespeare's England* (Cambridge: Cambridge University Press, 1996).

7. Kristina Straub, "Actors and Homophobia," in *Cultural Readings of Restoration and Eighteenth-Century English Theater*, ed. J. Douglas Canfield and Deborah C. Payne (Athens, Ga.: University of Georgia Press, 1995), 258; see also Straub, *Sexual Suspects*, 3–23.

8. Straub, "Actors and Homophobia," 259, 261; the internal quotation is from William Prynne, *Histrio-Mastrix: The Player's Scourge*, 2 vols. (1633; rpr. New York: Johnson Reprint Corporation, 1972), 1:168.

9. John Dryden, *All for Love*, ed. David Vieth (Lincoln: University of Nebraska Press, 1972); further references are to this edition.

10. See, for instance: G. S. Rousseau, "The Pursuit of Homosexuality in the Eighteenth Century: Utterly Confused Category and/or Rich Repository?" *Eighteenth-Century Life* 9 (1985):132–68; Randolph Trumbach, "Sodomitical Assaults, Gender, Role, and Sexual Development in Eighteenth-Century London," *Journal of Homosexuality* 16 (1988): 407–29; Harold Weber, "'Drudging in Fair Aurelia's Womb': Constructing Homosexual Economies in Rochester's Poetry," *The Eighteenth Century: Theory and Interpretation* 33 (1992):99–118. See also Carole Fabricant, "Rochester's World of Imperfect Enjoyment," *Journal of English and Germanic Philology* 73 (1974):338–50.

11. Jonathan Goldberg, *Sodometries: Renaissance Texts, Modern Sexualities* (Stanford: Stanford University Press, 1992), 121; see also Alan Bray, *Homosexuality in Renaissance England* (London: Gay Men's Press, 1982), and Alan Bray, "Homosexuality and the Signs of Male Friendship," *History Workshop: A Journal of Socialist and Feminist Historians* 29 (1990):1–15; Gregory W. Bredbeck, *Sodomy and Interpretation: Marlowe to Milton* (Ithaca: Cornell University Press, 1991); and Bruce R. Smith, *Homosexual Desire in Shakespeare's England* (Chicago: University of Chicago Press, 1991).

12. Goldberg, *Sodometries*, 122–23; see also Michel Foucault, *The History of Sexuality, vol. 1, An Introduction*, trans. Robert Hurley (New York: Pantheon, 1980), 101.

13. Goldberg, *Sodometries*, 119; see Bray, "Homosexuality and the Signs of Male Friendship," 1–5.

14. Consider, in this context, Otway's comedy on the same theme. *Friendship in Fashion* was staged in 1678. Betrayal of friendship is its central theme, and its thrust is to view such betrayal in contempt. See Robert D. Hume, *The Rakish Stage: Studies in English Drama, 1660–1800* (Carbondale: Southern Illinois University Press, 1983), 82–92.

15. Bray, "Homosexuality and the Signs of Male Friendship," 5.

16. Straub, *Sexual Suspects*, 20.

17. Nathaniel Lee, *The Rival Queens*, ed. P. F. Vernon (Lincoln: Nebraska University Press, 1970); further references are to this edition.

18. Lee's play and Dryden's are nearly contemporary: the latter appeared several months after the former in 1677 and was to a certain extent modeled on it. There has been some speculation concerning the personal relationship between Dryden and Lee. See David Vieth, "Introduction," *All for Love* (Lincoln: University of Nebraska Press, 1972), xxv.

19. Goldberg, *Sodometries*, 119.

20. See J. M. Armisted, *Nathaniel Lee* (Boston: G. K. Hall, 1979), 69.

21. *Cassandra: The Fam'd Romance, the Whole Work, in Five Parts, Written Originally in French and Now Elegantly Rendered into English*, by Sir Charles Cotterell;...(London: Printed for Peter Parker, at the Leg and Star over against the Royal Exchange in Cornhill, 1676), 13.

22. See, for instance, *Cassandra*, 109, 122, 141.

23. Although there was no Restoration edition of Marlowe's *Massacre at Paris*, Lee used the work as a model for his own ill-fated *The Massacre of Paris* (1678–79); see Armisted, *Nathaniel Lee*, 94, 119–20.

24. "Lee became 'distracted' and on November 11, 1684 . . . was admitted to 'Bedlam,' the Bethlehem Royal Hospital for the Insane." Armisted, *Nathaniel Lee*, 24. Lee remained there until spring 1688. Very little is known about the specific details of his illness.

25. Rochester, "The Disabled Debauchee," l. 40; in *The Poems of John Wilmot, Earl of Rochester*, ed. Keith Walker (Oxford: Blackwell, 1984), 99.

26. Backscheider, *Spectacular Politics*, 65.

27. Armisted, *Nathaniel Lee*, 30.

28. See Goldberg, *Sodometries*, 124; see also William Empsom, "Two Proper Crimes," *The Nation* 163 (1946):444–45.

29. See Backscheider, *Spectacular Politics*, 3–31.

30. Roach, "The Artificial Eye," 143.

31. See Diamond, "Gestus and Signature in Aphra Behn's *The Rover*," 519.

32. *Collected Works of John Wilmot, Earl of Rochester*, ed. John Hayward (London: None-such, 1926), 232.

33. *The London Stage: 1660–1800, Part 1: 1660–1700*, ed. William A. Lennep (Carbon-dale: Southern Illinois University Press, 1965), 238, 255, 265.

34. Montague Summers, *The Playhouse of Pepys* (London: Kegan Paul, 1935), 292–96.

35. Robert D. Hume and Judith Milhouse, *Producible Interpretation: Eight English Plays, 1675–1707* (Carbondale: Southern Illinois University Press, 1985), 134; Summers, *The Playhouse of Pepys*, 292.

6 "Be True to Yearning"

Notes on the Pioneers of Queer Theater

Don Shewey

Howard Crabtree, the musical-comedy performer and giddily imaginative costume designer who died of AIDS in June 1996, created his final opus *When Pigs Fly* as a tribute to the Dream Curlys of the world. You know, the ones who, in the high school productions of *Oklahoma!* got cast as the lead dancer in the dream-ballet sequence and got to wear a cowboy hat and pink tights cinched with a holster. All the nelly boys left adrift by adolescent social activities who stepped into their power dancing in musicals, sewing sequins onto faux-royal costumes, or staying up all night painting original backdrops for stage sets. All the pale, bookish, androgynous, flamboyant, odd-looking creatures either born with or socialized into "a talent to amuse," no less valuable to the world than other talent, though frequently less valued.

The history of queer theater was written on the bodies of its creators. The people who could pass usually did. They pursued "careers" in the "straight" theater where fellow out-to-you/closeted-to-them agents, casting directors, and friends counseled them carefully (as Noel Coward once did Cecil Beaton) on how to avoid appearing "obvious." Some of us, though, were so gay we couldn't help showing it. In the panel discussion "From the Invisible to the Ridiculous," Everett Quinton told an attentive audience that as a kid he liked to wrap a towel around his head and make faces in the bathroom mirror. For years, he thought he was insane, to the point of attempting suicide, until he was cruising Christopher Street one night and had the good fortune to pick up a man in whose theater company such passionate play was de rigueur. That was, of course, Charles Ludlam, who once said in an interview, "Gay people have always found refuge in the arts, and the Ridiculous Theatre is notable for admitting it. The people in it—and it is a very sophisticated theater, culturally—never dream of hiding anything about themselves that they feel is honest and true and the best part of themselves."

As Randy Conner documents in his extraordinary cross-cultural study *Blossom of Bone*, there have been gender-variant individuals since the beginning of recorded history. Sometimes embraced and sometimes reviled by their societies, they often found their place in houses of worship as priests and priestesses, devotees and attendants to temples in honor of revered deities. When the Inquisition and other medieval sex-negative crusades set about eradicating the pagan sensuality rampant just below the surface of ostensibly monotheistic religions, it simply reasserted itself in the semisecular realm of the artists. Theater in particular is the art form that most methodically assembles the elements of sacred ritual—consecrated space, designated time, community of celebrants, and preparations that consume 90 percent of the total energy of the enterprise.

The term "Queer Theater" first appeared, I believe, in Stefan Brecht's book of that name. Published in 1978, Brecht's loving, fanatical chronicle (compiled from copious diary entries) focused on a handful of phenomena from the gay artistic demimonde of the sixties and seventies: Jack Smith, John Vaccaro, Ronald Tavel, Charles Ludlam, the Hot Peaches, the Ballets Trocadero, and filmmaker John Waters. These creatures were sophisticated, ironic, prickly, highly cultured, eccentric—a far cry from any definition of queer theater that centers on such heartfelt but essentially white-bread plays like *Love! Valour! Compassion!* or one-man shows like *The Night Larry Kramer Kissed Me*.

In his book, Brecht quotes at length from an essay by George Denniston published in the journal *American Review* in 1973. Denniston recalled stepping out of a bar in the theater district at midnight and spying a fantastic androgynous creature. He was so captivated that, like Alice chasing the White Rabbit, he followed this person down the street into the doorway of a small theater, where he witnessed an otherwise forgotten queer-theater spectacle called *Whores of the Apostles*. The performance belonged, Denniston said:

neither to the masculine world nor the feminine, but to the world of the imagination. More specifically, to the imagination captured by yearning. Their play-acting was like the

125

make-believe of children, who with a few gestures and rags of costumes, skate as it were over sunlit ice, a ground of infinite possibility; with this difference, of course: that the grown-up actors had chosen a ground of the impossible, one would say the eternal impossible. Their blasphemy, their outrageous egotism, their sense of magic may have seemed demonic, but in fact they were priestly figures, they were acting out for us the wilderness of lust and crime against which we experience our social cohesion. In the biblical sense, they enacted the scapegoat. Their method, too, for all its wildness, was a spiritual method: be true to impulse and delight, be true to yearning. It leads to catastrophe, of course, but that was already behind them, for these were not ordinary people. Or put it another way: the catastrophe, already, is behind us all. It is the death of the heart to deny it. And since there is no other ground to dance upon, why, dance upon it!

Every gay homosexual queer knows the feeling of tumbling down the rabbit hole and finding yourself in Wonderland. For many of us, making theater was the initiation into experiencing queer self; for some, it was the other way around. Queerness and theater seem inextricably linked, twined around each other like flesh and spirit.

That was certainly true for me. Church was my first theater, a show we were always rehearsing for. At St. Joseph's Elementary School in Waco, Texas, the teachers taught us how to be Catholic. We learned how to dress for mass and special occasions like first communion. We learned our lines by heart, and the songs, and the choreography—when to sit and when to stand and when to kneel. The teachers taught us what sins were and how to confess. Being in church was really different from life in the trailer park where I grew up. In church, things were maintained with reverence and wonder and mystery. People wore special clothes and used a different language. Incense and candle wax dressed the air. From the moment I first saw them, I envied the altar boys who got to be part of the theater of church. They had roles to play, a few lines, they got to carry things for the priest, they got to dress up in special robes. I very much wanted to be one.

I was in third grade when it started, this craving not unrelated to my later craving to act, to go onstage, to get attention, to participate in a larger more colorful world that existed partly in the visible and partly in the invisible. I learned that behind the solemn ceremony there was humor and humanity. Kindness was available to a boy like me. All the priests looked at me and remembered when they too had been sensitive homosexual children who didn't belong to their families. They took me in and accepted me without question.

When I left home, I didn't bother going to mass on Sunday any more. At Rice

University, theater was an extracurricular activity, which meant it attracted only true devotees. There I found my calling. Theater became my church—not solemn/hush/behave church, but a community of purpose, humor, and a diffuse yet inviting ambisexuality. We did four shows a year, so at peak periods we stayed up all night building sets and sewing costumes, worked the box office between classes, and performed in the evening. Then at cast parties we'd get drunk and kiss each other. The campus was still closety in 1972–73; the only public sign of gay activity was in the basement men's room at the library. When I had an affair with a Greek Orthodox priest who was the musical director of our production of *Zorba!* our little theater community was scandalized.

After two years, I transferred to Boston University to study theater in earnest. The professional training environment deadened the spirit of theater for me, but Boston was a hotbed of gay political activism. There was even a gay student group on campus. For the first time, I found gay community outside the theater, and I brought my fervent new out identity to class with me. For monologues, I would sing "Does Anybody Love You?" from *Boy Meets Boy* or recite *suicide/when the rainbow is enuf* from *for colored girls who have considered suicide/when the rainbow is enuf*, blatantly imitating every inflection of Trazana Beverly's performance on the original cast album. I discovered soon enough that I wasn't cut out to be an actor. The whole going-to-auditions, looking-for-an-agent routine scared me. I didn't feel confident enough in my talent to withstand that constant torment. I found my niche writing about theater, first for the *Gay Community News*. I reviewed local productions, made pilgrimages to New York to see *Equus* and *A Chorus Line*, and began developing a gay analysis of mainstream theater.

Then a commercial production of Robert Patrick's *The Haunted Host* opened at a local theater starring this whirlwind force named Harvey Fierstien. This was the most out-out-out gay theater I'd ever witnessed. In the course of reviewing, interviewing, and getting to know Hurricane Harvey, I started to educate myself about a whole gay subculture Off-Off-Broadway that you never heard about unless you had grown up in New York reading the *Village Voice* and not necessarily even then.

In the 1950s and early 1960s, gay culture was a secret society of introductions, special knocks, passwords, highly codified behavior, a subterranean hothouse protected from and invisible to the bland, conformist, post–McCarthy era dominant culture. There were no openly gay bookstores, gay magazines, or gay talkshows. (Of course, there were gay bookstore clerks, gay magazine editors, and gay talk show hosts, though not necessarily openly so.) You couldn't go to the newsstand in Sheridan Square and pick up the *Advocate, Out, HX, New York Native, Honcho, Drummer,* and *My Comrade.* You would not find the word "gay" in the *New York Times,* or the word "homosexual" anywhere without heavy negative vibes. The Christopher Street clone hadn't been invented yet. No one paraded the streets with nipple rings or pierced septums. Theater in the West Village did not include *Dressing Room Divas, Nuns against Filth, Cute Boys in Their Underpants,* or *Vampire Lesbians of Sodom.* There were drag cotillions and skin shows where fairies congregated to entertain one another, but on the QT.

There were plenty of gay people creating important theater in the fifties and sixties and seventies who are never included in the pantheon when "queer theater" (or its cousin, "gay theater," or that imaginary being, "gay and lesbian theater") is discussed: Joseph Chaikin, Julian Beck, Jose Quintero, Ellis Rabb, Norris Houghton, Robert Moss, Richard Barr, Tom O'Horgan, Cheryl Crawford, Lyn Austin, Eva Le Gallienne, and Marshall Mason, to name only a few. William Inge, Tennessee Williams, and Edward Albee had no public identity as gay men, though all were tarred in the press for their homosexuality. What theater could be more "queer"/strange than Genet's? He had a tremendous impact on American theater in the early sixties, along with Samuel Beckett and Eugene Ionesco, but perhaps because his plays were much less homoerotic than his novels, he was not primarily perceived as a proponent of queer theater.

But queer theater happened because these paths had been cleared, the ground had been broken. Its emergence runs parallel to the gay liberation movement. The Stonewall Rebellion wasn't the conception but the birth of an out and proud social identity that had been gestating for a decade. Queer theater grew not from scripted plays written in isolation or from the championship of entrepreneurial producers. It grew from communities of people for whom theater was more than a career—it was a way to live.

The pioneer out gay theater makers didn't start from a theoretical or sociopolitical agenda. Their theater making was inseparable form their personal identities, their lives, their social circles, their senses of humor, their need for love and companionship. In contrast to previous generations of gay artists and artisans who had spent their lives making theater that rarely if ever reflected the dramas of their own lives, they wanted to be the same people at work that they were at home. They wanted to rehabilitate stereotypes of queers as weak sissies and psychotic bulldykes. But they didn't want to spend all their time consciousness-raising. As artists, they struggled to fashion intimate flashes of created life. Part of their priesthood was to live out an ideal articulated by Albert Camus: "Man's [sic] work is nothing but a slow trek to rediscover through the detours of art those one or two images in whose presence his heart first opened."

Only in retrospect is it possible to step back and see the wider context in which queer theater emerged Off-Off-Broadway—and to understand the courage it took to be that free. Since no manual had been written, the pioneers adhered to no coherent aesthetic, form, style, or content. They made theater that was outrageous and artistically ambitious. They also made three-character one-set plays and fifty-minute monologues. In general, though, "excess" was not a dirty word; few queer theater makers were minimalists. A lot of their work sifted through the debris of pop culture—deranging it, rearranging it, exaggerating it, taking it too seriously. That camp sensibility eventually entered the culture and got tamed in the process; nowadays, virtually all pop culture quotes other pop culture. Then it was a subversive strategy, cultural critique, and identity formation disguised as child's play.

In the sixties and seventies, queer theater artists worked almost exclusively in obscurity, without reviews or subscription audiences or advertising. Unavoidably, they were aware of another level of theater getting more attention elsewhere. Not just under the bright lights of Broadway either. From 1962 to 1971, for instance, the Ford Foundation invested more than $16 million in seventeen theaters around the country, thereby launching the regional theater movement as we know it. No such institutional support rallied the cause of queer cultural identity. Queer theater was built with the sweat equity and all-embracing vision of a small number of passionate individuals, including an African American fashion designer named Ellen Stewart, who started a coffeehouse and called it La Mama; a Methodist minister named Al Carmines, who started a poets' theater in the choir loft of the Judson Memorial Church; and especially a chubby opera queen with a lean mean cappucino machine who named his café after himself, Joe Cino. Legendary as the birthplace of Off-Off-Broadway, the Caffe Cino simultaneously provided a tinfoil and twinkle-lit platform for newly hatched queer playwrights such as Doric Wilson, H. M. Koutoukas, Bob Heide, Bill Hoffman, Lanford Wilson, Tom Eyen, Jeff Weiss, David Starkweather, Charles Stanley, and Robert Patrick. (Anyone who wants a vivid, thinly fictionalized, microscopically detailed description of life in and around the Cino need go no further than the nearest copy of Patrick's novel, *Temple Slave*, wherein all is revealed.)

I first learned about the Caffe Cino—and Patrick's down-the-Rabbit-Hole introduction to it—from his play *Kennedy's Children*, which had its pre-Broadway tryout in Boston while I was in college. The Cino had been closed for years, but Patrick's fictional account was so tantalizing that I sought out more information and found a motherlode in Albert Poland and Bruce Mailman's invaluable resource, *The Off-Off-Broadway Book*. And on my theater-going expeditions to New York, I started meeting some of the people who figured in this evolution of queer theater.

On one such jaunt, I interviewed two gay producers for *GCN*: Doric Wilson, who had founded The Other Side of Silence (TOSOS), the first theater company that called itself openly gay, and John Glines, who had worked with TOSOS briefly before starting his own company, the Glines. To my dazzled young eyes, they were bold, articulate, powerful impresarios of gay culture in the big city. In retrospect, I recognize that they were barely making it, struggling against many obstacles to put their shows on in church basements, or in Wilson's case, the bars where he made a living serving drinks.

The first time I ever stepped foot in a leather bar—although it was a warm, airless Sunday afternoon and there were no leathermen around—was to see Doric Wilson's *The West Street Gang* at the Spike. The play was set in just such a waterfront bar and ostensibly dealt with the need for gay men to protect themselves from marauding bands of juveniles who prowled the streets and stomped queers. But gay bashers weren't the only villains of the piece. The play also satirized self-appointed media spokesmen who exploit any gay controversy for their own ends. I had a bunch of mixed feelings about the show. One of the characters was "Arthur Klang," an obvious caricature of the *Village Voice* columnist Arthur Bell, whose coverage of sensational crimes by and against queers upset some gay readers, obviously including Doric Wilson. Bell was a friend of mine who had welcomed me into a circle of gay journalists that also included Vito Russo and Robert Chesley; in fact, I was staying at his apartment while visiting from Boston. I was confused by the intramural squabbling. Also, the script was schematic, the characters cartoonish, and the production qualities—the sets, the acting, and audience amenities—left something to be desired, certainly compared to *Equus* or *A Chorus Line*.

I came to understand, though, that this kind of theater was different from Broadway shows. It wasn't about stars or glamor or even literature especially. It was gay people talking to other gay people, without code, about the same things that were being discussed all over town across beer-splashed bars and breakfast tables (except that in those days, gay people didn't have breakfast; they had brunch). Street violence against gays and clashing views on what constituted "gay community" weren't being discussed in the *New York Times* or in Broadway shows in 1977. And I came to understand that the people doing this theater—including Doric Wilson as author/director/producer—were paying the rent with other jobs and doing theater for love and carfare, because it fed their spirits.

On another theater expedition, this time on assignment for the weekly *Boston Phoenix*, I spent a week hanging out with the Ridiculous Theatrical Company, interviewing Charles Ludlam and seeing their shows. The company had just moved into its first permanent home at 1 Sheridan Square, a somewhat clammy basement, downstairs from a Vietnamese restaurant and around the corner from the bar that launched the Stonewall Rebellion, which was then occupied by a mediocre diner called the Bagel And. Later, someone donated a supply of plush movie theater seats to the Ridiculous; at the time, though, the seating consisted of hard-on-the-butt, church-pew-like stone benches. In the delirium of inaugurating their new home, the company was mounting an ambitious rotating repertory of plays. In a single week, I got to see not only Ludlam's already famous rendition of *Camille* but also his version of *Hamlet*, *Stage Blood*, and *The Ventriloquist's Wife*, which he performed with Black-Eyed Susan and a foul-mouthed dummy named Walter Ego. In addition, Ludlam gave puppet shows in the afternoon: his award-winning *Punch and Judy Show* and something called *Anti-Galaxy Nebulae*, which was basically Charles and his lover Everett Quinton manipulating strange props and playing kooky music for an audience of seven, looking for all the world like two kids in a treasure-filled toy box. Charles invited me to spend a casual evening at the theater looking at somebody's slides from a trip to Europe. That evening sticks in my memory, partly because I ended up going home with the sexy lighting designer. But mostly I remember being surprised at the sweet and homey atmosphere of the gathering. In contrast to the flamboyant performers with their highly theatrical voices, outlandish costumes, and extreme makeup, the company members offstage were quiet, even mousy.

This experience unleashed a whole other confusion of thoughts for me. I could see that Ludlam was an ambitious, brilliant theater maker with the highest aspirations to art, toiling not on Broadway or in some well-funded institutional theater, but in his own jerry-rigged yet fully functional laboratory. Here was a theater ostentatiously made by gay people, using elements of gay culture (drag and camp and an inspired ability to synthesize disparate elements, to spin gold out of debris) but not directly addressing gay themes.

"We use artifacts that we find to try to make some kind of culture," Ludlam said to me when I interviewed him one afternoon, amid the chaos of set changes between shows, then added:

It's because the gay lifestyle has to be learned somewhere other than in the family unit. We throw our cards in the air and, leaving society's structure as is, form another outside of it. That's a complicated thing in itself. People who have to deal with that have a different worldview. If you have this point of view, you can be very disoriented and miserable, or you can use it as a creative tool and it becomes a tremendous advantage. I think art is a lot about making advantages out of your disadvantages. For instance, as a gay person, I obviously have feelings for me. If I play Camille, I make something very special and a little hard to understand available, accessible. Ultimately, I think that has more cultural impact than if I proselytized people who are already convinced.

Ludlam expressed decidedly mixed feelings about being labeled gay theater—not because he wanted people to think he was straight (although being devoutly Catholic, who knows what internalized homophobia lingered on?), but because as an artist he felt that most of what was called gay theater simply wasn't good enough. Nor was most straight theater. Nor was most experimental theater. Ludlam, like most great artists, had very high standards for himself and others. He said:

I set up my life and my art so that it doesn't have the pretentiousness other art has. There are two ways in this society to do art and justify it—one is to say it educates the public, and the other is to be high art, which replaces religion. But by doing Ridiculous art, you're claiming to be worse than you are: the classic ruse in comedy. By taking the role of the ne'er-do-well, I don't fall into traps. I can put ideas into the play, but I don't have to. I can be awful. Through parody, I can use the classics without being enslaved by them. And I throw responsibility for valuing things on the audience. Instead of "I fell asleep but it was opera," I dare the audience to have an opinion.

Ludlam wasn't the first to attempt to fuse high artistic aspirations with lowbrow popular forms. Many of the writers and directors and creators associated with the Caffe Cino and La Mama as well as queer theater pioneers Jack Smith, Ron Tavel, and John Vaccaro were well-read, extremely sophisticated and cultured individuals, making theater that operated on many levels. Nevertheless, Ludlam was both extraordinarily talented and exceptionally articulate about what he was doing. Both his theoretical essays and manifestos (collected by Steve Samuels in a useful volume called *Ridiculous Theatre: Scourge of Human Folly*) and his prodigious output as theater maker, had an incalculable effect on a succeeding generation of artists eager to be their gay selves and make excellent theater. Harvey Fierstein, Charles Busch, Tony Kushner, and David Greenspan—among many others—absorbed aspects of Ludlam's Ridiculous Theater and brought them to a wider audience than those who were fortunate enough to see Ludlam's own work.

It must be said that Ludlam assembled and cultivated an extraordinary company of versatile, highly resourceful, one-of-a-kind performers, who have carved their own profiles on the Mt. Rushmore of Off-Off-Broadway queer theater. They include Lola Pashalinski, Black-Eyed Susan, and Everett Quinton, who assumed artistic directorship of the company after Ludlam's death in 1987. Even Ethyl Eichelberger, a prodigious creator of his own solo "one-woman" extravaganzas, was never more powerful onstage than when he was directed by Ludlam. Sad to say, the Ridiculous is a company that has not simply been decimated, but virtually obliterated by the plague of our time. Its AIDS casualties include Bill Vehr, John D. Brockmeyer, and Georg Osterman, as well as Eichelberger and Ludlam himself.

As Ana Maria Simo pointed out in the panel discussion "From the Invisible to the Ridiculous," theaters such as Doric Wilson's TOSOS and Charles Ludlam's Ridiculous Theatrical Company coexisted in time and proximity with the lesbian theater she cofounded, Medusa's Revenge. Yet they may as well have been on different planets. They occupied completely distinct social circles and aesthetic realms, with no conscious or unconscious solidarity around any shared notions of something called "queer theater." Nor did they have or particularly seek a connection with feminist theaters in New York such as Womanspace, Interart, or Spiderwoman. Medusa's Revenge was formed out of a need for a group of Latina immigrant and working-class women to hold onto some kind of identity in a culture that reacted to their existence with a vacuum of validating images. Personal survival—of the soul and the spirit—drew them together, and out of that came their cultural production. Their suffering and their paradoxical freedom to create helped pave the way and to create at least a rudimentary model for the next generation of friskier, more culturally secure young dykes to follow—or depart from.

The WOW Café, which began as a festival and evolved into an ongoing theater, bloomed from the energy and talent of women such as Peggy Shaw, Lois Weaver, Carmelita Tropicana, Sarah Schulman, Holly Hughes, and the tribe who would eventually become known as the Five Lesbian Brothers. And as is so often the case, the basis for community was not only artistic but social and sexual. As Moe Angelos said in the panel discussion (quoting Carmelita Tropicana), women flocked to the WOW Café "looking for *poo-ssy*." (For an entertaining close-up picture of East Village lesbian life and the WOW Café, read Sarah Schulman's novel, *Girls, Visions, and Everything.*)

By the early eighties, an entire generation of queer artists had already established several working models of how to go about making queer theater. When

Harvey Fierstein won Tony Awards both for *Torch Song Trilogy*—each part of which had first appeared at La Mama—and then for his libretto for the Broadway musical *La Cage aux Folles*, it seemed like out gay theater had hit the mainstream and was here to stay. Still, outside New York, the resources, the know-how, and the like-minded company were not automatically at hand. Without a Ford Foundation flying artistic directors around to see how the others worked, pioneering gay theater companies such as San Francisco's Theatre Rhinocerous, Los Angeles's Celebration Theater, and Seattle's Alice B. Theatre had to do their share of reinventing the wheel—or, to give that effort a more positive spin, each had to evolve in a grassroots way out of its existing circumstances rather than reproduce the New York model.

Looking back over these notes, I cringe a little bit at my own tendency to idealize or romanticize queer theater, especially the aspect of art as a designated queer spiritual practice. If theater is the queerest art, why aren't its creators 100 percent queer? Obviously, many people who make theater and consider it a form of touching spirit are not gay. Is there a special kinship between sex and spirituality, eroticism and theatricality, that makes theater feel like home to gay people? As Jaffe Cohen of the comedy trio Funny Gay Males once put it, "High school drama club is basically a Head Start program for gay kids." You know . . . we like to make things pretty. We're not the only ones who make things pretty, though. Yes, the long lineage of artists as healers and shamans and shape-shifters includes many queers, but it doesn't exclude people who aren't queer.

Is the essence of queerness something that transcends sexual preference—or sexuality at all? Is it something that includes sex and art and is bigger than both? Is it something that is shared by most (but not all) gay men and lesbians and some straights (definitely not none)?

Posing these questions, I suddenly experience the folly of trying to write about gay culture as a separate entity. Like everything, it exists always in relation—not necessarily in opposition or antagonistic reaction—to other things. In the next breath, I recognize that these questions are far from resolved. They are alive in our work, in our conferences, and throughout this book.

One thing that might truthfully be said, though, is that the women and men who created queer theaters when none existed before, were looking for a place where their gayness was seen not as an embarrassment, a hindrance, or worse, but as the golden thread in the fabric of their lives—as Charles Ludlam put it, "the best part of them."

7 From the Invisible to the Ridiculous

The Emergence of an Out Theater Aesthetic

A conversation among Moe Angelos, Susan Finque, Lola Pashalinski, Everett Quinton, Ana Maria Simo, and Doric Wilson, moderated by Don Shewey

DON SHEWEY: The people on the panel represent the queer theater movement that started in the early sixties. Each of these people has been instrumental in either creating or further developing an out gay theater company. They're among the pioneers whose courage and passion and willingness to starve for their art paved the way for such a thing as a queer theater conference.

Our topic is the emergence of an out aesthetic; these artists really exemplify an out aesthetic, and speak from that out aesthetic, no matter what they talk about. I'd be curious to hear you start by speaking about your personal journey in your emergence as an out theater artist. Was there a time when you were in some version of the closet, and how did you get here from there?

Was there a difference between being out in your life and being out in the theater? What were those stages along the way for you? I'd like to suggest that we do this chronologically.

DORIC WILSON: I came to New York in 1958 from a ranch in Washington State. I did not come to New York in the cowboy style of the seventies. In the fifties, if you came from a ranch in Washington State, you came to New York trying to look like Noel Coward, and I looked as much like Noel Coward as I could. I've always been out. I grew up in a sort of pioneer family in a very unpopulated pioneer county, at that time, in Washington, the Five Cities.

There weren't any five cities when I grew up. There were only two cities. But my grandfather had more or less founded the county, and built the roads and what-have-you.

So, I had that wonderful old-time American arrogance of pioneers, that it didn't matter what I did, nobody had a right to say anything to me. So I came out in school. I came out because a friend who was gay killed himself when he realized that he was about to be discovered, and I decided I wasn't a good enough shot to kill myself, so I'd better come out. To be honest, that's more or less what happened.

I came to New York to be a set and costume designer, but I was so naive, I had no idea where one studies set and costume design. So I was used as an actor. I did any number of stock productions of *Auntie Mame* as young Patrick Dennis. My roommate at the time was a straight English actor and I wrote a play for a little theater workshop that we were in, an Adam and Eve play called *And He Made A Her,* and an actress in that company had just done a Tennessee Williams play at this coffeehouse on Cornelia Street in the Village.

Now, those of you who know New York City and know Cornelia Street know that it runs for one block. In the early sixties, what is now the West Village was almost part of Little Italy. It was not part of Bohemia.

So, the Caffe Cino was really more in Little Italy environment than New Bohemia. This actress, Regina Oliver, took me down to the Cino, introduced me to this short, impish, round man behind the counter: Joe Cino, who always had one hand on the arm of the cappucino machine or ringing a bell to start the performance, so I always see Joe Cino with one arm in the air. I started to hand him the play while he was making a sandwich and making cappucino. He opened the notebook, and he said, "Three weeks from now, on Friday," and closed the notebook and pushed the play away, and I turned to Regina and said, "What does that mean?"

She said, "That's when you open." From that point on, we all just did plays at the Cino. Lanford [Wilson], myself, Tom Ewen—we all wrote gay plays there, but it never occurred to us that's what we were doing. We also wrote bad plays there. Joe was completely open.

The other side of the coin was critics. In the sixties it was a problem if you were known as an out gay playwright. There were theaters that would not do your work. The most important of them was the Public Theater. Most of the Cino playwrights were not done at the Public Theater. But we had the Cino. So things were wonderful.

Most of our enemies at the time were not straight. They were other gays, closeted gays, higher up in the business. All the years I ran gay theater, I never had any trouble with a straight agent giving me submittals of actors for anything we did at TOSOS, but I had real trouble with the known gays. I hate to bring that up, but there it is.

LOLA PASHALINSKI: I went to the Cino often and it was wonderful. I am sort of of that era. I found myself queer in the fifties and going to places like the Cino was very important. I had a friend, Harvey Tavel, when I was twenty and he was eighteen and we stood on line at the Metropolitan Opera all the time, and formed a group of friends who did that for years, and that way I met his brother Ron. In the sixties, I had sort of come to a kind of impasse in my life, and one day Harvey called me and said, "Would you like to be a script girl for John Vacarro on a production called *The Life of Lady Godiva*? The year before, I had seen Ronnie's plays, *The Life and Times of Juanita Castro* and *Shower*, which had been produced in a storefront gallery on 10th Street and Third Avenue, and they were incredibly well run.

They were brilliantly directed by John, and he appeared in the second one, and they were so funny and so fresh and so daring and so erotic. Two women who played men's roles kissed each other, and I thought that was very wonderful. Before that, I had usually gotten my yayas out at *Rosenkavalier*, and this was different. I should say also that another influence in my life from when I was very young was Milton Berle, really.

So, I had these two things going in me, the Milton Berle thing and this other kind of romantic idea about lesbianism, from opera and all of that kind of stuff. And then there was Ronnie's play, and then I was asked to be a script girl, and then I walked into John's loft on Great Jones Street and I saw Maria Montez and Rene Ricard and a kind of world that was totally free. One day somebody dropped out. I was in the chorus line of nuns, and one of the nuns was out. John sent me up there just to stand in her place. And that was it. I never left. And then I became an actress, and here I am. I should say that in that cast was Charles Ludlam, and that's really why I became an actress.

EVERETT QUINTON: I was a really fucked up kid, and I was very insane because I learned to hate myself very early, very young. I thought I was nuts because I would go into the shower and in the privacy of my bathroom, I could be this drag queen. I would wrap myself in my towel and I didn't know anything, but I would just gesture and I would feel so free. But I thought I was nuts because of this, and I never had anyone to turn to because I was a terrified queer. I'm not terrified anymore, but then I was so afraid to be myself. I was digging myself into a very deep hole, and then I discovered Christopher Street.

I met Charles Ludlam next to the Lucille Lortel Theater. I was just cruising, and I met Charles Ludlam. That's my story. We went back to his apartment, and as we were walking, he told me he was writing the gay hero, and I was astonished, because I was living my life as a self-hating queer, and by this time, I had tried to kill myself several times because I couldn't face being queer—or not that I couldn't face it, I couldn't deal with other people's opinion of it.

I was not very courageous at the time. Charles was doing *Caprice* and it turned out to be the first play I was in. I remember seeing at a benefit for the company Georg Osterman, who was very beautiful, dressed as Bunny Bezwick in *Hot Ice*, and I was astounded that finally there was a place for me, that I was a drag queen, and that I was going to get a place to exist, free. Later we had a discussion with Georg about whether I was drag queen or an actor. Today I'm an actor, but I'm a drag queen actor.

I'm a drag queen, and that's my fundamental self, and in the Ridiculous, I got a place to stretch that. I found a place.

ANA MARIA SIMO: I came to New York in late 1973 and had already come out in college. I had gone to school in Paris, from sixty-eight to seventy-three, so I was a witness to a lot of political turmoil, and I was an activist, both in the gay movement and the feminist movement. The reason I left there was that a group of lesbians there wanted to start a space for lesbians, and we made some efforts, but it never happened because the French are not practical-minded and they can't make things happen.

So, I came here, and immediately I got involved through some New York friends in an attempt to create a lesbian space. It also didn't happen, but we did a lot of more American-style fund-raising and it was going to be called the Lesbian Life Space. But it didn't happen and it was very sad. I went home to do what everybody was doing: I was a typesetter, and as any typesetter at the time can tell, you did drugs. So, you typeset and you were in a state of stupor, saying, "What am I going to do with my life? I have a useless college undergraduate degree." Etcetera.

I had a girlfriend at the time who was an actress in the Spanish theater in New York, and she also worked at La Mama. She was a brilliant actress and a brilliant director. She was very dissatisfied with the roles that she was getting, as a woman.

She suggested the idea of the lesbian space and a theater where she could express herself and in a way, to help me out of a really pitiful situation, because I had no place. I was an exile from Cuba, and an exile from France, from two revolutions that didn't happen, and I was here. And the third thing, which was a career that wasn't happening here.

Out of that came the idea of Medusa's Revenge. It was her initiative to put me to work, so I would stop doing other things. We did our first play in September 1976. Both of us were exiles from Cuba. I had been here for three years; she had been here longer. It was a very abnormal situation for two lesbians, who were Latinas, who were recent immigrants, to take it upon themselves to do something that the natives couldn't do—because the idea was that if you were queer and you were a lesbian and you didn't have money, you couldn't do that kind of thing.

We did it. One of the reasons this is not known is precisely because neither one of us, or the women who came to work with us, were in the network of feminist theater or lesbian feminist activities. We were totally out of the loop in terms of our social class. We recruited for the theater by leafleting at the lesbian bars. I see Medusa's Revenge, in a way, as closer to what Doric Wilson was trying to do. That is, it was a community-based thing, although one of the two people there was someone who came from the theater. I came from a political background, but the whole thing was to recruit these women from the bars, and we got over fifteen of them who had never done anything. We ran a workshop for them to learn about acting and everything. I was not a writer then. I was the comanager. I would clean and stuff like that. I would do everything that's not artistic and I was very busy and fighting with the landlord. We were at 10 Bleecker Street, and we had the Yippies as the neighbors upstairs. There were people who were totally crazed, like one guy with a gun coming down a hall. I dealt with him. I was the bouncer. I was the person who would take the guns away and try to pacify them.

One day, the actors were doing improvisations and they felt that they weren't getting anywhere. I was cleaning the bathroom and I was asked if they gave me all their voluminous transcripts, if I could possibly write a play. (I had written fiction before, but I had dropped out of fiction, you know, when I started feeling angst.) I stayed home with a typewriter. I wrote the first scene of the play really quickly, and then I had this horrible writer's block the next month. I would be locked up in the house, cut off from things like acid and other things that I would preferably do, and I had to write this play, which suddenly, I just couldn't. Somehow—I don't know how—it got written. It was called *Bayou*, and it was very, very different from the feminist women's theater that was happening at the time, and a certain amount of women in the audience were walking out in a huff.

Medusa's Revenge operated from the fall of seventy-six to eighty-one, and WOW started immediately after, and a couple of items in the theater went to WOW. At the time, I remembered I felt relieved, because I felt the mission was in good hands, and it was continuing, and later I went on to become a playwright, mostly in the Latino theater.

A lot of the things that were thought about and kind of were in the area of Medusa's Revenge that I did there, I then did with the Lesbian Avengers in ninety-two, strangely enough, because that's a street group, so everything is done outdoors, but the same thing that I was working with in my own mind, the creative things in Medusa's Revenge, I think that I have been able to use in political work, perhaps because street activism has a lot of theatricalities. It has always attracted playwrights and people in the theater, and the idea of the power of words, not in the literal sense, but with mythmaking, poetic works, the power of graphics, of images, the power of street activity.

So I see a very coherent line for me from Medusa's Revenge, being a playwright in kind of legitimate, bona fide theaters, and then coming to lesbian activism. The difference when I started the Lesbian Avengers in 1992 with five friends, is that the space for lesbians is not indoors anymore. The symbolic value of doing something that marks our place in the city propelled me to the Avengers, and, actually, away from a lot of writing.

As a lesbian, I have plenty of indoors existence, and very little outdoors existence, and I love New York. This is my city, so I want to mark it. It's like an animal going to every little corner. I want my paws being there and being there, and I just was not satisfied with being a theater person and working indoors. I wanted to do some kind of outdoor theater/political things.

MOE ANGELOS: When I was probably about six years old, I saw a production of *Annie Get Your Gun*, and I was captivated by this idea that I could be a cowboy, but still be a girl, and I was given an *Annie Get Your Gun* outfit for Christmas. It had the holsters actually appliqued onto the skirt, which I found was not really very functional, and so I got real holsters and six-shooters.

So then we fast forward to 1980, and I had moved to New York and was going to NYU, studying theater, and I didn't like the theater anymore. I didn't have that feeling that I had as Annie with her guns, that I was really the cowboy. I dropped out of school, I was arrested in a political action in Washington, D.C., with Sarah Schulman among other people. It was the fall of 1981. After the trial was over and

I didn't have anywhere to go, because I wasn't going back to school, Sarah said to me, "You should come over to this women's theater festival. It's really great. There are going to be all these wild women from all over the world," and I felt, "yech, theater, but I'll give it another try." So I went over to Avenue A, to University of the Streets, at Seventh and A, which is now 7A Cafe, and at that point was an abandoned furniture store with a very big picture window which looked out onto those corners, and there was the WOW festival. I showed up on the first day and stayed for the entire festival.

I should mention that I was somewhere in this weird kind of closety, gross place in my life, where I couldn't figure out what was going on. I'm being very generous with myself there. I didn't want to figure out what was going on. There I was, surrounded by lesbians from all over the place, and they were doing really interesting theater, and most specifically, I saw the play *Split Britches*, by Split Britches, and I thought: "This is really good. This is interesting. I'm engaged with this again. This is exciting. And these women made this play themselves." And so I hung around, we got a space, I came out. That was one of the main things I actually got done at WOW: coming out. A lot of women come to WOW, as my friend Carmelita Tropicana says, "Looking for poossy." I, too, was looking for pussy, I guess, but my deeper, deeper self was speaking.

WOW was on 11th Street in a little, tiny storefront space during that early eighties era. There was a lot of performance going on. We would perform at WOW, and then we would run over to Avenue C and perform somewhere else, and then run back to Avenue A and perform someplace else, and it was a kind of round-robin of performance venues, which was very fertile. WOW was doing all kinds of stuff. We had a gallery space. We were very ambitious. We wanted to be everything for everybody, but it didn't work out. The most important thing is that like at Medusa's Revenge, women who never would have set foot onstage or written a word came to WOW somehow, looking for pussy, and managed to say something, or have an opportunity to have a forum to say things.

Now we're on 4th Street, still going strong, still producing work. We have no government funding, no funding of any kind except for the box office, which is modest, and we try and keep the prices low. We have an incredible volume of work, after all these years.

SUSAN FINQUE: I'm representing the West Coast. Let's deal with that, first. There are many, many people standing all over the world that could serve this panel fabulously—Marga Gomez, Brian Freeman. There are people who can no longer be here—Chuck Solomon and Martin Worman, who were original members of the

Gay Men's Theater Collective. And people like Kate Bornstein and Adele Prandini, who have put many, many miles on cleaning the toilets and staging the shows too, and my ex-theatrical partner, Rick Rankin in Seattle, also would have a tremendous amount to contribute here.

But I'm here, and that's really great. Back in 1990 in Seattle, we had a national theater festival for gay and lesbian artists. It started just days after Tim [Miller] and Holly [Hughes] were defunded, along with Karen [Finley] and John [Fleck]. And the media descended upon Seattle because at the same time, the then NEA director, John Frohnmayer, had come to see an opening of an opera. So it was quite the circus. Muriel Miguel was at that festival, and Kate Bornstein had brought *Hidden Agenda* there, and John Patterson, Rebecca Ransom, Sky Gilbert from Buddies in Bad Times, which is still flourishing in Toronto now. Split Britches brought *Little Women*. We said, "Gee, if we're going to bring all these artists here to perform, we better sit down and talk."

Don had asked me earlier, "When did you first see something lesbian? When did you know that there was something lesbian going on onstage?" I have a feeling I was a baby drag queen, because in my early years I used to stay in the bathroom, wrapped up in a towel to rehearse my synced performance with Julie Andrews on the record player singing, "How Do You Solve a Problem Like Maria," and at the time I was a tomboy. So, for me, it was very much a cross-gender role.

My first stage performance in another language besides English was as Yenta in *Fiddler on the Roof* at my temple, which we performed in Hebrew. At several points during the performance, I would turn to the audience and comment on the performance in English, which of course I was chastised for very strictly by the director, who was the rabbi, but as I look back, I realize that these were my initial dabblings in camp. I just felt like I wanted to have a more intimate relationship with the audience.

But perhaps more formalized exposure and involvement with what I identified as queer was, in my very first year of college, I had a relationship with Susan Griffin's play, *Voices*, which was originally written as a radio play. I say "relationship" because I read the play many times and held it in my hand for many years before I decided to do something with it, and I did something with it when my Shakespeare teacher at the time, Roger Stanley, would not cast me as Puck. I said, "Fine," and I dropped out of the theater program and I got involved with this play and directed it over in the cross-cultural studies program, in the women's studies program, which seemed to have an open ear and an open eye for doing other kinds of things like that, and then dropped out of school and went to San Francisco, where I was in a company called Caught in the Act, a theater collective of four short women, which was a sister company to the Gay Men's Theater Collective, and a lesbian theater company at the time called It's Just a Stage, which was under the direction of Adele Prandini.

Then I traveled the country in a vaudeville troupe called Professor Marvel's Miracle Pandemonium Revue, where I got my tap dancing skills under control, which I would certainly need in the years to come. Don, you should situate yourself, too.

DON SHEWEY: Although I see my role as the facilitator here, I'm happy to bring my story in. I thought about this in terms of just the smallest details of how I came out and the things that I looked to in culture for validation. I think that's where gay culture really meant a lot to me, and it took very small cues to give me that validation. I remember being thirteen years old and living in Aurora, Colorado, a suburb of Denver, and somehow finding Jean Genet's novel, *Our Lady of the Flowers,* in the public library, and crouching in the aisles of the library and reading this book about men in prison sniffing each other's farts, and this completely enflamed me and I would sit there and read it and hope nobody noticed, and I'd be totally hard and I couldn't bring myself to check out the book, but I would read it every time I went to the library. That somehow filled me. The same year—1967—*Hair* was on Broadway, and pop music was totally my life.

Nothing was more passionate and exciting to me than pop music, and the Fifth Dimension had recorded "Aquarius," and the Cowsills had recorded the title song, "Hair." I'd never seen a Broadway show—I was an air force brat and never went to the professional theater until I was a senior in high school. But I knew all these songs and bought the original Broadway cast album of *Hair.* There was a song called "Sodomy," which was also extremely exciting to me. But one thing had such a big impact on me. It was really just half a sentence on the back cover of the album that described a character who had a "thing" for Mick Jagger, and just the fact that there were gay characters in a Broadway musical relaxed something in me and allowed me to know that even in my kind of trailer trash milieu, if there weren't a lot of out queers, that somewhere out there in the world I had access to only by pop records, there was queerness.

The piece of that that came with me into my writing in theater, was being able to write openly about my desire for men. The first time I described an actor that I was hot for as "beautiful" in print, felt like a really big step.

The first professional writing I did was for *Gay Community News* in Boston, and that's where I started writing theater criticism. At the time, there wasn't a lot of gay theater to be had, and I was writing these insane reviews that were about

143

finding some queer perspective to write about Broadway try-outs of *Same Time Next Year* or *Pacific Overtures*. Then there was a commercial production, in a sort of Off-Broadway equivalent of a play by Robert Patrick called *The Haunted Host,* which they were producing with an actor I'd never heard of before whose name was Harvey Fierstein, and this became the thing I could write about. That was kind of a link for me to this world in New York theater that I then became avidly interested in.

As facilitator, though, I'm interested now in a couple of things that seem to be recurring themes in people telling their stories. One was that entering the theater or a sense of being gay in the theater was as much about how to live your life as a gay person as it was about any artistic aspiration.

Also, for a lot of people, the gay part of being queer in the theater had to do with cross-dressing, in some way. I'd like to hear a little bit more about the cross-dressing, or whatever else it was that made being out in the theater, be queer.

LOLA PASHALINSKI: It's interesting to me, personally, because for a long time, at the beginning of my experience with the Ridiculous Theatrical Company, Charles often cast me as the voluptuary or the earth mother or characters of that kind, and that was just fine. And it was a very pansexual company and one of the ideas behind it was that sexual identification is just a costume, like anything else. Actors have always done this. You put on a costume, you become another person, including their sexuality. But I was sort of in the closet, even in this most outrageous of companies, in a certain sense.

I mean, I was out as a lesbian, but when the time for me to be in drag—and this was something I had seen for a long time. My first theatrical experience in the theater was when I was fifteen years old, my parents took me to see Jean Arthur in *Peter Pan* and that was an incredible experience for me. And then all the opera-going and that kind of identification with men or boys when they're played by women—but when it came time for me to be in drag, I wanted to do it very, very much, because that was the Milton Berle side of me, the baggy-pants comedian, which at heart is really what I am. It's a male kind of clowning, but that was my sense of humor, which was what bound me to the company, because it was funny.

Still, when I was cast as Harry Feinschmecker in *Caprice* I struggled a great deal, because I was very uncomfortable. The role was great, and I enjoyed it very much, and I hope I did a good job, but underneath, I felt, well, they'll see I'm a lesbian. They'll think I'm not acting. They'll think it's just because I am a lesbian that I might be good in this, and it was very difficult for me, even though all my life I'd dressed in drag.

I'm in drag now. And most of the world, it seems to me, if you want to call it, is in drag, people wear pants. Everybody wears pants. The fear about being in drag, that it would expose me in a certain way and my masculine yearning, I think is because I didn't quite accept myself, not as a lesbian, but I didn't accept myself fully, or I hadn't fully accepted all of my sexuality. The sexuality of being a voluptuous woman on stage, that was a wonderful play-acting thing that I could enjoy, because I wasn't that kind of a woman, really. Later I became more accepting of myself for other reasons.

Just a couple of years ago I had the pleasure of playing Toby Belch in a *Twelfth Night* that was done at the Goodman by Neil Bartlett, and it was an entirely cross-dressed production. Women played all the parts except for Viola and Sebastian, who were played by two fourteen- and fifteen-year-old black American boys, and Feste, who was a black American male who played piano onstage through the whole play. That was when Milton Berle and my life sort of came together. It solved a lot of problems for me deep down inside.

I wonder about this next generation. I see Moe slide so easily between doing drag and doing a female role. I wonder how she does that, what that means to her and her psyche. Sometimes I think it's the position of gay people that they are pansexual, that they can be both, or they want to be both. It's either omnipotence or—there's a great line in *Eunuchs of the Forbidden City* where a eunuch says to the potential empress of China, "The eunuchs know men, and the eunuchs know women. They know them better than they know themselves." And "eunuchs" is a metaphor for "gay," I think. I am getting in trouble . . . But I'm interested in Moe and her generation and her own acting and how she does that.

MOE ANGELOS: Well, I'm not sure if I know how I do it. In *The Secretaries* where I played both a male and female in the same play, that very female, American secretary, was more drag to me. That was drag. The guy was easy. I've done that a lot before and I guess I can slip into that very comfortably, but, being that secretary with those nails and that hair . . .

LOLA PASHALINSKI: But Everett looks good that way.

DON SHEWEY: But Lola, I wasn't sure whether you meant that what was difficult for you about doing drag was a psychological thing or a professional thing, of not wanting to be seen as a "lesbian actor."

LOLA PASHALINSKI: Well, yes, there was all of that. It was partly psychological, partly because I wanted to avoid stereotypes of the man I was playing. I was not playing a Viennese count or a thirteen-year-old boy who's singing Mozart. I was playing a crude, vicious, patriarchal, overbearing bully, who goes into Caprice's

145

steam room and comes out gay, and I had two difficult things. I didn't want to be a stereotypical man, or I didn't want to be a stereotypical butch as the macho male, and I didn't know what to do about playing a gay man. I made him a stereotype.

DON SHEWEY: The other way around, which I heard from Everett, is that being a queen, which is, again, a kind of gay stereotype, was actually very freeing, a source of identity rather than shame. Is that true?

EVERETT QUINTON: It was important for me to be allowed to exist, in a theatrical sense. I remember seeing Charles put on his makeup to be Camille, and it was like something awakened in me. But Lola, I think it was important the way you played Harry when he came out of the steam room, because the way Charles wrote *Caprice* he didn't explain why the people were queer. People were just queer, and their mothers didn't hate them and their fathers didn't abuse them. They just were queer. So to have Harry come out and be this, it indicted these notions of—I don't know what the fuck I'm talking about! But I remember in *The Artificial Jungle* I was playing Zach Slade, a murderer and tough guy, and I wanted to do something faggy, and I thought, no, wait. Zach can't do that. Then I remembered Charles said inconsistency is what gives you life and freedom. It so freed me up, because I had thought, if I'm going to play a woman, I have to do it a certain way, and if I'm going to play a man, I've got to do it a certain way. Now I just go with the demands of the character, and the character takes me where I want to go. Some critics call me, "the butchest woman," and things like that, and I like that, because what I resist about, say, Kabuki drag queens, is how they pigeonhole women, as though there's one specific way to be a woman. I was often apologetic for being a drag queen in the theater, and today I'm not.

DON SHEWEY: When you say you were apologetic for being a drag queen, to whom? Or in what context?

EVERETT QUINTON: To anyone who had a problem with it. I would get so involved in trying to solve other people's problems that I would negate myself. What I do now is encourage people to be who they want to be on the stage. Bring it to life. You can't go wrong if you're telling your truth. If I try to apologize for my truth or tell someone else's truth, I'm fucked. I want to be queer in the theater, and be at peace with that and carry my own bags, and no one else's.

DON SHEWEY: Ana, I wanted to ask you: The drag and cross-gender stuff is something that is very much a feature of a lot of gay male performance, and also it's become a kind of nineties queer dyke thing. I wonder how it was when you were doing Medusa's Revenge, if women playing men was a big feature. What was the attitude about women doing drag in that company?

ANA MARIA SIMO: To answer that, I think I would have to talk about the differences among us. I hate the word "queer" because it's a word that homogenizes. It's very useful for academia, but troubling to me, to lesbians and to people who are not white. It's obvious that we have things in common, and it's obvious that a historian looking at all of this will say, "These people were all definitely part of something," but when you homogenize—and "gay and lesbian" is already homogenizing—there is a translation to that, which is "mostly gay, mostly white."

"Queer" is like the exaggeration of that, erasing the differences. We should find ways that acknowledge the similarities *and* acknowledge the differences. I don't have an answer. It torments me to say this, but I want to say it: Where I was in 1981 had absolutely nothing to do with the Ridiculous Theater in that I was never aware that the Ridiculous Theater was gay. To me, the Ridiculous Theater was a theater that was using a theatrical form that had always been used, which is, men in drag.

They had a budget and they had a theater. I was in a place with lesbians who were seeing theater both as aesthetic expression and as a way of creating a lesbian culture.

I went to and admired tremendously, the work of the Ridiculous Theater, which is wonderful. But I never thought we were on the same planet, or that we were in the same community. Recently, in the past few years, I started seeing in the *New York Times* and a number of places, that the Ridiculous was a gay theater. I see that word. There was a long stretch of time in which the media—maybe it was the media—wasn't saying, "This Ridiculous thing is gay, as Doric Wilson is." I never felt this was like me, because this was in the realm of culture, a culture that stretched sufficiently to incorporate them, but didn't stretch to me, because I was a lesbian, because I was not a white person, because I was an immigrant, because I have an accent. When I say this, I in no way want not to acknowledge the talent and the wonderful work that they were doing—or that we were doing—or that we all are together in the same community.

I am just describing a very disturbing fact, and it's not historical. It happens here, today. The social realities of our communities are not the same as its aesthetic reduction that we were queer.

So, in terms of drag, of course, it was done at Medusa's Revenge, but it didn't have the same meaning, at all, that it had for the Ridiculous.

DON SHEWEY: What meaning did it have?

ANA MARIA SIMO: It was just one of many things. Camp and drag were not the things that were propelling that theater. The company was all female and they played all the characters, including male characters, so there was cross-dressing, but not the same as drag.

The aesthetic was closer to European expressionism and to a Latin American tradition, and to our desire to find a lesbian culture. It was extremely political, in that sense. At the same time, we were very independent in that we were not politically correct in the terms of lesbian-feminist ideals all the time. We were very transgressive because we had scenes of violence between lesbians onstage, where someone would actually hit someone. We had scenes of torture, where someone was taken to a mental asylum. This is when people would want to throw up and walk away, because you were supposed not to show violence as a pattern among women.

There was definitely lots of cross-dressing, but it was not camp. It had nothing to do with the gay male aesthetic.

DON SHEWEY: I wonder if there was any consideration about fighting stereotypes of women as dykes as mannish women or wanting to avoid those stereotypes. Was that an issue?

ANA MARIA SIMO: That is not an issue when you are in an aesthetic that is more expressionistic, or that is like the theater of cruelty. That is absolutely not an issue there.

We were two Latinas running the theater, and one other Latina was a member of the cast. There were no African Americans in the group, showing the segregation that we had then, and that is worse today. Of the other fifteen women, it was mostly white, working-class women who were Arab American, Italian American, Italian-Puerto Rican, two or three European immigrants without papers.

So, we kind of attracted a certain population to the theater. None of them was in any position to be in the world of entitlement of the other theaters. It's kind of a cliché, but I think our lesbian and gay community has deep inequalities, and we refuse to see them, and we refuse to do anything about it. And I just want to say that I'm surprised to be sitting here, because in my real life, I would never be sitting here next to Lola. We were in two different worlds, and that is a fact I just want to bring up here, because we shouldn't gloss over those facts. It would be great if somehow we incorporated that and moved forward acknowledging that and seeing what do we do about it.

SUSAN FINQUE: I want to take a minute and sort of do what you just said, Ana, which is to look forward. There's a generational difference among us here on the panel, and we hear a distinctly different kind of growth toward our aesthetics from those of us who grew up in the fifties, as compared to those who grew up in the sixties and seventies. At Alice B., we talked a lot about shattering the notion of what gay and lesbian theater was supposed to be, by constantly twisting what the next show was, so that we were not only expanding and teaching our audience that gay theater wasn't peggable as soap opera, naturalistic plays that had homosexual relationships in them instead of heterosexual relationships.

The theater form itself was queer, which is a word that I like to use about form, instead of about my own identity. We have a perspective on the theater and especially on the artistic direction of generating material and interpreting material that is uniquely a gift to the art form, because I think that everything that happens on the stage is inherently some kind of drag.

Just to put on the costume becomes an "othering" of yourself, and as queer people, as gay and lesbian people, we have a perspective about how we make the work, and so we should be teaching. All of us should be teaching theater arts now, because we can do it better. In a class I'm teaching now, it's not teaching young men how to play women's roles and teaching young women how to play men's roles, but rather teaching young people how to understand the construction of gender, no matter where they start from, as an essential way of approaching the acting task.

I think we can go forward with some things in common, that being—if nothing else—that we wear a lavender pair of tinted glasses through which we see things differently, and we need to talk about what we see, and ways of seeing, ways of knowing that are different.

DORIC WILSON: Just a minor insert to that, and that is that since, I believe, the seventeenth century, the English word for putting on costume is putting on "dragging." So, there are people that say the word for drag queens comes from English for "costume."

DON SHEWEY: For costume, any kind of costume. Ana, you brought up an interesting irony or paradox of even the word "queer," and I'm realizing, just the way that you talk about feeling excluded from the term, how even the word "queer" has become subject to a kind of Orwellian shifting of meaning. In some ways, what could be more queer in the way we're using the word lesbian Cuban exiles making theater with other working-class women, in the sense that "queer" means "outside of whatever the dominant culture is," and yet, you're saying—if I hear you correctly—that you feel excluded from the way "queer" is being used in theory and aesthetics by academics.

ANA MARIA SIMO: I'm happily excluded, you know? I was just saying that the social realities of our experiences were very different, and that there's an irony that I am sitting here next to someone whose work I admire tremendously, who's an important actress, but whose work at the time had very little or nothing to do with Medusa's Revenge. And certainly the word "queer" doesn't mean what it used to. It's a very safe word for academia, but that was not the point that I was trying to make.

I'm not even interested in talking about the safe blandness of the word "queer." That's obvious to everybody. I was talking about the fact that in our so-called lesbian and gay community, there are different cultures, different races, and different social classes, and that we're constantly glossing over that fact and trying to put everybody in the same little slot.

DON SHEWEY: I'm interested, though, Ana, that you say that the word "queer" is safe and bland. That completely amazes me to hear you say that, because I thought the word "queer" . . .

ANA MARIA SIMO: It's become, it's become.

DON SHEWEY: It has become. That's what I mean by the Orwellian shifting of it, when something becomes like a brand name, it gets bland, whereas, didn't "queer" originally mean, specifically, "different"? And in all the ways you just mentioned—class difference, and culture and sexual preference. That's what "queer" always meant, often in a very inflammatory, derogatory sense. It's a funny irony, I guess, the way language gets trademarked, you know? A little "c" with a circle around it.

LOLA PASHALINSKI: I have to say something. I feel that there's a lot of variety in this panel, and that we're forgetting one thing: There's an aesthetic of theater which you could call "gay" or "queer," but I wouldn't want to, because I wouldn't want to label it. In other words, it was theater, that the theater and the art of theater came first. I think it's a label that Charles Ludlam resisted. He didn't want to be called a "gay theater." He was a theater artist. He used every device of the theater to do his work, and he broadened the boundaries of theater. He broke down plays. He played with forms. We're forgetting that politics doesn't exist only in direct political theater, but also in aesthetics. The kind of revolution Charles was involved in with a lot of other people was also an aesthetic revolution.

DORIC WILSON: I want to add two other points to that. Robert Patrick, whose ghost is hovering here while he is hiding out in California, brings up this very issue in his play *The Haunted Host*. A young man comes home with an older Off-Off-Broadway legend and asks that legend, do you write gay plays? And the character replies, do you mean do I write plays that go to bed with other plays of the same gender?

My history, though I certainly have always been out, and my theater has always been out, when I ran TOSOS, and when anybody interviews me, I can't help trying to avoid "gay playwright," and "gay theater." You want to change the words, fine, "queer," "fag," anything, mainly because what I love about Off-Off-Broadway is it is really your theater, my theater, his theater, your theater. It's the individual's theater. Yes, we need to be a collective—it's all right for conferences and so forth—but I think what's so exciting is all the theaters doing what they want to do. I vote for the diversity; the terminology is something that the critics, and with all due respect, academia is going to decide much later.

8 Queer Theater and the Disarticulation of Identity

David Savran

In the United States, the "gay nineties" witnessed an efflorescence of cultural productions by and about lesbians and gay men. Dozens of independent films were produced, from *Go Fish* to *Chasing Amy*, from *The Incredibly True Adventure of Two Girls in Love* to *Bound*, that feature lesbian protagonists. "Ellen" became the first sitcom to feature a lesbian hero while Ellen DeGeneres's own coming out provided fodder for countless editorials, sermons, and talk shows. k.d. lang, Melissa Etheridge, and the Indigo Girls all had their day over the airwaves and on video screens. Books by lesbian and gay writers, from Dorothy Allison to Edmund White, garner glowing reviews in the mainstream press. And in the theater, gay men and lesbians have been productive, visible, and honored as never before. *Angels in America*, having amassed the Pulitzer Prize, two best-play Tonys, and other prestigious awards, has chalked up a groundbreaking Broadway run, a national tour, and countless productions in regional theaters. But Tony Kushner is by no means the only widely produced out gay or lesbian playwright in America. Terrence McNally, Paula Vogel, Nicky Silver, Jon Robin Baitz, Paul Rudnick, Lanford Wilson, and Craig Lucas have all made the long trek uptown and remain among the most widely produced contemporary American playwrights. Downtown (or on the West Coast), meanwhile, Split Britches, Maria Irene Fornes, the Five Lesbian Brothers, Holly Hughes, Pomo Afro Homos, Carmelita Tropicana, the Ridiculous Theatrical Company, and David Greenspan (to name only the most well-established) continue to break new ground by producing work that is often far more experimental than that of their uptown kin. Although long a sanctuary for closeted lesbians and gay men, the U.S. theater is now *out* in a way it has never been before, populated by writers and artists who are now joyously, proudly—and matter-of-factly—queer.

A reclamation of a formerly stigmatized term, queer (as adjective or noun) remains for most cultural critics a deeply utopian designation: a locus of refusal, an unbinding of psychic and social energy, a destabilizing third term, a privileged mode of subversion. In Eve Sedgwick's theorization, it signifies less a fixed identity than a principle of polysemy: "'queer' can refer to: the open mesh of possibilities, gaps, overlaps, dissonances and resonances, lapses and excesses of meaning when the constituent elements of anyone's gender, of anyone's sexuality aren't made (or *can't* be made) to signify monolithically." And while sexuality and gender have historically been the privileged markers of that which passes for queer, Sedgwick emphasizes that "a lot of the most exciting recent work around 'queer' spins the term outward along dimensions that can't be subsumed under gender and sexuality at all," including "race, ethnicity," and "postcolonial nationality."[1] Queer also enjoys the distinction of being—at least in theory—gender-neutral so that it can describe male- and female-sexed bodies as well as anything else in between. Queer, in other words, represents an attempt to open up a vista of multiple, shifting, and gloriously polymorphous bodies, pleasures, and resistances and to problematize 1970s-style identity politics and the minoritizing discourses that are associated with lesbian feminism and gay liberation. To this extent, it is part of a new universalizing discourse that includes in its rainbow anyone willing to renounce the claims and prerogatives of heteronormativity. And although a utopian fantasy, queer remains a category which in practice has too often been dominated (much like the activist group Queer Nation, which did so much to disseminate the new queer politics and culture) by the persons, agendas, and styles of white gay men.[2]

Moreover, as Jill Dolan notes, "the insistent anti-hegemonic pose of 'queer' can also be a ruse for not taking responsibility for the vagaries of a movement, a style, a life."[3] Too often, a self-congratulatory queer identification functions as a substitute for a commitment to radical social change. And like the identity politics that it at once embraces and problematizes, a queer politic too often, as Wendy Brown notes, "may specifically abjure a critique of class power and class norms precisely insofar as these identities are established *vis-à-vis* a bourgeois norm of social acceptance, legal protection and relative material comfort."[4]

Although cognizant of its problems, I believe that "queer" remains a useful way for thinking about an American theater in which the boundaries between the traditional and the experimental have become increasingly porous, and in which ostensibly stable meanings and identities (sexual or otherwise) are routinely displaced by notions of mutability, instability, and polyvalence. At the same time, the flowering of a queer dramaturgy is a reminder that queer is a performative designation, one that privileges doing over being, action over intention. When applied to theater, it is less a fixed attribute of a given text than an effect produced by the interplay between and among text, actor, director, and spectator. Moreover, theater, in comparison with other arts (especially film), is queer in part because of its particular mode of address and its uncanny ability to arouse a spectator's mutable and mutating investments. More aggressively than film, theater challenges the Oedipal imperative that (according to the Freudian family romance) would definitively separate identification (with the parent of the same sex) from desire (for the parent of the other sex, and later, a surrogate for that parent). Delighting instead in confounding identification and desire, theater unleashes an Oedipal scandal.

The Particular and the Universal

In comparison with film and television, theater remains strictly marginalized. In the regional theaters, subscription bases continues to decline and with them, the adventurousness of most artistic directors.[5] And while Broadway is thriving, it does so increasingly by mimicking mass culture, either in the form of mind-numbing spectacles featuring singing cats, falling chandeliers, and dancing dinnerware, or plays like *The Heidi Chronicles* or *The Last Night of Ballyhoo*, whose style and themes aspire to "quality" television. Rarely is it able to sustain a so-called serious drama that is neither a revival nor a British import. And while serious drama does retain a foothold Off-Broadway, it does not have the same cultural capital as other forms of literature. American playwrights, with one exception (Eugene O'Neill), do not win Nobel prizes or become the figureheads of the literary world, the emblems of literature as an elite cultural practice, in the way that novelists like William Faulkner, Toni Morrison, or Thomas Pynchon do. Moreover, unlike poetry, with its dependence on small presses and a highly specialized and professionalized readership, theater is a manifestly commercial and public art. Enmortgaged to a slew of others who must realize the playwright's text, it has long been regarded as a bastard art—and the epitome of middlebrow culture.

Because of its marginal position, both economically and culturally theater is a particularly revealing example of the contradictions that structure what Pierre Bourdieu designates as the literary and artistic field. As he explains, this field is contained within a larger field of economic and political power, while at the same time "possessing a relative autonomy with respect to it, especially as regards its economic and political principles of hierarchization." It is this *relative autonomy* that gives the literary and artistic field both its high level of symbolic forms of capital and its low level of economic capital. In other words, despite its sometimes considerable prestige, it "occupies a *dominated position*" with respect to the field of economic and political power as a whole.[6] And the individual cultural producer (or theater artist), insofar as he or she is a part of the bourgeoisie, necessarily represents a "dominated fraction of the dominant class."[7]

The cultural producer is thus placed in an irreducibly contradictory position. On the one hand, this position licenses (and even encourages) him or her to critique hegemonic values insofar as it is the best way of accruing cultural capital. On the other hand, his or her class allegiance will finally (consciously or unconsciously) blunt this critique. Moreover, the more effective his or her threat, the less economic capital s/he is likely to amass. Because of theater's marginality in American culture, it seems to be held hostage to this double bind in a particularly unnerving way: the very disposition of the field guarantees that Broadway and regional theaters (unlike mass culture) are constantly in the process of trying both to undermine and reinforce hegemonic social values. More avowedly experimental theaters are under less pressure only because their budgets are so small and their less affluent audiences less invested in maintaining the status quo.

The select public that today attends professional theater, whether commercial or more experimental venues, is overwhelmingly middle-class and overwhelmingly liberal in its attitudes. Indeed, theater audiences are in large part distinguished from the audiences for film and television on account of their appetite for works both formally and thematically more challenging than the vast majority of major studio releases or prime-time miniseries. Moreover, since the 1988 controversies over NEA funding for exhibitions of Robert Mapplethorpe and Andres Serrano and the subsequent attempt by the Endowment to revoke grants to the so-called NEA four (all of whom feature queer content in their work), theater, as a liberal form, has been distinguished from mass culture in part by its many (often sexualized) representations of gay men.

In television and film, lesbians and lesbian eroticism provide a kind of spicy divertissement that is arguably less threatening to the many straight men who produce and consume these works than male homoeroticism. Even a film like *Bound*, with its triumphantly lethal lesbians, manages to control and contain these resistant subjects (to some extent at least) through the scopophilia of the cinematic apparatus. Unlike mass culture, however, theater capitalizes on spectacularizing gay men and gay male bodies while simultaneously producing them as subjects. For despite their many differences, *Angels in America* and *Love! Valour! Compassion!* set the standard for a putatively queer Broadway theater that allows spectators to participate in something that has all the trappings—but little of the substance—of a transgressive project.

Angels works actively to undermine the difference between public and private, and indeed, to queer American political culture, but its millennialism (not unlike that, ironically, of the Christian right) functions to reassure spectators that History has a meaning and is nearing fulfillment and that they can awaken from the nightmare of the past. Although in its reinvention (and opening up) of gay domestic drama *Love! Valour! Compassion!* does not question the opposition between public and private, it is, like *Angels*, committed to a utopian vision of community and a teleology of redemption. Yet unlike *Angels*, it does not attempt to reimagine gay male subjectivity or problematize racial, gendered, or class-based norms, preferring instead to exploit, proudly and voyeuristically, the buffed bodies and physical endowments of (the actors playing the roles of) upwardly mobile gay men. Like the identity politics to which they remain indentured, both plays restrict transgression to the cultural and sexual realms and respectfully forswear any critique of an expansive liberal pluralism that is all too ready to accept these men as producers and, most especially, consumers of cultural diversity.[8]

In short, this putatively queer theater too often titillates bourgeois audiences, queer and straight alike, and reassures them of their hip, liberal values. At the same time, lesbians, as both playwrights and characters, remain virtually invisible on Broadway and in the regional theaters. They flourish downtown in more modest arenas where their presence (like that of their gay brothers on Broadway) has become virtually a prerequisite for that variety of edgy performance that challenges the canons of realism and bourgeois social values. Yet despite its relative marginalization, the downtown performance circuit is able to offer artists like Holly Hughes or Split Britches a measure of control over the means of production that their brothers uptown sacrifice to the more corporatized interests of the large producing organizations.

The success of gay men on Broadway and in regional theaters is in part the result of the work of their many distinguished—and closeted—forebears. Although the Western theater, at least since its professionalization during the Early Modern period, has been relatively hospitable to a wide variety of social and sexual dissidents, gay men in particular have played important roles in the U.S. theater since World War II. Although critics dared not reveal the sexual orientation of several rather eminent theater artists during the late 1940s and 1950s (and the height of McCarthyism), some relished casting not-so-subtle aspersions against at least one playwright whose writings, in the words of an anonymous reviewer for *Time* magazine, read "too frequently as if the chapters of *Psychopathia Sexualis* had been raided for TV skits."[9] By 1961, however, prominent critics like Howard Taubman (of the *New York Times*) began to acknowledge "the increasing incidence and influence of homosexuality on New York's stage" and decry the "indirection" practiced by playwrights that, he alleged, "distorts human values." Noting that homosexuality is "a fact of life" and that "[n]othing human should be alien to an enlightened theater," he argued that the problem is less its avowal than its disguise. It is the latter that produces those malodorous closet dramas that turn a woman into an "unpleasant," "exaggerated" grotesque and a man "into a ragingly lustful beast or . . . a limp, handsome neutral creature of otherworldy purity."[10] Five years later, Stanley Kauffmann (also in the *Times*) virtually named names by observing that "three of the most successful American playwrights of the last twenty years are (reputed) homosexuals." (It hardly required a private detective to fill in the names Tennessee Williams, William Inge, and Edward Albee.) And like Taubman, he argued for a tolerant, liberal theater in which the "homosexual dramatist must be free to write truthfully of what he [*sic*] knows, rather than try to transform it to a life he does not know."[11]

Taubman's and Kauffmann's positions are demonstrably homophobic insofar as they demand that these—implicitly male—homosexual writers, unlike their heterosexual brethren, are fit to write only of what they "know," that is, homosexuality. (According to this prescription, a sort of cultural nationalism *avant la lettre*, a male writer should write only about men, an African American writer only about African Americans, and so on. And isn't there something more than a little absurd in assuming that a writer could survive and prosper in the United States during the heyday of "Father Knows Best" and "The Donna Reed Show" without knowing heterosexuality?) Most important, their argument is based upon an association of homosexuality with the "distorted" and "neurotic" and heterosexuality with the universal.[12] While the homosexual artist should be restricted to writing about perverts, the heterosexual is free to explore all kinds of identities. The former gives a skewed version of society while the latter offers an ostensibly more balanced assessment.

Yet a mere glance at social histories of the Cold War era suggests that the portraits of U.S. culture limned by Williams, Inge, and Albee are far less distorted than Taubman and Kauffmann suggest.[13] Indeed, the representations of discontented marriages, of characters who "represent something different from what they purport to be," and of "the lurid violence that seems a sublimation of social hatreds" describes all too well the very real disturbances that underlay the Cold War consensus but which the arbiters of culture (and producers of "Father Knows Best") routinely preferred to disavow.[14] Indeed, the gay male playwrights of the 1950s and 1960s achieved their renown (and notoriety) in large part because of their ability to construct plays that, for most theatergoers at least, were read as all-too-true fictions.

Yet the continued association of the heterosexual with the universal and the homosexual with the particular has been an obstinate mythology that was bolstered by the emerging gay commercial theater of the late 1960s and 1970s. The very plea for tolerance advanced by *The Boys in the Band* depends on the construction of the gay male as a deviant subject who should be embraced by an expansive liberal pluralism on condition that he lock his perversions away and minimally disrupt the sequestration of public from private. In relation to this tradition, the greatest and most radical contribution of the new queer theater of the 1990s (and in particular of *Angels in America* and *Love! Valour! Compassion!*) has been its reconstruction of the gay man as a universal subject. In these texts, homosexual subjectivities are produced as representative not of the perverse but the normative, not the subversive but the national.

This project is particularly unmistakable in Kushner's "Gay Fantasia on National Themes," with its queering of U.S. political culture, but it is also dramatized in a running gag in *Love! Valour! Compassion!* in which James discovers a book that "gives the names of all the gay men and lesbians in this country in alphabetical order, from the pre-Revolutionary period (Pocahontas, I think her name was) right up to now, someone called Dan Rather."[15] These two plays thereby work to fulfill what Monique Wittig describes as the Proustian project of making "'homosexual' the axis of categorization from which to universalize."[16] At the same time, however, even this universalizing project must be recognized as producing a false universal insofar as the new queer in these texts remains a white, middle-class subject whose racialized identity is clearly foregrounded by the presence of Belize and

Ramon (who represent an idealized fantasy in each play: perfectly radical politics and perfectly fuckable body, respectively). Intriguingly, this false universalism enables a queered national identity also to pass as an international identity. For *Angels in America* and *Love! Valour! Compassion!* represent the two most widely produced U.S. plays in western European theaters during the 1996–1997 season.[17] In a world increasingly held hostage to an American-style globalized economy and in a Europe increasingly seduced by *la mode américaine*, these texts would seem to epitomize a new queer culture whose very Americanness is the proof of its transnational character.

While Kushner and McNally win Tony awards, a more avant-gardist mode of performance has been institutionalized in alternative venues. Dominated by lesbians rather than white gay men, this queer theater is thoroughly deconstructive in its strategies. Rather than attempt to universalize the queer subject, it delights in deconstructing subjectivity, or rather, in revealing the disruptions and divisions that structure all subjectivities. For Holly Hughes, for example, performance is a privileged medium for examining the processes by which identities are socially produced. All her work stages the Other within the self (or the Other that structures the self) and remembers a lost, forgotten tongue (like her "mother's invented French") that can be used to articulate (lesbian) desire.[18] Calling attention to the indispensability of narrative for the construction of subjectivity, Hughes uses the stage—standing, as she puts it, in the beams of "light shining out of [the audience's] eyes"—to dramatize both the contingent nature of performance and the performative nature of identity.[19] Like the work of so many other downtown performers, Hughes's is highly self-reflexive and is designed to cast the audience as a collective before whom the performer testifies and, thus, as an active, if silent, accessory to the production of her identity. It is queer, however, less because of its subject matter than its method. For it testifies to the fact that during the late 1980s, self-identified queer performers appropriated and expanded the techniques of deconstructive performance developed during the previous decade (by the Wooster Group, Robert Wilson, and Mabou Mines, among many others) in order to take possession of a mode of self-presentation that at once asserts and problematizes (queer) identities and desires. For Hughes is as much concerned with absence, with that which defies representation, as she is with trying to carve out a space for an autonomous, dissident subject. At the same time, her deconstructive politics lead her not to look for an escape from an oppressive (in this case, heteronormative) culture than to use the contradictions always already at play within heteronormativity to undermine its epistemological priority and privilege. Much like the subversive readings of Freud that proliferate throughout queer theory, the new queer performance attempts less to prove that perverts are normal than to demonstrate that all desire is perverted. Simultaneously, it dramatizes the recognition that performance (as a staging of the Other within the self) is, by definition, a rather queer occupation.

If one can consider the new queer theater (stretching from the WOW Café to Broadway) to be in any way a unified category, it would seem that its distinctive importance in U.S. culture is the result of its ability to consolidate the apparent contradictions between the universalizing and the deconstructive in provocative ways. For the more closely one analyzes this opposition, the less securely it seems to hold. Thus, for example, despite their commercial successes, both *Angels in America* and *Love! Valour! Compassion!* rehearse many strategies that place them at odds with the conventions of domestic realism. Both exploit direct address; both shuffle temporal sequence; both dramatize a mixture of memory, fantasy, and desire; both intercut scenes in an almost cinematic way; both feature drag; both spectacularize the male body; both demonstrate the volatile relationship between the private and the public. At the same time, both plays—like those of their more avant-gardist kin—work to foreground and problematize performance itself. Both attempt to reimagine community and to universalize a queer (white) subjectivity. So too, the deconstructive strategies of the more avant-gardist work function both to particularize the subject and to produce him or her as the paradigm of subjectivity *tout court*. By enacting a problematic associated with a particular, abjected identity, Holly Hughes simultaneously dramatizes the impossibility of stabilizing any and all identities. By performing a fragmented history of black gay men and the particular issues facing them, Pomo Afro Homos illuminate the difficulty of producing any affirmative (racial or sexual) minority identity. Whether in its uptown or downtown guises, then, the new queer theater has become a metonym for postnaturalistic performance in the United States, representing in a particularly clear and incisive form both the situation of theater as a bastard (which is to say, hybridized) art and the necessary slippage (both on- and offstage) between self and Other.

Writing and Reading Out

The ascendancy of a deconstructive queer theater in the United States and of a universalized queer subject in some respects marks a significant historical break with the gay and lesbian theater that emerged around Stonewall and is best exemplified by plays like *The Boys in the Band* and *Last Summer at Bluefish Cove*. For although many queer playwrights acknowledge their debt to this work, they are also insistent on problematizing the relationship between the sexual identity of the cultural producer and his or her work. This became particularly clear at the "Reading and Writing Out" panel that I moderated at the CLAGS Queer Theater Conference. The works of the writers on the panel, Janis Astor del Valle, Maria Irene Fornes, Joan Shenkar, Nicky Silver, and Chay Yew represent an extremely heterogeneous grouping. And while Silver's project is arguably the most universalizing and Fornes's the most deconstructive, all these playwrights have produced work that disrupts a facile opposition between these terms. Despite their diverse backgrounds, ages, ethnicities, races, and points of view, all agree that identity—sexual or otherwise—is always a problem.

Fornes understands it to be so vexed because it is in large part unconscious; it is "so delicate and so elusive" as to be virtually inaccessible to the writing subject.[20] Astor del Valle argues that identity is "ever-evolving," while Yew notes that he "never intended to be categorized" and that he "hate[s] being categorized." Shenkar, meanwhile, observes that "when you sit down to face that blank sheet of paper, you are reduced . . . the best thing you can do is to erase yourself." Rather than affirming a preexistent, full subject, writing produces the writing self as an empty appendage to a pluralized text.

In elaborating on the idea of self-erasure, Fornes notes in a provocative metaphor that writing "is like your fingerprints." For any writer, writing remains a unique and enigmatic enterprise—unique because all fingerprints are different and enigmatic because "you have no idea what they look like." And fingerprints, although quite literally at one's fingertips, usually remain unknown, or taken for granted. Yet they are also *the* distinctive signature of the individual. "Wherever you go, you are leaving your mark," leaving a trace behind that can be used to identify you. Both alien and incriminating, fingerprints are a privileged marker of identity which for Fornes is an "elusive," "mysterious," and irrecoverable property, "so hidden from yourself." And although writing clearly bears a privileged relation to the production of identity, it does not function to stabilize it or lend it coherence. Writing, she adds, is a "search inside, . . . but you search inside you for an imaginary other." Writing, like performance, is a quest less for the self than for an Other who stands in for the self, for a fantasy double (that is, a theatrical character or persona) that always manages to elude the subject. Writing, in short, represents not a stabilization but a disarticulation of identity.

If theater is the queerest art, perhaps it is so because of the ability of writing and performance to disarticulate and disrupt identity—whether the identity in question is that of the playwright or the spectator. And while the slippage between playwright and text is, as Fornes alleges, a function of the fact that at some level the writer never knows what he or she is making, the disarticulation of the spectator is produced rather differently, by the specificity of the theatrical apparatus. In comparing theater with film, Christian Metz emphasizes that although the former has a materiality and a facticity that the latter (being "closer to phantasy") lacks, the most crucial difference between the two lies in their construction of the spectator.[21] Since the "spectator is absent" from that peculiar mirror that constitutes the film screen, "it is always the other who is on the screen; as for me, I am there to look at him [*sic*]." Unlike the theatrical spectator, the cinematic spectator takes "no part in the perceived" (1982: 48). He or she, rather, is occupied with looking and so "*identifies with himself,* with himself as a pure act of perception," which is to say, discovers "himself" as the one who watches the Other silently in the dark (1982: 49, emphasis in original). (Countless critics of Metz, beginning with Laura Mulvey, emphasize that because the spectator is masculinized by the apparatus, Metz's use of masculine pronouns represents far more than a figure of speech.)[22] As a result of the spectator's identification with the camera, the cinematic apparatus succeeds in resuscitating "a kind of transcendental subject" whose "presence often remains diffuse, geographically undifferentiated, unevenly distributed over the whole surface of the screen; or more precisely hovering" (1982: 49, 54). Metz emphasizes that unlike theater, in which the spectator identifies primarily with characters onstage, the cinematic spectator's identifications with characters are only "secondary" or "tertiary" (1982: 56).

While Metz's analysis of theatrical spectatorship is clearly based upon his familiarity with realistic or naturalistic theater, he is, I believe, correct to discern that empathic identification—or disidentification—with characters tends to be more important in theater than it is in film.[23] Even in plays that clearly attempt some kind of Brechtian distanciation (like *Angels in America*), the spectator must, if the play is going to work, identify with some of the characters. At the same time, I would like to suggest that identification in the theater is always extremely unstable and unpredictable. For theater is also distinguished from film on account of the relatively nonhierarchical nature of the stage picture. Even the most carefully composed tableau does not focus the spectatorial gaze quite as definitively as the cinematic shot (at least in Hollywood narrative cinema). Rather, the theatrical image is more dependent on a dialogical relationship between setting and human subject, between container and the thing contained, and directors, designers, and actors constantly exploit the knowledge that the spectator's eye will wander over the stage. In fact, isn't spectatorial pleasure in the theater in part the result of the spectator's necessarily errant eye?

This concept of errancy is important, I believe, because it accounts both for the quality of the primary identifications with characters that the spectator makes and for the tacit contract between actor and spectator. For when Metz describes actor and spectator as "the two protagonists of an authentic perverse couple," he means that in theater the actor actively (and exhibitionistically) consents to a scopic relationship, deliberately presenting him- or herself to the spectator (1982: 63). The actor, moreover, always vies with the other actors for the spectator's attention (and usually empathy as well). At the same time, plays, unlike novels (except in rare instances), do not use a narrator to provide a seamless narrative voice or to adopt a coherent attitude toward the dramatic action. Even when they do (as, for example, in Paula Vogel's *How I Learned to Drive*), the narrator often functions as a dramatic equivalent of a red herring, opening up rather than foreclosing multiple points of view. As a result, the spectator's identification with characters remains more errant and more unpredictable than in narrative forms. In fact, theater spectatorship, I believe, provides a particularly powerful paradigm for a destabilized position in which identification is almost indistinguishable from desire. For how, in watching *Cat on a Hot Tin Roof*, for example, can one separate one's identification with Maggie or Brick (against the tyranny of the commodity and the nuclear family) from one's desire for these gloriously spectacularized and fetishized creatures? And it is precisely this confusion of identification with desire that renders theater the queerest art, the one most liable to disturb the illusion the spectator is likely to harbor that his or her sexual identity is stable and unambiguous. For sexual identities remain the most unstable of all identities—in part because of the polymorphous nature of desire itself, in part because they are (usually) among the least visible of identities, in part because, as Judith Butler rather famously points out, they are always predicated on a repudiation. Butler emphasizes that in the production of a putatively queer identity, what is disavowed is not "something like heterosexuality or bisexuality," but rather "a set of identificatory and practical *crossings* between these categories that renders the discreteness of each equally suspect."[24] For Butler is most concerned with valorizing these "crossings" not only because they acknowledge the necessarily plural constitution of all subjects (who always take up multiple positionalities), but also because they enable the formation of political communities and coalitions. "[I]t may be," she suggests, "only by risking the incoherence of identity that connection is possible."[25]

It seems to me that the possibility, nay, the necessity of multiple identifications and desires that theater authorizes—across genders, sexualities, races, classes—renders it both the most utopian form of cultural production and the queerest. For the spectator is always impelled by the very nature of theater to take up multiple positions and to desire multiple partners, to identify or conjugate—secretly, in the dark, in one's fantasies—with many characters, to enjoy what Butler calls "the *pleasure* produced by the instability" of erotic categories.[26] And this instability is redoubled by the fact that the spectator is never able definitively to separate a character from the actor playing the role. So one always identifies with and desires both a clearly designated absence (a character) and a material presence (an actor). Moreover, since the theatergoer is always more or less conscious of the rest of the audience, s/he always retains more of his or her social being sitting in the darkened theater than the filmgoer does. As a result, the theater is the site, as Metz notes, in which "a true 'audience'" is constituted, "a temporary collectivity" made all the more efficacious both by the physical presence of actors' bodies as well as by the actors' awareness that they are being overseen, that they are participating willingly in the formation of "an authentic perverse couple."[27]

Whether on Broadway or off, the new theater of the 1990s that both deconstructs and universalizes the queer subject, represents a utopian project dedicated to spectatorial pleasure, to the crossing of identifications and desires, to a queer colonization of the public sphere, and to community formation. And the ascendancy of this new theater is clearly connected, I believe, to other recent developments: to the rise of queer nationalism and queer theory, and to the escalating struggle for lesbian and gay civil rights. At the same time, one must be wary of claiming premature victory. For despite its success, queer theater remains a marginal form of cultural production that characteristically addresses those already sympathetic to its cause. Moreover, this theater, as I have argued, tends to privilege white, bourgeois subjects, producing them as the axis from which to universalize. As a result, it prefers to naturalize commodity production and consumption and almost invariably ignores the increasingly inequitable distribution of wealth in the United States.

For the new queer theater is clearly an expression of those identity politics that, having displaced the New Left during the early 1970s, remain dependent, as Brown notes, "upon the demise of a *critique* of capitalism and of bourgeois cultural and economic values."[28] And one might here recall that that heady moment in the early 1990s when—in the wake of Queer Nation, *Paris Is Burning*, and Madonna's *Sex*—everything seemed suddenly queer, was impelled by far more than a renewal of AIDS activism or a salutary backlash against the Christian right. For that moment (memorialized in texts like *Angels in America, Love! Valour! Compassion!* and Sedgwick's *Tendencies*) coincides with what I would call a national identity crisis that is itself linked to the collapse of historical communism and the attenuation of the opposition between East and West. For it was in that moment that "queer" emerged as a utopian trope which (in contradistinction to the often anticapitalist program of the earlier gay and lesbian liberation movements) appropriates corporate strategies to reimagine a nation of sexual outlaws who are defined at least as much by what they consume as by whom they fuck.

Despite its universalizing tendencies, the new queer theater is only beginning to redress the long history of the exclusion of women as playwrights, directors, and designers. For almost invariably, gay men have achieved levels of visibility and power in the theater that are routinely denied to women, whether straight or lesbian. At the "Reading and Writing Out" panel I moderated, this gender inequality was vividly and cruelly reenacted. Silver and Yew sat on one side of me while Astor del Valle, Fornes, and Schenkar sat on the other (I did not plan this partitioning). As Dolan describes the scene, two "sides" quickly emerged and as they became "more ideological," it looked "as though a schoolyard brawl was about to be staged."

Silver and Yew laughed and whispered when the women talked, and Silver began each of his comments with a parody of something one of the women before him had volunteered. Schenkar's and Fornes's faces expressed their displeasure with Silver's camping, and in their remarks took care to distinguish themselves from this category "queer," especially if Silver was the defense's exhibit A.[29]

Not only were Silver and Yew far less amusing than they imagined, but also far less articulate than the women they mocked. Unfortunately, however, this ugly performance was hardly a unique event. Rather, an offstage and more subtle and insidious version of it holds sway in countless theaters across the United States. And this denigration of women tends to be echoed by the relative exclusion of lesbians and gay men of color from major administrative and artistic positions in prestigious theaters (the New York Shakespeare Festival is the most prominent exception to this rule). Until women and people of color are able to procure the same highly visible forums as white gay men in which to present their work, a truly universalized and democratized queer theater will remain a utopian fantasy.

Or perhaps, to shift the terms of the argument, the problem is less a matter of the identity of the cultural producer than of the political character of the project

DAVID SAVRAN

s/he undertakes. For the makers of queer theater I listed above are so categorized on the basis of their avowed sexual identities. But if queer theater is, as I suggest, largely a formal designation, why not include John Guare, Mac Wellman, and Suzan-Lori Parks among its luminaries? Why must a queer theater remain fixated on the illusory stability of that most unstable of identities? And why not acknowledge the fact that a writer's work will always exceed, and often belie, his or her avowed identity? White men—whether gay or straight—are quite capable of producing a theater that is not only queer, but also feminist, antiracist, antihomophobic, and anticapitalist. The problem is, they haven't.

Notes

My thanks to Framji Minwalla, Alisa Solomon, and Scott Teagarden for their valuable feedback on this essay.

1. Eve Kosofsky Sedgwick, *Tendencies* (Durham: Duke University Press, 1993), 8–9.
2. See, for example, Maria Maggenti, "Women as Queer Nationals," *Out/look*, no. 11 (Winter 1991): 20–23, and Guy Trebay, "In Your Face," *Village Voice*, August 14, 1990: 37–39.
3. Jill Dolan, "Building a Theatrical Vernacular: Responsibility, Community, Ambivalence, and Queer Theatre," *Modern Drama* 39.1 (1996):2.
4. Wendy Brown, "Wounded Attachments: Late Modern Oppositional Political Formations," in *The Identity in Question*, ed. John Rajchman (New York: Routledge, 1995), 207.
5. See, for example, Barbara Janowitz, "Theatre Facts 93," insert in *American Theatre*, April 1994, 4–5.
6. Pierre Bourdieu, "The Field of Cultural Production, or: The Economic World Reversed," in Pierre Bourdieu, *The Field of Cultural Production: Essays on Art and Literature*, ed. Randall Johnson (New York: Columbia University Press, 1993), 37–38.
7. Editor's Introduction, in Bourdieu, *The Field of Cultural Production*, 15.
8. For a much more detailed critique of *Angels in America*, see David Savran, *Taking It Like a Man: White Masculinity, Masochism, and Contemporary American Culture* (Princeton: Princeton University Press, 1998), chapter 5.
9. Review of Tennessee Williams, *One Arm*, *Time*, January 3, 1955, 76.
10. Howard Taubman, "Not What It Seems: Homosexual Motif Get Heterosexual Guise," *New York Times*, November 5, 1961, II.1.
11. Stanley Kauffman, "Homosexual Drama and Its Disguises," *New York Times*, January 23, 1966, II.1.

166

12. Kauffman, "Homosexual Drama," II.1.

13. See, for example, Elaine Tyler May, *Homeward Bound: American Families in the Cold War Era* (New York: Basic Books, 1988).

14. Taubman, "Not What It Seems," II.1; Kauffman, "Homosexual Drama," II.1.

15. Terrence McNally, *Love! Valour! Compassion! And A Perfect Ganesh: Two Plays* (New York: Plume, 1995), 69.

16. Monique Wittig, *The Straight Mind and Other Essays* (Boston: Beacon Press, 1992), 61.

17. My thanks to Marvin Carlson for pointing this out to me.

18. Holly Hughes, *Clit Notes: A Sapphic Sampler* (New York: Grove Press, 1996), 171.

19. Hughes, *Clit Notes*, 2–3.

20. Transcript, "Reading and Writing Out," Queer Theater Conference, April 27, 1995.

21. Christian Metz, *The Imaginary Signifier: Psychoanalysis and the Cinema*, trans. Celie Britton, Annwyl Williams, Ben Brewster, and Alfred Guzzetti (Bloomington: Indiana University Press, 1982), 43; all other references will be noted in the text.

22. See, for example, Laura Mulvey, *Visual and Other Pleasures* (Bloomington: Indiana University Press, 1989).

23. I am using identification here in the sense defined by Laplanche and Pontalis as a "[p]sychological process whereby the subject assimilates an aspect, property or attribute of the other and is transformed, wholly or partially, after the model the other provides. It is by means of a series of identifications that the personality is constituted and specified." J. Laplanche and J.-B. Pontalis, *The Language of Psycho-Analysis*, trans. Donald Nicholson-Smith (New York: Norton, 1974), 205.

24. Judith Butler, "Imitation and Gender Insubordination," in *The Lesbian and Gay Studies Reader*, ed. Henry Abelove, Michèle Aina Barale, and David M. Halperin (New York: Routledge, 1993), 310, my emphasis.

25. Judith Butler, *Bodies That Matter: On the Discursive Limits of "Sex"* (New York: Routledge, 1993), 113.

26. Butler, "Imitation and Gender Insubordination," 308, emphasis in original.

27. Metz, *The Imaginary Signifier*, 64.

28. Brown, "Wounded Attachments," 206, emphasis in original.

29. Dolan, "Building a Theatrical Vernacular," 9–10.

Playing from P.S. 122 to Peoria

A conversation among Holly Hughes, Deb Parks-Satterfield, and
Paula Vogel, moderated by Cynthia Mayeda

CYNTHIA MAYEDA: A couple of weeks ago, I was moderating a panel at the Public Theater on the state and future of Asian American theater, and one of the panelists, David Henry Hwang, a playwright who wrote, among other things, *M. Butterfly*, was talking about his *M. Butterfly* experience. I was asking the panel to talk about what they thought Asian American theater was. Was it about the subject? Was it about the maker? Was it about the interpreters, and David said what I thought was a very provocative thing. And that was that when *M. Butterfly* was on Broadway, he had no question but that that was an Asian American play.

When that same play became a film, he said he didn't think it was Asian American and I've been chewing on that since, and as prologue to today, it reminded me that it is not only about a venue, about a locale, but about who, as well as the where. A couple of days after that, I found myself on Broadway, seeing *Love! Valor! Compassion!* with my very best friend in the world, and as we walked out, we were both actually quite deeply affected by the evening, and a little surprisingly, and he said to me . . . he's a gay white man, he said, "I have to admit, I kind of resisted this experience, but there was something very powerful about knowing you were on Broadway, well into the run, seeing a full audience, a very mixed audience, and not feeling like I had to take care of everybody else."

Everybody was on their own, and most people having quite a lovely evening in the theater. I offer those observations as two of the things that I've been thinking about in preparation for today.

We're going to see if we can get to the heart of the question, which, as posed, was how locale, how environment, how politics—I will add personnel—production values, affect a work, and how we make choices. I will pose a question to get us off the dime, a hypothetical, and my colleagues will talk about it.

So here's the hypothetical. Paula Vogel has written a play, a two-hander, starring, guess who? Deb Parks-Satterfield and Holly Hughes, about race issues in the lesbian community, and I'm producing this play, and am delighted to learn that we have several choices about where we might start this tour, and as a good producer, I want to make sure that you get the venues that you think are most advantageous to this work. Of course, it's a premiere.

So, Paula is particularly interested and anxious to make sure that it's in what she thinks of as the right place at the right time, and this is going to be a great opportunity in Holly and Deb's career, so they want to make sure they appear in the right place at the right time.

I'm going to give you three choices—you don't have to just choose one—but I'd like you to talk among yourselves about what you think, given your own experiences with your own work, what you think the pluses and minuses might be of these three places. The first is a regional theater in the Midwest in a small metropolitan area, not major, but not rural. It is a metropolitan area. There's a substantial subscriber base with a typical subscriber audience. They've seen a lot of work, seven plays a year, over 120 jillion billion years. The artistic director is a heterosexual male whose interest in this play is as sincere as possible. This is not about exoticism. It is not about a UNICEF card, you know, one gay/lesbian play, one African American play—it's not about that. He's genuinely interested in providing a nice mix of opportunities for his audience members. So, that's Theater A.

The second choice is Alternative Space B in New York City. It's artist-run. It's been there since the early seventies. It has an audience you recognize, a very serious arts crowd, mixed audience, regarding sexual orientation, and the production values are a little slim. There's never quite enough money, but somehow the work always gets made, with a great deal of integrity.

And the final choice is a gay and lesbian community festival, not an arts festival, not a cultural festival, not a theater festival, but a community festival where there is, very obviously, an arts component, and this is the possibility for kind of the centerpiece of the arts component, and this is in San Francisco. This is the second annual festival. So, it's had an experience of one year, a little rough around the edges. Very eager, and an audience you might expect. So what do you think? Paula, maybe you could start, as maker of the work.

PAULA VOGEL: May we talk about a choice that's not on the list?

CYNTHIA MAYEDA: Absolutely.

PAULA VOGEL: All right. I would choose to go to Perseverance Theater in Juno, Alaska. I will tell you why. I've been a little perturbed right now by what I would call a kind of New York chauvinism that is expressing itself in terms of the making of art and in terms of the expression of lesbian art, and that there's been a tendency to create myths and clichés about the audience outside New York that has nothing to do with my experience, which is, for the past ten years, I've been doing all my premieres in Perseverance Theater, Juneau, Alaska, population thirty thousand, in a state in which there are approximately, oh, some ninety different ethnicities, and in which there is a kind of coalition in this theater company.

It's the only company I've ever worked with that has a sweat lodge in back of the theater. And it's extraordinary to have your work discussed in a way that the work is not ghettoized. It is seen as part of the continuum that may go from the Greeks to Sam Shepard to Kabuki, whatever, and that is actually where I would propose to start this. One of the things that is difficult, in terms of the three choices, and one of the things I wanted to address today is that when we're talking about creating work in the gay and lesbian theater environment, I am assuming that it is feminist, one in which gay men support and form a coalition, and which is multicultural.

Now, I'm realizing I'm probably in a time warp that comes from having, in essence, been raised by a feminist gay brother, and possibly it's coming from the fact that most of my theatrical experience has been in small towns, rather than in New York City, and a coalition is necessary in a smaller town, a coalition is necessary for any kind of survival to happen, which is not ignoring difference, but particularly from your hypothetical, it seems to me then that the place to do it is not New York City, in which we tend to get into kind of entrenched camps, and in which it's okay to be a gay man and be misogynist, or to be a gay male critic and be misogynist.

It's okay to denounce work in terms of victimization and not go and see it, as a woman critic, because you don't want to give press to the subject of AIDS, in which it's okay not to critique your own position of privilege. So, I would say outside New York, for my choice. I don't know how you would both feel.

170

DEB PARKS-SATTERFIELD: When I think of the first venue, I would want to know what this subscription audience had seen before, because if the things that they were seeing were *South Pacific* and *My Fair Lady* and that kind of stuff I would really be concerned about coming in there with my black queer ass, you know? I hear what you're saying about small towns, but when I think about that first hypothetical venue, this heterosexual man has the best intentions and everything, but would we possibly be looked upon as exotic flowers, do people want to do a voyeuristic thing? Or would this audience have been exposed to other types of theater? So that we were just not stepping up in there and going "Hi! I'm queer!"

CYNTHIA MAYEDA: So, if the audience were really virginal, in that way, I think what I hear you saying is that wouldn't be a place you'd want to begin, or that wouldn't be a place you'd want to take this play?

DEB PARKS-SATTERFIELD: I don't know. An audience like that sounds like a challenge. One of the reasons I perform is that there's this give and take with the audience, and the hardest thing for me is, when you're doing something, and people have got that trout face. During a performance like that, I almost want to stop and say, "Well, did you like it or did you hate it? What's going on with the face here?"

PAULA VOGEL: They're going back to the sea.

DEB PARKS-SATTERFIELD: Right. I sort of start doing that tap dancing thing: please, please like us! Then you find out they did like it, but were undemonstrative.

PAULA VOGEL: Well, I think one of the basic things we should be negotiating is that wherever we perform, there's a backdoor exit onto the alleyway . . .

HOLLY HUGHES: Right, and a car waiting.

DEB PARKS-SATTERFIELD: So I'd have to know what came before we got there.

CYNTHIA MAYEDA: What do you think, Holly?

HOLLY HUGHES: First of all, I've had bad experiences and good experiences at any kind of theater. I've been censored at lesbian theaters. I've had every kind of experience. So, I think from just describing the theater and the demographics and the works there, it's impossible to tell what you're walking into, and one thing that I would take very seriously is other people's experience with that specific theater, so that Paula had had a relationship with this theater would be great. That would seem like a really great place to incubate something, and you already have a little bit of history there. The other thing that I would worry about, would be something about how my presence in a project would affect the people that I'm working with and the theater that I'm working with, and how well they could deal with that, and by that I mean being sort of a marked woman, from my NEA history.

I may not be at the forefront of this, but the fact is that people who have presented me have gotten death threats, bomb threats, funding cuts. People that I have been working with have had their funding jeopardized. I have experienced doing a play that looked at issues of racism in the lesbian community, that I did in Minneapolis, San Francisco, and in this city [New York City], and in San Francisco I was working with young women who were nineteen years old, and I had wanted the theater to really make sure that their families knew who I was.

They couldn't seem to find nineteen-year-old lesbian actresses in San Francisco—that's a whole other panel discussion—and as a result, at the opening of the play, we had one really angry mom in the theater, yelling at me that I had ruined her daughter's life. Worse things happened. Somebody just got fired at the Portland Art Museum in Oregon for trying to bring me. I'm concerned about how this affects the people that I work with. Without becoming paranoid—although it's impossible to become paranoid in this day and age, I even think that it's healthy nowadays to be paranoid—but that would be a question that I would raise.

CYNTHIA MAYEDA: Well, given that, and given everything else we've talked about, but especially given that, I want to make sure that you get the right venue for this piece, so maybe I should go back and see what I can do, in addition to finding the three I've already found. So, tell me what qualities might be the right ones. I've heard somebody say that you probably should have a relationship with the venue already. I wonder how Paula feels about it?

PAULA VOGEL: I think another thing is important about this. One of the things in the hypothetical that I would already feel uncomfortable with is the whole notion of authorship of a piece like this, because this sounds to me like a collaborative piece, which is not hierarchically written, and so one of the questions I have—and this varies from company to company—is whether or not certain companies allow artists to come in and create a process which is not, here's three weeks of rehearsal, boom! Wham, bam, thank you, ma'am. Let's get out the subscription copy, etcetera and so forth. But that you can actually come in as artists and say, "No, we want a different relationship with the designers. We want a different relationship with the actors. We want to create a collaborative process."

Some companies are good about that, and other companies are, "Uh-uh. Here's our train schedule, and we've got to make the trains run on time." How is it that something like, for example, Anne Bogart's *The Women* is created? How does a company say, "How do you want to approach this as artists?" Is there that kind of leeway there?

Just like you're saying, I've had wonderful experiences with well-intentioned heterosexual artistic directors inviting me in, and I've had horror stories where I thought that I was going to be tarred and feathered by—well, I might as well mention names—Wired Women Productions in St. Louis. I thought I wasn't going to escape with my life. So, the question I have is how much input do we have as artists in the theater company itself?

CYNTHIA MAYEDA: Please forgive me if this is naive, or maybe even ignorant: That's not an issue that necessarily is about sexual orientation, or where sexual orientation plays a larger role than it may for a heterosexual audience. Am I right?

PAULA VOGEL: That's correct. It's not actually an issue of orientation. It's an issue of how do you let artists in, how much of a home are you going to provide? But it is one of the crucial things, in terms of a successful project.

DEB PARKS-SATTERFIELD: I can echo that. What's been interesting for me and my group, as we travel around the United States is that our worst times have been with white lesbians producing us.

PAULA VOGEL: No kidding.

DEB PARKS-SATTERFIELD: Yes, which is really sad. We go in there with the expectation that they are going to make this home for us, that it's like, we're lesbians, you're lesbians, we're different colors but so what? Let's all do this! And what the experience has been is somewhat inhospitable, and the more successful venues that we've worked at have been run by white gay men, where we were shocked that we were treated better than by the women, who we figured would just embrace us.

CYNTHIA MAYEDA: Deb, does that vary, depending on whether you're in Peoria or New York or . . .

DEB PARKS-SATTERFIELD: I don't think it has anything to do with the size of the city. I'm not going to name any names, but we were in Oakland, and . . . but I'm not going to tell you where, though. Is there a backdoor here? All right, good. The hair on the back of my neck is standing up.

So, we were in Oakland and Oakland isn't a little tiny town. There's this Mom-and-Mom-running-the-storefront sort of attitude at some of the lesbian places that we've traveled to. You know, a here-you-are-at-Kinko's-at-four-in-the-morning-Xeroxing-things kind of attitude. Where you look at the flyer and someone picked the type that's going fifty different directions, and it expresses a sort of lax attitude about producing someone that's coming in. There's not a welcoming space made for you. With that attitude, it doesn't seem to matter what size the town is.

CYNTHIA MAYEDA: I don't know if you were all here for the last discussion, but I was totally fascinated by Tony Kushner's statement that he wanted the audience to know at least as much as he did so that he and they could go further. And I thought, well, that's interesting, in light of the fact that we're about to talk about venues—whether you're in a major metropolitan area and you're at a gay and lesbian theater or you're at a large regional theater in the same city. What do you think about that?

PAULA VOGEL: That goes back to what you were asking about what came before us in the season? What kinds of plays are being done on that season? I think about Perseverance Theater in Alaska, where they do *The Importance of Being Earnest* in logging camps. I think of Omaha Magic, of Megan Terry and Joanne Schmidman, and I think about that as a model. This is what Omaha, Nebraska, thinks theater is. That is fabulous. They sent me an audiotape of the postplay discussion of *And Baby Makes Seven* that I couldn't go to, and I've never heard such brilliant dramaturgical criticism as that coming out of their subscribers, and then in the middle of the discussion, somebody said, "Well, what did you think about the potatoes?" And I went, *what?* And they said, "What do you think about how we used the potatoes in *And Baby Makes Seven*?" I went, wow, I wish I could have seen that production. Then they start talking about the soap bubbles.

God knows what they did, but it sounded like a place I'd like to work. To me, the proper space is a space in which, depending on the show, if it's always queer theater, it's always feminist theater, it is always black theater. Because the theater should be as changeable as our identity, and as destabilized as our identity. That, to me, is what the notion of theater is, and there are certain places, regardless . . .

CYNTHIA MAYEDA: But also part of the community.

PAULA VOGEL: Part of the community. It is their daily bread. That's what they do; they go to the theater.

HOLLY HUGHES: One time I was in another place that will remain nameless.

PAULA VOGEL: Oh, god. Come on.

HOLLY HUGHES: I knew I was going to have a bad experience there. It was some place where you're supposed to do a work in progress and then show it. Where the artists were living, we didn't have any TV sets, because they assumed we'd be working all the time. We did find where the TV sets were housed. So, in those brief moments when we weren't creating our works of genius we could watch . . . The play was going to be a fifteen-minute work-in-progress of, like, stream-of-cappucino nonsense. We didn't know. Or maybe it could have been fabulous. But for our fifteen minutes they were charging eighteen dollars. And I asked about this and they said, "Well . . ." and it was in a rural part of a certain part of the country, and they said, "Well, we wanted to keep out the riff-raff." And I thought, of course, I'm not going to have any audience that's going to understand it.

I like a broader range of people, and I think looking at the ticket prices and who is this accessible to is a really important kind of question. And what kind of community outreach has been done? What does the community mean? What is the function of this theater? I've seen really amazing experimental theater done in places like St. Louis.

PAULA VOGEL: Yes, that's another thing to talk about on this hypothetical project: not just, what have they seen before? But how much are the ticket prices? What is the outreach? There are companies that I would not like to go to—like a certain theater company in Orange County—where you feel like they should put holy water at the aisles when you go in. I mean, there's plush velvet seats and people sit like it's the mass. It's impolite to cough, to laugh, to eat mints, all that kind of thing. In that kind of rarified atmosphere, I think we probably wouldn't be very happy . . .

HOLLY HUGHES: It should be a dump . . . in some ways. Really. But a nice dump.

DEB PARKS-SATTERFIELD: But, you know, we've been taught a religiosity around art, whereas before everybody just went to the theater. It was no big deal, and now it's like you get dressed up, you sit in a plush seat with your hands folded on top of your desk. And we've been taught to act that way and to view it that way.

CYNTHIA MAYEDA: I'm going to push a little bit. Let me bring us back a half step. We're going to assume that we've been out on the road for a while so . . .

DEB PARKS-SATTERFIELD: Too long.

CYNTHIA MAYEDA: And I'm picking up on the "dump" statement. We have an opportunity to go to Broadway. *Angels* just closed. *Love! Valor!* hasn't opened, and there's an empty theater, and if I don't have an opportunity to reconnect with the three of you, I'm just going back to conversations we've had earlier. So I'm definitely going to tell the Nederlanders we're totally uninterested, because I heard you say, "It's got to be a dump." I heard you say, "The ticket prices have to be low."

PAULA VOGEL: Well, we were talking about places where I think something might be originated, finding some place that's comfortable, where you really feel like you can incubate something, which might be different from where you'd be willing to present something.

CYNTHIA MAYEDA: Okay, let me just put a button on this. It is the premiere. It hasn't incubated anywhere except in your hearts and heads, to this moment. We haven't had an audience, and I still get a call from Jujamicyn and they say, "We understand you're about to do this, and there's a chance you don't have to leave town, but why don't we do it on Broadway? It sounds to me like there might be an audience for this show." Do I have your permission to say, "No way. No. Ticket prices are too high and we haven't incubated it and we don't know who is coming—the same audience may have seen *Miss Saigon* that afternoon, and this is . . .

DEB PARKS-SATTERFIELD: And now we move to the whore section of acting.

CYNTHIA MAYEDA: I'm not sure. I'm not sure.

DEB PARKS-SATTERFIELD: But, I mean, give me plush. Give me plush! If I had an opportunity like that, I would go ahead and be a ho'. To pass up an opportunity like that, I think, would be silly.

CYNTHIA MAYEDA: Well, I guess I'm asking you whether you have to be a whore to go do it?

DEB PARKS-SATTERFIELD: Well, that's just me.

CYNTHIA MAYEDA: Do you all three agree?

PAULA VOGEL: I don't recognize that reality, that that would happen, that lesbian play about racism?

CYNTHIA MAYEDA: Elaborate.

PAULA VOGEL: I would not pass up an opportunity, because I would assume all the way along that as we were moving into Broadway that I would wake up in my bed the next morning, and it's all been a fantasy or a dream. I would go along for the ride, because I don't believe that it would happen, and I think it would be interesting to try. I'm willing to try anything once, and I think that for us, as lesbians on Broadway, it would only happen once. It would happen one night, and it would be closed the next day.

CYNTHIA MAYEDA: Great opening night party, though.

PAULA VOGEL: This is kind of like contemplating what life is going to be like in the twenty-second century. Lesbian theater is so far from even making inroads into Off Broadway. We'll all be back at the Perseverance Theater the next day.

DEB PARKS-SATTERFIELD: Yeah, it's like hoping that you win the Lotto. It's like, give me the chance to say, "Gee, I got all this money, I don't know what to do with it."

CYNTHIA MAYEDA: I was just also trying to honor what I heard you say earlier, and I was trying to figure out if I could get those things to be copacetic or if . . .

PAULA VOGEL: I think there's something that's been happening right now, and this is something that I'm actually very perturbed about, because there's been a code name tossed around, which is a way to break up coalitions happening across race, class, gender lines, and that is, as the funding pie gets smaller and the NEA is phasing itself out of existence, we are now saying "community theater" as if saying "amateur . . ." you know, "amateur night." To me, great theater is always theater that creates community. I've been hearing artistic directors who have been running their companies on a five million dollar budget suddenly have to go for grants where they have to do community outreach, and they come to me as if I'm going to be sympathetic, saying, "Well, I didn't get my degree in social work," and I'm like, "I'm sorry, why is it that creating a community and opening up dialogue is suddenly amateur?"

You've heard this. And that doesn't mean that a company that has a five million dollar budget can't be creating community . . .

DEB PARKS-SATTERFIELD: Yes, but they have the option not to create community theater.

HOLLY HUGHES: That's right. That's right. They've had the option not to. There are—and again, this is an individual thing—there are people who recognize that theater should be a right for every member in the community to participate in. One other thing to push this, because I've got a lot of attitude about this: I would actually want to go into a place where we say, "The audience knows as much as we do," in which every member of the audience has either written a play or is thinking about writing a play, has acted, has directed, wants to be, in essence, in my community, as an artist. And there are places that, not only in terms of what went before, but where the membrane of the stage is very thin between the audience and the performers, otherwise, we end up being performing trained dogs with large ticket prices.

I don't want that kind of exclusion. So when we're talking about that, the attitude of that theater company, in terms of inclusion for their audience members in the process of what we're doing as work, is important to me.

One of the things I like to do—I don't know where I first got the idea. I think somebody suggested doing it, and then I found I got sort of hooked on it—is to do performance workshops, as well as doing a performance, which is teaching what I do, teaching how to shape autobiographical material for performance and storytelling workshops. I'm really indebted to Tim Miller's ideas about some of these things, and one of the great things that happened is that I've found I'm actually less interested in writing for other voices than helping other people write for themselves now.

It also helped dissolve something that was really horrible for me about touring, which is the isolation of it. These workshops provide a limited sense of the community that you were in at different times. I mean, I did a workshop in Houston last spring, and it was a surprising demographic. I'm always surprised that it was mostly men that came to the workshop, and it turned out it was mostly men that were in the audience.

But the big-budget theaters address a community, too. It's the same community that's addressed when they talk about "community values." It's white. It's heterosexual. It's middle class. Their spiritual practice is golf, you know?

CYNTHIA MAYEDA: The only thing I'd offer is that in my experience, this is not about the size of theaters, and that's sometimes disappointing or alarming or even shocking that there can be very tiny theaters that sort of masquerade as being "of the community," and claiming to be really fully integrated, and it's as much bullshit as it might be if they have a subscriber base.

HOLLY HUGHES: That's right.

CYNTHIA MAYEDA: I think we all should be aware of that.

PAULA VOGEL: Right. It's not about the size of the budget. It's really about the way that that theater organization is working on the inside.

CYNTHIA MAYEDA: And the way they interface with the community, too.

PAULA VOGEL: Yeah, I'm as concerned about how, for example, the interns are being used in a theater company, as whether I'm going to feel comfortable there, and how they're talking to younger artists who were working in that company is a factor, in terms of finding a really great place to originate work, I think.

CYNTHIA MAYEDA: And is it important to you who the interns are? In other words—now I'm coming back full circle—it's the three of you taking this on the road, and is it important to you that you're in a place where the interns are not all heterosexual?

DEB PARKS-SATTERFIELD: Well, yeah. To walk into a place cold and look around— for me and my girls to look around and see that we're the only raisins in the oatmeal, that's scary to me. You walk in and you're looking around, and thinking: okay, if I can't have a brown face, let me see, I'll take a kind of red one. Okay, you look around for that. And if the interns aren't even different colors, different genders, and so on, that's very scary. But it's especially scary where it's all white lesbians who think that they have put together some sort of integrated utopia, when actually, it's all white lesbians who all sort of look the same. And sometimes they're in an area where they could actually buy a building for really cheap, because it's all these brown and red and different colors of people all out here—it's in the ghetto.

That's why the building is cheap. So for that group to not reflect the community that they're in is frightening to me.

CYNTHIA MAYEDA: Right. Maybe this is just a finer point, but I'm just curious, why do you think that when your hosts are gay white men, they're more hospitable?

DEB PARKS-SATTERFIELD: I don't know. I really don't. I don't know. We had incredible experiences at Highways in L.A., and in Boston, with Abe Rybeck. They were amazing to us, and they didn't know us. You send out your stuff and somebody sees it and they think, okay, I'll have them down here and you don't know what to expect. We had bad experiences with black gay men and we were totally floored by that. Come on. This can't be happening, you know?

HOLLY HUGHES: And horizontal hostility is such a horrible problem, and the closer you are, the worse it is, the more painful it is.

DEB PARKS-SATTERFIELD: Yeah, very painful.

HOLLY HUGHES: It's very, very painful.

PAULA VOGEL: Likewise. I've had some experiences with women producers that have been wonderful, and I've had other experiences . . . One woman producer developed, I think, a bladder problem because Phyllis Nagy and I were in the building. She didn't want to use the toilet. Do you know what I mean? I'm glad. I'm glad she developed a bladder problem.

CYNTHIA MAYEDA: I think with that, we're going to kick the door open. May I? I'd like to turn to our friends in the audience.

AUDIENCE QUESTION: You talked about theaters' hospitality or inhospitality in making a nest for you, and I'm wondering, what does making a nest for you involve?

HOLLY HUGHES: One of the things that I would hope is that the people that you're working with want to be doing what they're doing, and that it matters deeply to them. It's incredible work, work in the theater. There's no nine to five about it. So, you want to work with people who want to work with you and are clear that this is their passion.

DEB PARKS-SATTERFIELD: Sometimes you run into people who say that they want to do that, but they're really fried, they're really burned out. They really don't want to do this. I had an experience with a woman who said to us, "We consider our space a Wiccan temple"—this is true—"We consider our space a Wiccan temple." And that they didn't do any advertising because if people were meant to find this place, they would find it. I was flabbergasted by that. Luckily it was in Minneapolis. I knew a lot of people there, so we had a decent audience.

PAULA VOGEL: Anna Deavere Smith came up and did this amazing workshop—I was just amazed, watching her with this group of artists. And at the end of it she said that she thought that any artistic director or anyone in the community had really only one obligation, which is only to do work that you love. Love the people you're working with. Do work that you love. Circle Rep provided a really wonderful nest for me. You talked about hospitable gay white men. I stop and think about Lanford Wilson or Bill Hoffman just being excited, just being excited that you're there.

DEB PARKS-SATTERFIELD: And wanting to have you there.

PAULA VOGEL: It makes you really want to pay back with generosity. It makes you want to do the best that you can for that, and that's not anything that is about sexual orientation, gender, or race. It's generosity.

AUDIENCE QUESTION: The discrepancy you're describing between spaces run by gay white men and spaces run by lesbians—is the difference a matter of resources? Men just have more of them.

CYNTHIA MAYEDA: That's a good point.

DEB PARKS-SATTERFIELD: I understand what you're talking about. But on the other hand, being a lesbian, I sometimes get really tired of hearing that. I don't know how to describe it. But it's an attitude almost like: here are these pitiful people over here who are just trying to make something happen. We are these lesbians, and then over here, the boys have more stuff, so then they can do a better job. It's still a question of working someplace where it's obvious that the people don't want to be there anymore, whether they have resources or not. I mean, we've worked in places where the girls had stuff: a nice space, nice equipment. They had this. They had that. And still something just wasn't happening there. For whatever reason, we weren't treated well.

PAULA VOGEL: I'm going to make the pitch for Perseverance again because . . .

DEB PARKS-SATTERFIELD: I want to go there!

HOLLY HUGHES: Yeah, let's go there.

PAULA VOGEL: Let's do it! People often laugh at this, but everybody in the staff there basically rotate jobs. So if you're artistic director, you're going to spend a weekend running the box office, or you may be cleaning up the bathroom. And I know this sounds very strange, but it's important to me as a writer to know I have to participate in making sure that the space is cleaned up.

HOLLY HUGHES: There's a hierarchy in the way things are done in theater.

PAULA VOGEL: So I come back to this. There are lesbian companies filled with volunteers who are generous, who are excited, and who are working on a shoestring, and actually, I think the most interesting thing is actually starting where money can be the problem. Money can be the problem. Because then you don't have to share your resources in the same way in creating a work. I don't really think this comes down to a money issue, in a way, and I don't think this really comes down to the orientation, necessarily, of the artistic director, but I'm talking about creating a circle, and that this circle includes the audience, the circle includes the community, and that's going to just have a ripple effect. Circles grow outward; the ideal place to find a nest is in the center of that.

AUDIENCE QUESTION: You mentioned earlier that sometimes you're the only raisins in the oatmeal. What is the up side to that? I'd like to see Holly go to Harlem and us go to, I don't know, Teaneck.

DEB PARKS-SATTERFIELD: More can happen, yes, but I also know how much pressure there is. Sometimes we go into a place and we look out there and we do not see ourselves reflected at all. I understand both sides of it. I think, yes, it's daring and it's a good thing to do, but then on the other hand, I would still like to have a little bit of comfort to look out and see different colors. Even though we had a bad experience in Oakland, the audience was mostly large, black women, and that was a trip. Here we are, these big black girls doing all this stuff about being fat, black, and queer, and here are all these fat, black, queer women in the audience. I cried. It's only happened once. Once.

HOLLY HUGHES: I agree that there should be more cross-pollination, but it should expand just beyond the places that you or I go to. Also, how do we fight the problems of tokenism, you know, that they tend to find the lesbian of the moment.

DEB PARKS-SATTERFIELD: Yeah. Flavor of the month.

HOLLY HUGHES: I remember once Danitra Vance telling me that her show was really taking off at La Mama just after Whoopi Goldberg had been launched, and everybody telling her she should be more like Whoopi Goldberg. And the idea that there could be one funny African American woman at a time. One of the things that's been great in the last few years, is that there have been more lesbians touring. So I don't face what I faced when I first started touring: that I might get presented by very, very nice people, and they'd have a little party for me afterward, and then they'd start telling me how relieved they were that I wasn't butch, that I wasn't ugly, I wasn't angry, which, clearly . . .

PAULA VOGEL: Did they use the same bathroom facilities?

HOLLY HUGHES: . . . which clearly would become untrue in a minute.

AUDIENCE QUESTION: How do you like performing at universities?

DEB PARKS-SATTERFIELD: I've had great experience at universities. Some of the campuses we've been on have a climate that reminds me of the late sixties, early seventies. They're just eager for it, you know? We usually sell out at universities, and they just adore us.

CYNTHIA MAYEDA: You two agree? It's a mix?

PAULA VOGEL: Mix.

HOLLY HUGHES: It's a mixed bag. I've had great experiences at universities and terrible ones. There was one performance I did where the presenter was crying in the dressing room afterward, that now she's not going to get tenure, after my show.

CYNTHIA MAYEDA: Back to what you said, Deb, about facilities—this has been haunting me forever. A few years ago I did the NEA site visit at the Public Theater, and I was going on a tour and we were passing through the green room on the way to something else, and of course I couldn't help but take note of how pathetic it was, and how it was like jillions of other green rooms. It stuck in my throat because the week before I'd been at a university in the Southwestern United States, on a tour with a group of grant makers, and they were showing off their new facility, which was incredibly impressive, and when we got to the green room—this is honest to Christ the truth—I started to cry because it was so amazing, and I knew that I had been in the greatest not-for-profit theaters in America and had never seen a green room that came even close. I don't know if I'd seen a rehearsal room as nice as their green room was.

HOLLY HUGHES: Most of the theaters in the poorest universities I've been to have been, generally, so much better than all but the premiere performance spaces.

PAULA VOGEL: The university where I'm working has an incredible facility, which I do not participate in. We have an abandoned little cafeteria where you can still smell the hamburgers, and I love that space, because my experience is that new work is born in the manger and not at the inn, that there's usually no room at the inn, and I feel very, very comfortable in the dump.

CYNTHIA MAYEDA: And with that, quite arbitrarily, I'm going to bring this to a close. I do too many panels, and I always feel honored, but I rarely enjoy it as much as I have today. It's been a terrifically fizzy conversation. And let me say that I'm sure the next time this panel meets, rather than "From P.S. 122 to Peoria," it will surely read "From P.S. 122 to Perseverance."

Apple Island and the Performance of Community

Stacy Wolf

Performing Womyn

Apple Island, a self-described "women's cultural and art space" in Madison, Wisconsin, sits along one of the city's major roads, dotted with car dealerships, a lumber yard, Jiffy Lube, and occasional working-class taverns. Located about a mile east of the capitol building, a fair distance from both Madison's other theaters and from its gay bars, the inconspicuous, industrial brick building with little marking identifying it as a lesbian space requires foreknowledge (or at least high motivation and interest) for a potential spectator even to find the door. Its activities and performances inscribe an audience whose spectating practices belie identity politics even as the space tries to institute them.

A small sign adorns the outside of the refurbished warehouse, featuring the space's logo—an apple on the crest of a wave. Suggestive of nature, movement, and Eve, the image both reappropriates the symbol of patriarchy's bad girl and the symbol of her desire for knowledge, and links that image to a more traditional female affiliation with water. The logo emblematizes Apple Island's attempt to rework the feminine. The name also emphasizes the idea of a safe and separate space. There are no numbers on the building, and the inside, which looks like an office building with its freshly painted white walls and hardwood floors, offers no directions to the space itself, which is around the corner and in the back. You have to *want* to get to Apple Island to get there.

Apple Island's location parallels a similarly teleological lesbian identity, based on self-knowledge and self-naming, and necessarily implicated in representation. As Judith Roof points out, "Identifying as a lesbian already requires a circle where experience and representation define one another."[1] In its structuring of its audience, Apple Island does not problematize that identity, but relies on assumptions about what it means to "be" a lesbian as it represents itself as a (lesbian) community and cultural space. Ultimately, that representation, that discursive construction, is more significant than the "reality" of Apple Island's audiences. In other words, even though some of the performances allow men in the audience (Apple Island even hosted country western line dancing for men), and even though heterosexual women may partake of activities without renouncing men, Apple Island identifies and defines itself as a space for lesbians.

I want to describe Apple Island as a site of cultural production and to look (in part, ethnographically) at the various ways spectators use the place.[2] As one location in Madison where lesbian identities are performed (onstage and off), Apple Island and the attendant discourses of Madison's "women's community" construct a notion of lesbian identity through cultural production. These local configurations of lesbian identities and of a lesbian community are, I think, very useful fictions that (seem to need to) elide difference to maintain their hegemony. At the same time, they provide a significant venue for alternative cultural production through performance. Georges Van Den Abbeele writes that there is "an element of demagoguery or mystification at work in the seductive appeal to community."[3] Community is seductive in all venues, but maybe more so in one that is based on "identity." Aware of both the seductiveness and the demagoguery of the call to and desire for community (and locating myself as seducer and seduced, as demagogue and follower), I hope to demystify its workings in this context, and to, as Van Den Abbeele suggests, "develop a more just logic of community."

"The Personal Is Political" of Place, Space, and Money

Architecturally and spatially, Apple Island looks more like a community center than a performance space. Inside, it is simply a large, rectangular room, which is rearranged according to the needs of each activity or performance. A small, raised stage is often set up at the far end of the room or halfway in on the right. Sometimes the floor is cleared, as for a dance, and sometimes folding chairs are set up around or facing the stage. The room is equipped with a few lighting instruments. The walls are decorated with prints and posters of art by women, and the snack bar offers coffee, juice, and soda (no alcohol), and cookies, ice cream, and brownies. Near the entrance on the right is a table covered with flyers and a bulletin board advertising upcoming events for women, at Apple Island as well as in Milwaukee and Chicago.

Apple Island advertises some of its events by listing them in *Feminist Voices*, a local monthly newspaper, and by posting flyers in several local merchants' windows. But only three sites provide complete information about these activities: A Room of One's Own (Madison's feminist bookstore); "Her Turn," Sue Gold-womon's[4] weekly program on the local community radio station; and Apple Island itself. Both the bookstore and the radio show present themselves as community centers, posting or announcing notices about local lectures, concerts, and conferences. While there is public access to information about Apple Island, it mostly circulates subculturally through a network of mutually supporting organizations and businesses. The close connection among Apple Island, A Room of One's Own, and "Her Turn" fosters not only a sense that there is a bounded community of insiders, but also that this community has certain concerns, interests, tastes, and desires.

To comprehend much of Apple Island's publicity, potential spectators need a political and cultural context. Apple Island's photocopied flyers address themselves to a specific audience derived from a specific community. The flyer for *Peg's Passing*, for example, shows (what we assume is) Peg's face and the event's time, date, and location (Apple Island). To know that this was a dance and party that commemorated the anniversary of the death of a local feminist activist, you had to know who Peg was and know enough about her or the hosts of the event to assume what kind of event it would be. In this instance and in general, a complex interplay of identity and knowledge construct Apple Island's potential spectators.

Mainstream newspapers do not review performances at Apple Island.[5] When reviews do appear in *Feminist Voices*, they are emotionally charged, intensely personal, almost confessional accounts of the "reviewer's" experience at Apple Island. Reviews are hardly necessary to attract an audience, as the communication circle works well. Also, the critical stance of reviewing could open up readings that members of the Apple Island community would consider inappropriate: functioning to reproduce its own community, Apple Island's preferred spectator sees its performances and representations in one way.

Many of Apple Island's events are fund-raisers: a dance for the local women's ride service, a performance to raise donations for women with disabilities, a concert to send two women to France to study with a political guru. Indeed, such support for specific local organizations and community members connects performance with a specific idea of the political, which here is a woman-centered one. Furthermore, many performers present work at Apple Island for free. Donating their time and talents, the performers' bodies enact their politics. These bodies are iconic, not representational; they reproduce their political and social identity. Whatever the subject of a performance, the act of performing is understood as political. The content may include references to a specific issue or cause, but the very enactment by definition includes (gender) identity politics. In this respect, the personal is always political in Apple Island performances.

Admission is by sliding scale—spectators pay what they can. In the moment when the spectator decides what she will pay, a different kind of personal becomes political (and public), and the political, personal. This action differs strikingly from a spectator buying a ticket at a theater where prices vary according to seat location, and free choice reflects one's desire to pay for quality (proximity to the performance)—and also for some cultural capital. At Apple Island, where money is seen more for its sustaining function and less for its exchange value, a spectator must classify herself according to her *ability* to pay; the underlying ideology holds that each spectator wants to pay as much as she can to support the community.

In or Out?

Apple Island and its audience participate in a struggle over the meaning of Madison's women's community, a struggle inflected with theoretical, academic debates about identity, politics, and gender. Apple Island is read through its place in Madison, a university town where queer theory and ideas about the performance of identity increasingly pervade the intellectual landscape where Apple Island opened in 1991. The space's insistence on a strict correlation of sex and gender, on an unquestioning essentialism of identity, strikes one as almost preceding queer theory. I don't want to reify a division between theory and practice, nor do I want to represent Apple Island as anachronistic, but the language spoken there— notwithstanding contestation of the place's meanings and uses among those who frequent it—is one that regards gender as a stable and knowable category. Woman signifies Oppressed; Empowerment is the strategy of change.

I have gathered perceptions of the internal debates over meaning through conversations within and outside Apple Island, extended interviews with performers and spectators, and by sitting in on a discussion about the place in a "Lesbian Culture" class.[6] Most of the women to whom I spoke saw Apple Island as representing Madison's most vocal and visible "women's community." They described its aesthetic and ideology as "cultural feminist," but did not always agree about whether that term carried positive or negative valences. The sense that Apple Island is a community space requires a spectator to see herself as inside or outside that community. So, not surprisingly, everyone to whom I spoke first talked about her perception of her own inclusion or exclusion, often defining that in terms of her sexual identity or of her intellectual and/or emotional sympathy with lesbian-feminist[7] politics. And although many performers and spectators questioned the very idea of a coherent women's community, they consistently used the term. Like the ways in which representation by sheer repetition becomes reality, the repeated use of the phrase "women's community," even when accompanied by rolling eyes or a two-fingered gesture indicating quotation marks, makes us believe there is such a thing.

Perhaps. "confederacy" idea?

The powerful fiction of community sets up an expectation of insiderness at Apple Island. For some, it's an offer of a safe space; for others, it's an oppressive or exclusionary one. Stephanie, for example, who works at the university Women's Studies Research Center and receives monthly flyers from Apple Island but has never been there, noted "a double message of inclusion/exclusion." She said, "Clearly, if they send flyers to everyone [at Women's Studies], they're trying to be welcoming in some way, [. . .] but the flyers themselves are peculiar in that they carry almost no information unless you already know the language." She told me that before our conversation, she could not decipher what Apple Island was. She said, "I knew only that Apple Island was some kind of space where something related to women went on, that I was supposed to be (and wanted to be) interested in, but where I knew, vaguely, that I couldn't go." She added, "It really seems that their flyers are more antipublicity than anything else." How does Stephanie know that she "couldn't go" to Apple Island? And why can't she? As a straight feminist interested in performance and familiar with the language of feminist theory, is she unable, by virtue of her sexuality, to recognize the codes of lesbian-feminism?

Despite, or maybe even because of, Apple Island's exclusions, I am interested in tracking the use value of such a cultural "community" site for variously positioned spectators. Apple Island is just one among many gay and lesbian theaters that flourished beginning in the 1980s. Some have a more national profile, like the

WOW Café in Manhattan, Theater Rhinoceros in San Francisco, and Alice B. in Seattle. Many university towns have a performance space that may be explicitly dedicated to gay and lesbian work or that may offer an alternative venue for self-consciously politicized, left-leaning performances, such as Esther's Follies in Austin, Texas, or the Mickee Faust Club in Tallahassee, Florida.[8]

Apple Island clearly provides a vital and significant cultural and social space. It is supported and frequented by an active, self-identified, mostly white, lesbian-feminist audience community. For the women who attend regularly, there *is* a women's community, a real one, which emerges quite naturally from the personal, politicized practice of individuals gathering there. Naomi, for instance, who goes to Apple Island almost every weekend and whose friends have performed there, said that the place is welcoming, not exclusionary. Well aware of what she called Apple Island's "folklore of censorship," she said simply, "It's inaccurate." Katie, another habitué, said, "I'm thirty-eight, and Apple Island feels more like my community than anywhere else." Insiders view the women's community in positive terms; only women who feel excluded for whatever reasons denaturalize the boundaries and make explicit what they see as particular expectations about the performance of identity.

But "being" a lesbian isn't enough. Jenny, for example, a lesbian and practicing-but-not-identifying feminist,[9] has felt excluded for reasons completely opposite to those of Stephanie. She is a folk singer and guitarist who, after performing there several times, said, "Those Midwesterners are so damn polite!" During one of her concerts, she repeatedly called to the audience, "You guys aren't dead, are you? You can laugh and talk." Accustomed to performing in mixed bars to much less attentive audiences on the East Coast, Jenny said that when performing at Apple Island she missed the danger she enjoyed when she was misread as a potential pickup by men when she performs in mixed bars. At Apple Island, where her sexual identity was apparent and expected, she felt no charge. Although her identity could position her as an insider, she rejected Apple Island because it felt too safe.

I have often felt compelled to perform a particular lesbian style to be read as an insider at Apple Island, never quite knowing whether the performance was for an audience or for myself, or whether by enacting insiderness, I might feel it or prove it to be impossible to feel. Nonetheless, in months of attending Apple Island, always nervous that my academic motives would be found out, I never felt like an insider. But I began to perceive the appeal of the place. I began to see hopeful gaps in the cultural feminist ideology. Something in Apple Island's refusal to drop feminism and join the perhaps more chic nomenclature of queerness, and in its insistence on the realness of community, earned my respect. Although, as Biddy Martin asserts, queer theory tends to characterize gender identity as boring, staid, and resoundingly stable, while it represents sexuality as free, performative, fun, and fluid, Apple Island, I hope to show, refuses the distinction and the dismissal.[10]

Performing Lesbians

During the first two years of its existence (1991–93, the years of my research), Apple Island housed both performances and meetings. The performances perpetuate an economic and ideological network, reinforcing the community's sense of its own existence. The events and their publicity flyers can be read intertextually through the discourses of cultural feminism, lesbian separatism, and local history and folklore. They illustrate what cultural feminism is made to mean in this space. Posters are often phrased as invitations—"come join us"—or stating that a performer will "share" her music with us. "Woman" stands as an unproblematized signifier, unmarked by other identity categories.

Most of the performances are original, conceived by the performers, and employ performance art, solo monologue, and stand-up comedy. Musicians frequently play, often as part of a bill of a variety of acts. Some pieces explore ways of women's self-empowerment. Kate Ryan, a local artist, performed an original series of monologues called *Class Work*, advertised as "a hurtling narrative spanning the continuum from the fourth world to the first." In the performance, Ryan played a number of characters in her family and community to recount her often painful experiences with class divisions and expectation.[11]

Published plays are rarely but occasionally produced, as in the case of Velina Houston's *Tea*—notable, too, because men were allowed to attend and because the play represents heterosexual Asian American women. The producers of *Tea* rented Apple Island, although publicity does not differentiate among producers. Yet *Tea's* very presence was the exception that proved Apple Island's rule of white, lesbian-feminist solo performance.

Many performances deal with issues of women's spirituality and rituals, such as one called *The Joy of Spinning*. Like most of the shows at Apple Island, this performance consisted of four different pieces by four different performers. The most provocative featured three women costumed as spiders. They carried a huge spool of yarn and danced and climbed all over the space, creating a web around themselves and the audience. They alternated movement with storytelling, and self-consciously noted that the physical web signified the power of stories and the danger of being caught in one's own autobiographical fictions. The stories themselves were about each woman's relationship to stories: Beth's mother told her lies about the family to keep it intact; Julie created stories about another girl-child to escape the pain of her own abuse. These two performers employed radically different styles. Beth hilariously imitated her mother's ludicrous tale-telling. Julie's tone was serious and understated, allowing words themselves to capture the power and pain of her story. I refer to these performers by their first names not because I know them personally, but because Apple Island, productively and problematically, conflates performer and character.[12] Whether the stories are autobiographical or fictional one never knows, but either way they embody a truth, a lesson to be learned. The audience applauds as much for their willingness to share themselves as for the performance.

The Spectator's Self-Story

Because of my perceptions of my identity and my (precarious? nonexistent?) relationship to the "women's community" in Madison and to Apple Island, my "field-work" continually produced anxieties. I also found myself attending events at Apple Island alone, an irregular experience for this, and most theater spectators.[13] When I went to see *The Naked Truth* in March 1992, I was glad that I had been there before, so at least I knew where to go.

The story: Women are hanging out in the hall. One woman is seated behind a table, selling handmade cloth purses. Everyone looks at me. I think, "They don't think I'm a lesbian." I pay my $5 at the door, smile at the woman taking the money, act like I think I belong here, and go into the main room. It's packed and I don't recognize anyone. I feel curiously relieved, as if glad to be there anonymously. The woman next to me, in her fifties, studies her program with concentration and seems to be here alone, too. I want to ask her why she came here, what she thinks about this scene, but I don't. I think, "How would I ever be brave enough to bring a tape recorder here?" and, "Maybe no one will talk to me because they know I'm critical of this place and don't order my books at the women's bookstore."

Laurie, one of tonight's performers whom I know through mutual friends, comes up, touches my arm, and says, "Hi, I hope you like the show."

I know I'm supposed to feel okay here. I'm a woman, a lesbian, a feminist, a theater person. Why do I feel scared? Why do I feel like they might discover that

I'm not authentic, that my motives aren't pure, that I really wanted to go to the movies tonight?

Everyone knows everyone—it seems. There *is* a kind of community here. I can feel it. I think about having gone to the Madison Civic Center to see the Ballet Trocadero de Monte Carlo the night before. Even filled with a crowd of gay men, lesbians, and ballet aficionados, the Civic Center's lobby and the Oscar Mayer Theater felt official, marked by cultural capital and by being public. There, people talked with companions in pairs or groups of a few; spectating seemed a private event in a public place. At Apple Island, the groups keep moving and shifting; people are introduced to each other and it seems that most of the audience knows the performers. It's noisy until the house lights go down and bright general stage lights come up.

Laurie and Jean present a four-part piece about being female. In the first, Laurie speaks directly to the audience, describing various points when she felt "between lives." She tells poignant stories with sardonic seriousness. Throughout Laurie's tale, Jean crouches behind a table and manipulates Barbie dolls as puppets, as if to illustrate Laurie's stories. The puppets do not illustrate Laurie's narrative, but rather enact other, seemingly related stories, so that the connection between the puppets' actions and the spoken text is indirect but evident. For example, when Laurie describes how she always felt torn between wanting to be a performer and feeling like she should have an office job, the two identical Barbies appear to go for a walk and then beat each other up. Laurie's stories tend to be serious, and everything the Barbies do is ridiculous, in part because they're Barbies. I think the performance is compelling, and I smile to myself, relieved.

In the second part, the two lie on the floor in sleeping bags as we hear the song "Tender Shepherds" from *Peter Pan*. Are they children? Are they in *Peter Pan* with a woman playing a boy? In the third section, Laurie and Jean play old women and dress in layers of mismatched clothing. The soundtrack plays an old recording of a woman teaching birdcalls. I'm confused, and worse, don't find these sections engaging. Then, in the last part, the two stand naked with a slide of trees projected onto their bodies and the wall behind them. Women and nature? Women returning to nature? What does anyone else think it's about, and what about it? Everyone else laughs and seems to like it, but I don't think the piece is intentionally funny, unless it's a parody of the idea of woman-as-nature.

But here at Apple Island, does it matter what the performers do? How are rules and expectations of performances different here? Would the audience love them no matter what? Is what is represented—as David Román and Tim Miller argue—

beside the point?[14] Like them, I want to understand artistic choices and values within a notion of gay/lesbian/queer community and from a perspective that considers use value as fundamental. The audience's utter support, then, can be read as a subcultural de Certeauian tactic. Since a critical, distanced, "objective" stance is a strategy of dominant ideology, when the audience accepts the performers and refuses to adopt a critical stance, they subvert the dominant. As Román and Miller assert, "Community-based queer theater allows for its terms—community, queer, theater—to coexist without competition or hierarchy." At the same time, I'm skeptical of many of the artistic and political choices and values in the "community," which should include me, but doesn't.

Laurie and Jean's piece, which is self-consciously ironic in some places and sentimentally self-empowering in others, makes a fascinating juxtaposition with the next performer, a singer-guitarist, dressed in jeans, high-top sneakers, and a white T-shirt, who tells us what each song is about and what to think about it. Spectators cheer. Is that because they agree with her? Or because they know her? Is it comforting (or for me, discomforting) to be told what to think? Or is it what she thinks that troubles me? She sings, she says, in honor of "nearing the end of the five-thousand-year rule of the patriarchy, during which men have done unspeakable things to women." I'm stunned by the simplicity of the statements, which she presents as political analysis, not demonstration slogans. I write on my program: "I don't feel safe here," and then, "(why do I shift into the lingo?)"

Ann, an undergraduate I recognize from performance art classes, presents the next piece, in which she is dressed as a housewife in a space marked as a kitchen by curtains hung on the back wall. She cuts up vegetables rhythmically and steadily, while we hear the sound of a siren continually getting louder, then receding, then a loud explosion, someone screaming, followed by Barbra Streisand singing, "Happy Days Are Here Again." I feel moved and chilled, then surprised at my own reaction. Am I too afraid and cynical here? Am I trying to make myself feel like an insider?

After Ann's piece, a woman who seems to be in charge announces upcoming events, including a concert by a singer from Chicago who will be at the Michigan Festival[15]—a reference that is immediately understood.

I think, I know this language. I can enter. I can elect to be part of it. Yet why does it feel exclusive? Why do I feel like I don't have access, that I'm not an insider? Is part of the pleasure of this place the sense of insiderness it provides? And then, is all cultural criticism either trashing or celebration?

A dance follows the performance, but I leave before it starts. Almost all events include a dance, which encourages all who attend to participate beyond spectatorship and to become physically and socially active. Indeed, the dance—the performance of oneself—is part of the performance. As Richard Bauman writes:

Each speech community will make use of a structured set of distinctive communication means from among resources in culturally conventionalized and culture-specific ways to key the performance frame, such that all communication that takes place within that frame is understood as performance within that community.[16]

Performances that typify the Apple Island community in Bauman's sense might be regarded by outsiders as therapy sessions, overly experimental interpretive dances, or simply bad singing. And while any culturally unfamiliar performance may be dismissed by a new, inexperienced spectator, the performances at Apple Island presume that spectators share a specific *identity,* not merely a particular cultural knowledge. In practice, then, spectators' ability to understand and appreciate the performances becomes an insiderness: spectators join and are embraced by this speech community through their engagement with its terms of spectating, and at the same time, through this exchange, the community's social solidarity is asserted. Unlike other performance sites, where resistant meanings may provide moments of pleasurable spectating, Apple Island's communicative frame guarantees that resistant spectatorship immediately transfers to resistance to the community "as a whole." And because performance here is political and personal, resistance is understood (within the community) as personally and politically incorrect. For insiders, though, this tacit policing is essential to their stability as a (sub)culture. For, as Ulf Hannerz writes, "by participating in keeping its particular traffic of meaning going," new members of a subculture "contribute to maintaining it as a supportive environment for the perspectives of those involved."[17]

The conventionalized and specific markers of lesbian-feminist performance at Apple Island that create this "particular traffic of meaning" can be contrasted in both address and tone with those of queer performances, which, as Judith Butler argues, are directed outward. Because the aggressive reappropriation of the label "queer" is always haunted by a homophobic history and the possibility that the label will be used again to shame, queer performances are marked by what Butler calls "the increasing theatricalization of political rage."[18]

Queer performances—such as those by the Five Lesbian Brothers, Holly Hughes, Split Britches, and the Mickee Faust Club of Tallahassee—as Román and Miller explain, usefully and necessarily "preach to the converted." But, I would suggest, their process of "conversion and transformation" ideally eschews the strict, presumptive identity politics of Apple Island. Apple Island's celebration of the feminine, in contrast, embraces traditional (white) femininity, gently infusing it with a positive valence, a self-affirming tone. Performance here is directed inward, toward the already existing community; it functions primarily to sustain the community's sense of its own existence.

A typical flyer advertising a birthday party reveals how Apple Island inscribes a particular audience. First, Apple Island announces itself as "a haven of independence," emphasizing a separatist ideology where women's culture flourishes in isolation. Apple Island, as the poster says, is for women; the event features a women's band and the grand (door) prize reinforces this circularity by awarding the winner with one year's admission to Apple Island. The photograph of potential spectators also encourages a specific spectatorial identification: four women, stereotypically marked as lesbians, with short hair, hands in jeans pockets, androgynous clothing, and a rather defiant but joyful expression.

The word "free" appears three times on the poster, once stating that personal-care attendants are admitted free of charge, and twice more in reference to the space being alcohol, smoke, and scent-free. What's free at Apple Island is meant "to increase accessibility." Cast in the language of accessibility, not rules or prohibitions, these announcements specifically encourage women with disabilities and women who don't smoke, drink, or wear scented products to attend. But this rhetoric of freedom belies its own regulatory function, its restraining of women who do smoke, drink, or wear perfume. As Alisa Solomon writes, "This noble attempt to create a counterculture becomes an unintentional imitation of the oppression it's determined to replace."[19]

Apple Island's insistence on creating a safe space perpetuates the false ideal that there can be one. Iris Marion Young analyzes the connection between feminism's quest for a romanticized safe space and the debilitating assumptions of identity politics that coalesce in such a desire for community. She argues that feminists who desire community "will tend to suppress differences among themselves or implicitly to exclude from their political groups persons with whom they do not identify."[20]

I need not rehearse here the well-known arguments against identity politics' reliance on essentialist notions of identity.[21] At Apple Island such identity politics are so pervasive that they can be invoked connotatively, not denotatively. For example, the word "lesbian" almost never appears on publicity materials, and I don't think I have ever heard the word spoken in the place (the closest would be a singer who talked about "coming out" and "loving women," but she never used the l-word). Instead, "womon" and "womyn" signify the intended community, specifically gendered, sexed, and politicized. They rely uncritically on the sex-gender system, cementing sex to gender, gender to sexuality. Thus, while the lesbian identity politics of Apple Island are prevalent, definitive, and unspoken, they subtextually speak what Jean-Luc Nancy calls "the myth of their own community."[22] Young sees this mythmaking as a misdirected utopian impulse, an ultimately stultifying imperative.

Many spectators' comments and many of my own experiences at Apple Island bear out these critiques. For example, Cathy, a theater graduate student, commented that at one concert she resented being told by the performers what the songs were about and how to interpret them. She felt her autonomy and agency as a spectator denied. As (what I would call) a Bakhtinian spectator, she wanted to provide her own accent on terms like "oppression" and "patriarchy." But in Apple Island's context, the terms functioned monologically, as unmovable signifiers. At the same concert and in a similar Bakhtinian vein, Martha explained that she didn't feel like she could make jokes or be parodic there. Spectators note the conventions of the speech community. They are not outsiders by language but by ideology.

Uses, Struggles, and Gaps

While I agree with these critiques of identity politics in theory and in practice, and have demonstrated Apple Island's peremptory identity politics, I also would like to explore how their very presumptuousness may offer a way to rethink the terms that Apple Island (and identity politics) inexorably links: lesbian, performance, and politics.

Katie King suggests complicating "cultural feminism" to read it in terms of women's cultural production.[23] She critiques the habitual conflation of cultural feminism with the antipornography movement, a collapsing which I've not only witnessed in conversations and classrooms but have perpetuated. Because Madison's sites of (cultural) feminist cultural production, namely, Apple Island, A Room of One's Own, and "Her Turn," also often express an antipornography position, I have been tempted to forget the other aspects that are worthwhile. I would like to take up Teresa de Lauretis's call to "risk essentialism," to specify the actions in a feminist community, to redraw "community" as a productive site: here, as a productive site of culture, of performance.[24]

In the shift from gay and lesbian to queer studies, some modes of feminist cultural production that either privilege gender over sexuality or that link the two are seen as passé before they can even be analyzed. I'd like to suggest a model of queer studies cultural criticism that allows for multiple sexualities, but also asserts that gender matters.

Another poster from Apple Island points to this possibility. This one belies a singular notion of lesbian identity by representing two completely different lesbian styles. On one hand, the spelling of "womyn" and the picture of Judy Fjell signify cultural feminism. She appears in a spiked haircut and upturned collar, holding an acoustic guitar—all local markers of a gentle, clean-cut, woman-identified folk singer. She also played at the Michigan Womyn's Music Festival (which, several years ago, decided to admit only "women-born women"). But on the same flyer, the "Girls in the Nose" express a parodic mode, reappropriating the label "girl," wearing dark lipstick and seductive sequined halter tops, and loving the camera in a tone completely different from the women on the birthday party poster. Despite Apple Island's lesbian hegemony, queerness seeps in as style.

Whatever spectators' perceived location in the lesbian style wars (meaning leather or flannel, spike heels or workboots, miniskirts or jeans, lipstick or not), or whatever their perceived location in Apple Island's inside-outside dichotomy, they all make various uses of Apple Island's discourses, practicing what de Certeau calls poaching.[25] De Certeau argues that readers do not absorb a text in its entirety, but rather pick and choose what to take in and what to ignore. For de Certeau, the critic should not ask what a text is about, but rather analyze various readings of a text to illuminate underlying assumptions about specific positionalities and reading practices. In this way, consumption of a text is theorized as the production of meaning, positing an active, invested reader rather than a cultural dupe.

I would suggest that a differently articulated spectatorial poaching operates in a location like Apple Island, which is circumscribed by a community imperative. Even as spectators seem to be merely describing Apple Island or its productions or events, they are already interpreting, already actively reading, already reworking the meaning of "women's community" and by extension, "cultural feminism." Louise, for example, who has been both a performer and a spectator at Apple Island, feels that she cannot be included in Apple Island's community because she doesn't sleep with women, even though she identifies herself as a "political lesbian," and even though she has in fact participated in Apple Island's community on both sides of the lights. Louise's comments are significant because they clarify a nuanced identity that some critiques of cultural feminism may elide; that is, while cultural feminism is often accused of being antisex, Louise sees Apple Island as being precisely about sexual practices. Louise would say that she is describing the community and its boundaries, but I would suggest she is very actively poaching community iconography.

The Spectator's Second Self-Story

Perhaps the activity that best exemplifies Apple Island's refusal of political and performative divisions is country western line dancing, a weekly and very popular activity. Participating in country western line dancing forced me to reconsider what I meant by describing Apple Island as "cultural feminist," and how I imagined community boundaries.

Responding to a flyer that said, "Beginners welcome, no partners necessary. Doors open at 7:30, dancing at 8 P.M.," I went to Apple Island to do country western line dancing, careful not to get there too early. A few minutes before 8:00, there were no signs of life and the unmarked doors were locked. After a few minutes a woman opened the door. "Is there dancing?" I asked, thinking that no one was there, and that maybe it had been canceled. "As soon as the instructors get here," she answered, a bit snappishly. Like the last time, I felt inappropriate and outside.

I walked in, tentatively, trying to convince myself that I didn't care if I felt awkward. There was no one at the table taking money, and a few women were standing around in groups talking, and a few others took chairs off the stacks and sat along the edges of the room. A moment later the instructors entered and began setting up. Soon a woman came in to take money from people. It was a sliding scale and I was prepared to pay $5, but she gave me change as if I had paid $3. Again, I didn't know if I was supposed to say something, offer to pay more, or what. I kept quiet and took the change.

Not simply a class or a dance or a performance or any easy way to pick someone up, country western line dancing is all of these. Many women at the event know each other and know the instructors, blurring the distinction between the instructors-as-performers and the audience. Because everyone dances and because Apple Island is a place where lesbians can perform our sexuality overtly, everyone becomes an actor. Country western line dancing functions as what folklorist Roger D. Abrahams calls a "display event"—the public world of a subculture, performing for itself its "technique of bonding and boundary-making."[26]

While the physicality of the dancing suggests a lesbian identity which is jaunty, blue-jeaned, and a bit sweaty, the language of the teacher-leaders indicates the specific discursive construction of lesbian identity through a number of assumptions and in-jokes. For example, the two instructors apologize at the beginning that a few of the songs will contain masculine pronouns. They mention in passing that they learned country western line dancing "at Michigan." They move through the dances very slowly, stressing that "There are no mistakes, just variations."

During the evening, there is both an insistence on finding a mate, on being coupled, and a constant reminder that "no partners (are) necessary." The dances are learned individually, but an easy variation makes it into a couple dance. Also the turns and crosses of many of the dances put bodies in close proximity to one another. The leaders constantly make sexual jokes and comments: "You'll like this part because you can look at how tight her jeans are," and "This is the part where you can give her a little wink or a smile." The floor patterns and instructors' patter put into action the point Elspeth Probyn makes: "Desire points us not to a person, not to an individual, but to the movement of different body parts."[27]

As an active, embodied, highly structured activity, country western line dancing requires both disciplining the body and making it a spectacle for female consumption (one best represented, perhaps, by k.d. lang, who serves both as a lesbian icon—bold, brazen, and inimitably sexual—as well as a reference to mainstream fashion which increasingly incorporates a historically lesbian style). Country western line dancing refuses easy dichotomies of lesbian identity and style. Involving not just Birkenstocked, flannel-shirted separatists or lipstick lesbians, county western line dancing in Madison reconfigures cultural feminism in a rhetoric that is both sexualized and politically correct.[28] It is seductive, encouraging insiderness in a space that might otherwise exclude the very same spectators: me, for example. In this respect, Apple Island makes room for variations on what is meant by "lesbian." As Valerie Traub writes:

In its singularity and self-identity, "lesbian" is a politically necessary but conceptually inadequate demarcation: to my mind, less a person than an activity, less an activity than a modality of pleasure, a position taken in relation to desire . . . better used as an adjective ("lesbian desire") than a noun.[29]

Spectators' uses of Apple Island are always about community, and always about the expectation of identity affirmed. And I'm no different. If, as James Clifford writes, "Insiders studying their own cultures offer new angles of vision and new depths of understanding. Their accounts are empowered and restricted in unique ways,"[30] my account is, I think, empowered and restricted by my own uncertainty of my in/outsiderness in relation to Madison's women's community. And I must take to heart Ed Cohen's urging that theorists who dismiss identity categories accept that political change comes from people's emotions and their willingness to put their bodies on the line.[31] I wanted, in my experiences, conversations, observations, and analyses to find the personal and political woven with the theoretical. But maybe it's impossible to say "women's community" without saying it longingly. It implies, I think, a utopian space where no one I know lives.[32]

Notes

1. Judith Roof, *The Lure of Knowledge* (New York: Columbia University Press, 1992), 120.

2. I attended a number of performances and activities at Apple Island from its opening in 1991 through 1994. All the performances I describe took place during that time, as did the interviews I conducted for this research. I've changed the informants' names.

3. Georges Van Den Abbeele, "Introduction," in *Community at Loose Ends*, ed. Miami Theory Collective (Minneapolis: University of Minnesota Press, 1991), ix.

4. Sue Goldwomon's name and its spelling indicate her affiliation with a cultural feminist perspective that reworks language to eliminate references to men.

5. One exception is Kate Ryan's piece, which I'll discuss later.

6. The class was taught by Jill Dolan at the University of Wisconsin-Madison in the summer of 1992.

7. See Adrienne Rich, "Compulsory Heterosexuality and Lesbian Existence," in *Powers of Desire: The Politics of Sexuality*, ed. Ann Snitow, Christine Stansell, and Sharon Thompson (New York: Monthly Review Press, 1983), 177–205.

8. For a more extensive exploration of the recent growth of gay and lesbian theaters, see David Román and Tim Miller, "Preaching to the Converted," in this volume.

9. Perhaps the most populated identity category of the late-twentieth-century United States, this refers to a woman who behaves as a feminist according to "feminist common sense" but who will not "label" herself a feminist. In other words, this is a woman who says, "I'm not a feminist, but . . ."

10. Biddy Martin, "Sexual Practice and Changing Lesbian Identities," in *Destabilizing Theory: Contemporary Feminist Debates*, ed. Michele Barrett and Anne Phillips (Stanford, Calif.: Stanford University Press, 1992), 117. Martin also spoke to this issue during her talk at the University of Wisconsin-Madison on November 19, 1993.

11. Ryan, like the producers of *Tea*, rented Apple Island's space. Her piece was also funded by the Dane County Cultural Affairs Commission and was the first performance at Apple Island that has ever been reviewed in the *Wisconsin State Journal*. I think this occasion speaks less to a possible shifting ideology at Apple Island and more to Ryan's particular political, theatrical, and financial affiliations.

12. I would contrast this conflation with the also original performances of the Mickee Faust Club in Tallahassee, Florida, another community theater that might be better described as queer rather than lesbian. Like Apple Island, the Mickee Faust Club presumes an audience that knows many of the players, but unlike Apple Island, performers' genders and sexualities seldom align with their characters'. Insiderness in Faust's community, I might suggest, emerges in part from spectators' knowledge that the performers constantly play across identities.

13. Susan Bennett notes how most people go to the theater with others. See her *Theatre Audiences: A Theory of Production and Reception* (New York: Routledge, 1990).

14. Román and Miller, "Preaching to the Converted," originally published in *Theatre Journal* 47.2 (May 1995):175. It is reprinted in this volume.

15. The Michigan Womyn's Music Festival is an annual five-day national, cultural, feminist event.

16. Richard Bauman, *Verbal Art as Performance* (Prospect Hills, Ill.: Waveland Press, 1977), 16.

17. Ulf Hannerz, *Cultural Complexity: Studies in the Social Organization of Meaning* (New York: Columbia University Press, 1992), 71.

18. Judith Butler, *Bodies That Matter: On the Discursive Limits of "Sex"* (New York: Routledge, 1993), 233.

19. Alisa Solomon, "Dykotomies: Scents and Sensibility," in *Sisters, Sexperts, Queers: Beyond the Lesbian Nation*, ed. Arlene Stein (New York: Penguin, 1993), 215.

20. Iris Marion Young, "The Ideal of Community and the Politics of Difference," in *Feminism/Postmodernism*, ed. Linda J. Nicholson (New York: Routledge, 1990), 300.

21. Identity politics, which may have begun with the statement of the Combahee River Women's Collective, asserts that the personal is always and fundamentally political. Based on the belief that we can best understand our own oppressions, it encourages political alignments by identity. Identity politics have come under attack as reductive and not politically useful, and more cultural theorists argue for coalition politics, or alignments based on similar political agendas, not personal identities. See, for example, Judith Butler, "Performative Acts and Gender Constitution: An Essay in Phenomenology and Feminist Theory," in *Performing Feminisms*, ed. Sue-Ellen Case (Baltimore: Johns Hopkins University Press, 1990), 270–82; bell hooks, *Talking Back: Thinking Feminist,*

Thinking Black (South End Press, 1989); Peggy Phelan, *Unmarked: The Politics of Performance* (New York: Routledge, 1993).

In brief, visibility is predicated on labeling, which is predicated on self-knowledge, supporting an overly coherent and rigid concept of identity, and, as Diana Fuss notes (*Essentially Speaking*, Routledge, 1989), an overly coherent and rigid concept of politics. Peggy Phelan has questioned the use value of visibility politics, noting the New Right's ability to regulate bodies on the basis of identity categories that keep them visible. And Judith Butler has pondered the possible consequences of no longer naming lesbian identity as such. Butler explains that in order to come out of the closet as a lesbian, one must perpetually recreate the closet; that is, by naming one's identity as "lesbian," one judges and condemns other lesbians who are in it but who just haven't said it. Judith Roof (*Come As You Are: Sexuality and Narrative,* Columbia University Press, 1996) argues provocatively: "Identification represents a conservative trend, a reluctant and perhaps understandable difficulty with leaving behind the comforts of the story, the reassurance of assimilation, and a belief in the liberatory value of the mere fact of being a lesbian, since in a very real sense, being a lesbian does represent some kind of victory" (1996: 155). In her more recent book, *Bodies That Matter*, Butler argues that identity labels are necessary, but that they can never be more than a fragile fiction (1993: 230). In other words, she says, we must use them, but understand their limits.

22. Jean-Luc Nancy, quoted in Van Den Abbeele, *Community at Loose Ends*, xv.

23. Katie King, "Producing Sex, Theory, and Culture: Gay/Straight Remappings in Contemporary Feminism," in *Conflicts in Feminism*, ed. Marianne Hirsch and Evelyn Fox Keller (New York: Routledge, 1990), 87.

24. Teresa de Lauretis, "The Essence of the Triangle or, Taking the Risk of Essentialism Seriously: Feminist Theory in Italy, the U.S. and Britain," *Differences* 1.2 (summer 1989):13.

25. Michel de Certeau, *The Practice of Everyday Life*, trans. Steven Rendall (Berkeley: University of California Press, 1984), xii.

26. Roger D. Abrahams, "Shouting Match at the Border: The Folklore of Display Events," in *And Other Neighborly Names*, ed. Richard Bauman and Roger D. Abrahams (Austin: University of Texas Press, 1981), 305.

27. Elspeth Probyn, "Queer Belongings," in *Sexy Bodies: The Strange Carnalities of Feminism*, ed. Elizabeth Grosz and Elspeth Probyn (New York: Routledge, 1995), 14.

28. Although, problematically, country western line dancing, in practice here and as a reference to the straight version, reinscribes Apple Island's hegemonic whiteness.

29. Valerie Traub, "The Ambiguities of 'Lesbian' Viewing Pleasure: The (Dis)Articulations of *Black Widow*," in *Out in Culture: Gay, Lesbian, and Queer Essays on Popular*

Culture, ed. Corey K. Creekmur and Alexander Doty (Durham: Duke University Press, 1995), 131.

30. James Clifford, "Introduction: Partial Truths," in *Writing Culture: The Poetics and Politics of Ethnography*, ed. James Clifford and George E. Marcus (Berkeley: University of California Press, 1986), 9.

31. Ed Cohen, "Who Are 'We'? Gay 'Identity' as Political (E)motion (A Theoretical Rumination)," in *Inside/Out: Lesbian Theories/Gay Theories*, ed. Diana Fuss (New York: Routledge, 1991), 84.

32. I would like to thank Framji Minwalla and Alisa Solomon for their thoughtful responses to an earlier draft of this essay, and Jill Dolan, Phillip Zarrilli, and Sally Banes for their many-faceted support on this project. Thanks, too, to the many women at Apple Island who spoke to me in the course of this research.

11   "Preaching to the Converted"

David Román and Tim Miller

Not long ago, I was performing *My Queer Body*, one of my full-evening solo pieces, in the beautiful Yale Repertory Theater. This show explores the stories that our bodies carry and how the huge losses to AIDS challenges our deepest selves. The performance, I hope, is a journey through the most intimate pleasures and pains of being in our bodies in these difficult and juicy times. *My Queer Body* ends with a rousing call to claiming ecstasy and an image of a fabulous queer future replete with a black lesbian president. That's it in a nutshell. There is one point in the show when I wander naked out in the audience, exposed by the glare of the follow spot as I get close enough to see people. I look them in the eye and acknowledge them as the community occupying that theater for that evening. I see their glasses. Feel their hair (maybe indulge in a quip about their haircare products). Notice the audience's wisdom. Discreetly, of course, cruise a boy. At a certain point, I sit on one of the audience member's laps and look in their eyes. My butt naked on their laps. I try to speak clearly to them:

I'm sitting here with you now. I see your eyes. I see myself in your eyes. I could try to tell you some more sweet or scary stories like I was doing up on stage in those big red theatrical lights. But it wouldn't really matter what I did. Cause, right now sitting with you, whatever I do is gonna be wetter and messier and more human and more complicated than when I stand up there on the stage and think I'm gonna take you nice people into a volcano.[1]

I said these words as I sat on the lap of a young man who was sitting on the aisle (take that as a general warning). I looked into his face. Into his eyes. This young man began to shake. His face quaking. His eyes overflowing. He was trembling intensely but he was present in his gaze and really making contact with me. I was scared too. I wasn't sure what was going on for him. How intense was this for him? What unknown boundary had I crossed? Have I fucked somebody up? The performance continues:

I sometimes feel this border between my body and some friends who are really sick right now. It's like this nice coastline on your arm here. It's a border I want to cross, though. A coastline I want to pull people to. Maybe you have brought a special life preserver and you can teach me how to use it and we can throw it to all our friends who are sick and we can pull them back to shore. I want to hold these bodies really close so that not one more slips away. (1993: 326)

Anyhow, finally I got back onstage where I belonged. I trusted that this momentary connection had been okay for this young man. After the show, as is my fashion, I immediately came out on the stage to talk with people. I like to leave the stage lights up and encourage folks to come up onstage. They can say hello to me or to each other. Before too long there were about a hundred or so people up on the stage of Yale Rep. They hauled themselves up onto the lip of the high stage or found the stairs and were chatting with each other, looking around, saying hello to me. I like to have people feel that the stage is a place where they are welcome. Their feet belong there too. Many people shared with me their experiences of the performance or made contact in some way that was important for them. The young fellow I had been with in the audience came up and we hugged. I asked him if sitting on his lap had been all right. He said it was, and explained that, because of the many things going on in his life as a queer man, our connection had been very intense for him. The performance had opened up some things within. We hugged again and he went off with his friend. Then a man came up to me and held my hand. He told me his lover had died of AIDS that morning in the hospital. In his arms. He told me he hadn't known what to do with himself. He chose to come and see my performance. He told me that the piece helped him in a deep way to be with his feelings of loss. It helped him claim the life that is in him for his future, the life that still breathes in his body. We talked for some time. Holding hands. Tuning in.

Now, clearly, this was a very charged gathering of people in New Haven. I'm not saying this was a typical night. But every night I step out onto a stage or performance space, I assume that many of the people that have assembled are in a dynamic and challenging experience as they enter the theater. For many of them, their presence is literally a matter of life and death: while one audience member may be dealing with the upheaval of just having come out, another may well have buried someone that morning. Mourning and celebration are the two poles of this life. I know they are often hovering quite near the surface of the community that gathers to see my work. These charged feelings are quite present in the theaters that I step out into, asking spectators to shout out a favorite place on their bodies. I know I am a queer performer presenting my homo-content work in a time of crisis. My work is also filtered through a complex set of political events around the right wing's attempt to censor lesbian and gay artists. Perhaps this makes these human gatherings for the work more pregnant with feeling and need. The call to community more pointed. I want to feel the full blast of the humanness of the situation. I want, as a performer, to be pulled and challenged. I want to serve, in some small way, this most human of gatherings. At this point in my life, I look at an audience and simply expect that people have just been to a funeral, or have just had delicious sex, or may recently have been queer bashed. I imagine each person carries these wounds and pleasures very close to them as they take their seats.

As the light comes up and I begin to speak, the beauty of these gatherings makes me feel many things. I feel humbled by their openness. Energized by human presence. Shamed by their authenticity. Emboldened by this challenge.

I.

Among the many dismissive responses to lesbian and gay theater and performance, in the popular press and even among lesbian and gay people, the accusation that lesbian and gay artists are preaching to the converted is perhaps the most frequent. Surprisingly, it is also the one dismissal that lesbian and gay artists, intellectuals, and cultural workers have failed to forcefully rebut or theorize about. The ubiquity of the "preaching to the converted" dismissal becomes evident with any perusal of theater reviews (of works as celebrated as Tony Kushner's *Angels in America* to new works in community-based venues from emerging queer artists and playwrights) or any eavesdropping of gay people's own assessment of lesbian and gay theater.[2]

Such foreclosing comments are made without reflection by a variety of critics and spectators alike. Mainstream theater reviewers, for example, often dismiss queer artists who address queer issues for queer audiences as having a limited scope of address. Generally these critics see community-based work not as theater but as propaganda; queer theater, from this perspective, has little or no artistic value and queer audiences have little or no critical acumen. And yet queer spectators, too, participate in this kind of conjecture. Work that is explicitly directed toward a queer audience and performed in a community-based or queer-friendly venue is underattended, undervalued, and mocked—by lesbians and gay men—for its alleged naiveté or predictability.

Such a contradiction—that, on the one hand, gay people harbor no critical distance from gay art, and that, on the other, gay audiences are themselves hypercritical of gay art—helps sustain the accusatory and shaming force of the "preaching to the converted" dismissal. In either case, the idea that an artist is preaching to the converted sets into motion a no-win discursive dynamic that implicates both the artist and the audience. The dismissive "preaching to the converted" response assumes that queer artists are didactic and queer audiences are static. Mainstream reviewers who employ the phrase position queer people as needing to be preached to, while queer people who employ the phrase position queer audiences as defiantly against being preached at. Regardless of how the phrase is employed—whether it be to insist that queer artists are propagandists and queer audiences are infantile, or to insist that queer artists are didactic and queer audiences bored with it all—lesbian and gay theater that supposedly preaches to the converted is never understood as a valuable, indeed viable, activity. Instead, the uncontested phrase shuts down discussions around the important cultural work that queer artists perform for their queer audiences. The result is yet another occasion of queer disempowerment, one which undermines the idea of building a community culture around an ongoing series of events and gatherings.

This collaborative essay is not meant to argue defensively against the "preaching to the converted" accusation. Rather we see our essay as a means to argue *for* preaching to the converted, as we understand the phrase: first, as a descriptive work which names the potential affinities between the two terms of its locution—preacher/congregation, performer/audience; second (however much it historically has been deployed as derogatory), as a descriptive essay for community-based, and often community-specific, lesbian and gay theater and performance.

Lesbian and gay theater, like many other marginalized identity-based community theater movements, comes out of a history of political struggle. Enabled by the post-Stonewall liberation politics of identity that galvanized lesbians and gay men to come out and demonstrate to the world that "we are everywhere," lesbians and gay men established community-based theaters where lesbian and gay playwrights, actors, technicians, and others involved in the production of performance could both develop and refine their work without fear of reproach. Moreover, lesbians and gay men interested in theater that spoke explicitly about lesbian and gay issues now had a theater within the public sphere where subcultural codes, vernaculars, and customs could be articulated and shared, negotiated and contested. In New York City, for example, this process began as early as 1958 with the founding of the Caffe Cino and continued with the emergence in the 1960s and 1970s of other Off-Off Broadway theaters such as La Mama, the Judson Poets Theater, the Glines House, and the Playhouse of the Ridiculous. In these Off-Off Broadway houses, lesbians and gay men were able to begin offering alternative representations to the standard fare of mainstream representation, which Don Shewey identifies as "frivolous fairies, psychotic bulldykes, and suicidal queens."[3] The founding of a new generation of lesbian and/or gay theaters in the early 1980s, such as San Francisco's Theater Rhinoceros, New York City's WOW Café, and Seattle's Alice B. Theater, extended the cultural work of their predecessors and were essential to developing both lesbian and gay artists and audiences locally, regionally, and nationally. Together these people forged their energies to simulate and enact a sense of queer history and queer community. At once a place for queer art and queer gathering, lesbian and gay theater remained primarily a theater of, by, and for lesbians and gay men.[4] The idea of forging community, however tentative or utopian, rested on the assumptions that community is a political necessity and a viable possibility. The history of lesbian and gay theater accepts the notion of community as axiomatic and stages the struggle to sustain and expand community as one of its primary objectives.

The current critique of the mythos of a lesbian and gay community from post-identity politics theorists, public sphere analysts, queer activists of color, sexual radicals, and others who find loosely utopian community constructions to be, at best, problematic, puts pressure on lesbian and gay performers, theaters, and supporters to articulate more clearly both the feasibility of our objectives and the limits of our political projects.[5] And while it is fashionable to negate the significance of these early community-based theaters as simply reifying the culture of the (white) queer ghetto, as having been the result and symptom of the accumulation of (bourgeois) public space, and as having thus served their primary purpose, these negations may be premature and may inadvertently contribute to the closing of these important community institutions. The financial vulnerability of many of these theaters leads people to believe that their social function has been achieved and that the work at these theaters is no longer necessary. In part, there is truth in both these assertions. Lesbian and gay issues are no longer confined to a cultural ghetto; (white) gay male culture at least has made some dent in mainstream culture, and (white) lesbian chic continues to hold some market trend, although less securely and always as market trend. Still, the mainstream interest in queer culture, in particular queer theater and performance, is fragile and not systemically structured into the institutions that produce and finance mainstream production. Therefore, it needs to be said early on that the financial vulnerability of the queer arts is most often the result of an antiart sentiment endemic in contemporary U.S. culture and, more directly, of the cultural wars fueled by the ongoing crisis of the National Endowment for the Arts; it is not the result of the artistic failure of queer artists.[6]

Moreover, given the development of lesbian and gay playwrights and performers—Tony Kushner, Claire Chafee, and Han Ong, among others—through the regional theater system, it is tempting to arrive at the conclusion that lesbian and gay artists no longer need to work in exclusively lesbian and gay spaces to succeed. Thus the argument that the artistic merits of community-based lesbian and gay theater outside the regional theater circuit are wanting puts into motion a binarism between established theater venues and community-based venues that valorizes the former over the latter. Such a high culture-low culture distinction reveals its insistence on canonical prejudices and fails to account for the distinct audiences each system develops and markets. Certainly, much of the work produced by community-based lesbian and gay theaters is inconsistent on all levels of the artistic process—script, performance, and production—and is often, regrettably, predictable. Cross-dressing and drag, staples of lesbian and gay community-based theaters, are no longer, in and of themselves, politically subversive or stunningly theatrical. Like the well-made play, staged transvestism has become for lesbian and gay theater what it has often been historically, a theatrical convention capable of subversiveness and theatricality, but not necessarily inherently so.

And yet, despite these occasional artistic shortcomings, it would be a great disservice to dismiss the work of community-based lesbian and gay theaters as trivial. Many audience members derive great pleasure from the very conventions others may find objectionable. One can never gauge the effect of the first experience of these conventions on the spectator, nor can one conflate all spectators' experience into a unified response; in other words, one person's experience of subversion may be another's experience of boredom, and vice versa. Equally important, much of the significant cultural work occurring in lesbian and gay theater spaces results from the social dynamics of queer gatherings. The context and space of performance, for many queer spectators and participants, informs most forcefully their experience of the performance. In many ways, what is represented onstage is beside the point. This is not to suggest, by any means, that the artistic process does not matter. Many of us continue to expect important work to emerge from these institutions. Rather, the point here is that the context of the performance plays a crucial role in the aesthetic experience of our theatergoing. Community-based queer theater allows for its terms—community, queer, theater—to coexist without competition or hierarchy.

Still, it needs to be understood that the focus on the establishment of lesbian and gay theaters in the United States is only part of the story of the development of lesbian and gay theater. Individual lesbian and gay performing artists, for whatever reasons, are not always presented by local community-based lesbian and gay theaters. Many of these theaters understandably prefer to work within the available pool of artistically talented and interested people living in their communities. It is not always economically feasible, artistically necessary, or politically viable to bring outside lesbian and gay talent into local community-based lesbian and gay projects. Queer solo performing artists offer a special challenge, since they generally need to rely on producing venues outside their immediate local community for their work to reach other audiences. Presenting institutions such as San Francisco's Josie's Cabaret and Juice Bar, and New York City's long-standing alternative performance space, P.S. 122, begin to accommodate this need with their support of lesbian and gay solo performing artists. While they may not be specifically lesbian and gay-identified venues, the participation of these presenting institutions in the development of lesbian and gay performing artists is a crucial and often unacknowledged factor in the history of lesbian and gay theater. Queer-friendly and supportive presenting institutions provide an invaluable service in the development of an audience for lesbian and gay performance and in the nurturing of emerging and established queer performing artists.

In cities with neither a lesbian and gay theater nor an established queer-friendly performance venue, individual presenters play a central role in supporting queer artists and audiences. Howie Baggadonutz, for example, is one of the primary presenters of regional and national queer artists for his community of

Portland, Oregon; his efforts have enabled Portland to emerge as one of the most significant and lucrative harbors of queer performance on the West Coast. Sometimes these individuals are affiliated with a local college or university, which ends up sponsoring the cultural event, often at the request and with the labor of the student lesbian and gay organizations. But these college and university connections are themselves vulnerable to university politics and procedures, student interest, and student matriculation. Nonetheless, colleges and universities continue to be some of the most prestigious gigs for performing artists. Their role in developing queer performance, while provisional, helps emerging and established performers get not only work, but also grants, residencies, and even, on occasion, teaching appointments.

Lesbian and gay theater develops from, and is sustained by, the community-based labor of lesbian and gay theater establishments, queer-friendly and supportive presenting venues, and individual lesbian and gay presenters. These cultural workers enable queer people to gather into the space of performance. Once gathered into this space, spectators, artists, and technicians enact, even if only temporarily, community.

The provisional and fragile community engendered by performance solicits from those assembled a dynamic (and impossible to determine and assess) relationship to the many aspects of the theatrical occasion. Theater audiences, as Susan Bennett has demonstrated, bring any number of expectations to the theatrical event.[7] Lesbian and gay theater audiences, moreover, bring to the theatrical occasion a specific social paradox. On the one hand, the support of many lesbian and gay audiences for community-based theater results from the desire to be in a crowd of other lesbian and gay people. This desire rests on the comforts of identity politics and easily adapts to the primacy of sexuality in identity construction. And yet, on the other hand, many spectators also attend community-based events in order to defy the politics of sameness. Rather than upholding an uncritical stance toward the notion of queer community, many queer spectators set out to put pressure on this concept. This desire never rests, but rather prefers to unsettle the comforts of identity politics in the very space of its enactment. Thus, the impulse to seek community comes out of a series of relational and often contradictory tendencies ranging from the desire to be part of a community, however fabricated or temporal that concept of community may be, to the desire to test individual identity in opposition to the very concept of lesbian and gay community itself. Queer theater audiences are dynamic social gatherings that cannot be readily reduced to a monolithic, static whole.

Queer theater audiences, like all theater audiences, defy simplistic categorizations and resist overly determined preconceptions concerning why we are even at the theater. At the theater, queer people gather to see old friends or acquaintances who may be in the audience, on the technical crew, or performing onstage; we go to the theater to flaunt old and new lovers, cruise the crowd, or savor the moment when the theater darkens and we can safely and discreetly hold our beloved's hand; we go to the theater to parade our fashions and attitudes, to affirm our tastes, ideas, and values, and in order to be absorbed into a critical mass of subcultural resistance to the heteronormative muscle we must continually encounter in our daily lives. But we also go to the theater for other reasons. Some of us arrive at the space of performance to defy queer collectivity even as we paradoxically enter into it; we enter into the space of performance as nonwhites, transgendered, disabled, differently sized, celibate; we enter into the space of performance, as we enter other queer public space, disidentifying with the theatrical representation, the body in performance, the assembled crowd. Some of us arrive at the theater with or without these aspirations or reservations; we enter into the space of performance because we know that magic and transformation sometimes happens here and our curiosity gets the better of us. We remember that performance puts into motion any number of emotions that circulate within the space of performance and that, occasionally, this dynamic transference of energy invigorates our lives, persuading us to return again and again to the theater.

II.

The idea of "the converted" assumes an inert mass of people which absorbs performance uncritically and passively, without explicit interaction, and with immediate approval of the representation imbedded in performance. The charge that queer artists are preaching to the converted reveals an arrogance on the part of the accuser who assumes a knowledge of the people gathered in the space of performance. This charge assumes that a stable and static mass has arrived fully into an imagined state of conversion—a condition that, though not articulated, is both assumed and belittled. To claim that artists are only preaching to the converted implies a fixed position for the audience assembled that trivializes the ever-changing and never immediately apparent needs and desires of queer spectators. Imagining an audience as "the converted" relies on a binarism which insists on an either/or: either you are among the converted, or you are not. When critics write that performers are preaching to the converted, they locate audiences across an invisible but understood border of conversion—spectators have gone over to the other side, have arrived, and have achieved a fixed state of grace. This state of grace is nothing less than an irreversible state of loss. The cult of the converted is beyond redemption.

When the "preaching to the converted" dismissal is directed toward queer performance it trivializes spectators' specific histories regarding queer identity and community. The dismissal disregards both the communal needs of the assembled crowd and the specific issues of the individual spectator. To dismiss queer performance as preaching to the converted presupposes that we, the already allegedly converted, no longer need occasions, events, and rituals where members of our community profess and perform to us their beliefs so that we in the assembled crowd can take these performances and incorporate their insights into our own continuing struggle to live in a deeply homophobic world. To dismiss queer work as preaching to the converted negates the terror of homophobia as it is experienced always and differently by queer people, it dismisses the emotional and political benefits of queer people's gathering together in shared public space, and it assumes a political stability for lesbians and gays that is as naive as it is politically dangerous.

If the converted exist—that is, if there is an identifiable critical mass of queers who together compose a congregation of people converted into believing in the necessity of queer identities and communities, culture, and politics—then "the converted" needs to be understood as a dynamic assembly that both individually and communally enters into the space of performance to sustain the very state of conversion. Truth be told, however, the converted are never wholly converted. Rather, like the process of coming out, which is a lifelong project of continuous self-identifications and revelations, there is no definitive moment of absolute conversion. Instead, to be among the converted is to be open to a series of conversions, it is a way of being that implies a constant state of negotiation and need depending on the specific psychosocial and sociohistorical occasions of our daily lives. Conversion, understood from this perspective, demands a continual testing of one's identity, if only as a means to affirm it. It implies vulnerability—and its occasional companion, consent—to a barrage of occasions that challenge queer identity and queer community. Abuse and coercion also linger alongside the vulnerable. Interesting, then, that despite the history of libelous conjecture of queer people's imagined recruitment of the young, the inflammatory "preaching to the converted" dismissal is never rephrased as the less condescending but at the same time more threatening accusation that queer artists are "preaching to convert."

Somewhere, conversion has occurred prior to performance; it's a done deal before you even enter the space of performance. Once in, there is no turning back.

III.

There is, of course, an extremely strange irony to this "preaching to the converted" dismissal. There is an almost obsessive desire on the part of many mainstream and academic critics to completely separate theater from its roots as sacred storytelling. The interweaving of ritual space ("church," if it doesn't make you nervous) and theater is thousands of years old. This convergence appears in one form or other in most cultures around the world. Sacred space and theater space so frequently overlap. Their precincts have often had the same street address. How big a leap is it really from some Greek chorus queen who was a servant of Dionysis doing a summer stock *Oresteia* in the fourth century B.C. to that performance at Yale Repertory Theater? (A theater which occupies, I might add, a former Calvary Baptist Church!) These spaces and choruses speak to each other. There are church services in theater auditoriums. Performances in sanctuaries. The spaces themselves and the people who performed the rites were sometimes the *same*. In some cultures today, they still are the same. These varied roles of priest, storyteller, shaman, and performer are knitted together across time, and their job descriptions spring from some of the basic stirrings and needs of human life: The story must be told. The dead must be remembered. The creation of the world must be explained. The feast requires song and celebration.

The roots of these communal tasks so often lead us to the performers and the preachers. From the medieval church music-drama and morality plays, to the retelling of Arjuna's questioning of the gods on the battlefields in a thousand performances of *The Mahabharata*, this overlap has been a crucial springboard for world drama. With the various fracturings of more recent history, this relation between preacher and performer often grew more and more contentious. In the Roman Catholic world the clergy was disturbed by the proliferation and popularity of these nonliturgical church dramas. Pope Innocent III (1198–1216) prohibited theatrical performances in churches. Gregory IX backpedaled a few years later, saying these popular church dramas were tolerable as long as their goal was "ad devotionem excitandem" (to excite devotion).[8] Even though words like "to excite devotion" could be variously interpreted by church artists (could maybe even spell big box office!), this edict did create an acceptance of theatrical expression as sacred drama.

Enter. Stage left. The Renaissance. With a flourish.

Theatrical texts and presentations begin an exile from their parallel life as identifiable liturgical text. Keep the preachers out of the play. And the drama out of the sermon. The precincts are now across town from each other. Some of this separation can be traced to an understandable alienation from mainstream Christian cultural background experienced by many artists and intellectuals. But, within that alienation, there is a deeper mistrust of any kind of spiritual system that suggests higher power, shared belief, or community purpose. Theater has created a set of new liturgies with a spiritual function addressing the big questions: What happens when we die? How do we explain terrible events? Is moral action possible? But these new secular themes rest on a highly policed, if perhaps artificial, separation. This policing can be quite strict, in fact. The most censure I ever felt from an extended community of theater artists was not in one of my many naked homoerotic solo performances. It was when I collaborated with Episcopal priest Malcolm Boyd on a series of "performance art sermons" at Saint Augustine-by-the-Sea Episcopal Church in Santa Monica, California.[9] In crossing the church-theater separation—or the priest-performer split, for that matter—I felt like I had broken a deeply rooted rule of maintaining a totally secular posture as a theater artist.

This schism of spirit from the theater can be especially problematic for lesbian and gay people, who often have had an inscribed role both in sacred ritual and storytelling. In *Another Mother Tongue*, Judy Grahn, the lesbian poet and cultural historian, charts this duality:

This participation is a natural inheritance, for theater began as the ceremonial dramas and rites whose purpose was the reenacting of spiritual events for the benefit of tribal and village people. And it was the Gay shamanic priesthood who was in charge of these ritual dramas. The faggot sorcerer with his fagus wand and his costumes representing the god-forces and animal spirits of the universe in which his people lived took center stage and gave direction in the ceremonial theatrical functions and tribal origin stories. The formal traditional theater retains much of its original purpose as rite, the reenactment of transformation. The curtain, or veil of vision or consciousness opens to display a second world, a state of being different from the everyday one. It is a world which the audience agrees to enter by contracting both emotionally and intellectually to believe in the story being told.[10]

The preacher's voice has had a huge influence on the performer's voice in the United States. Theater here, especially solo performing, also has been powerfully affected by an extreme valorization of individual speech and public assembly; a forceful public speaking ability is a valued skill. This cultural inheritance has been one explanation for the explosion of solo performance here. In other English-speaking nations, it is often noted how comfortable Americans are holding forth with their opinions. The veiled comment here, of course, is that we won't shut the fuck up. But the important truth is that we do place value on having our voices heard. The American ego places importance on speaking your piece and doing it in a compelling manner. This tendency, when mixed with the rich legacy of feminist autobiographical performers of the 1970s who dared to attach importance to individual experience, has created a powerful new theater of witness and testimony.

It would seem that the supposed need to separate the sacred from the theatrical, the sermon from the soliloquy, is in fact an odd obsession. For lesbian and gay people it is often a censorious one. For queer people, the act of being witnessed is inevitably both sacred (that is, transformational) and performative. From the ritual and theatrical life-action of "coming out" to the urgent necessity of telling the tale of who we are, the lesbian and gay experience is often chartered by a set of initiations and gestures that are designed to be participated in and witnessed. The solo performer, in this cultural situation, often exists in a complex vortex of expectations and roles: emcee, sacrificial lamb, minstrel, priest, and entertainer. S/he may be experiencing simultaneously the needs of the self and community as they manifest themselves in his/her experience, and may try to notice where these needs overlap—to locate the site of a potential conversion or transformation. This could take the form of a renewed commitment, or a call to action. It could dare a journey within, make possible a time for focus, or demand a certain consciousness.

Many performers are accepting this set of challenges and are daring to make community calls. These manifestos are often unequivocal calls to action. They are often programmatic and specific. The artist might even go as far as to provide useful recipes for confronting and transforming internalized racism, self-hate, or shame. This has been especially true of a host of queer performers who have cut through the so-called neutrality that was often put forward as the jackpot in the pantheon of values that an artist should strive for. These artists have found instead a more engaged and direct mode of expression. The necessity of responding to AIDS and the right-wing attacks on lesbian and gay culture has demanded a variety of more immediate expressions in performance. Michael Kearns's charged reclamation of his sexual self in the face of AIDS in his solo, *Rock*, provides spectators with techniques to do the same. Annie Sprinkle, in *Post-Porn Modernist*, leads us through her exploration of her body and includes us in a participatory ritual at the end of her performance. At the conclusion of *Fierce Love: Stories from Black Gay Life*, the Pomo Afro Homos look the audience directly in the eye as they exclaim that "our stories must be told; our lives, forever real, must be cherished; and our love, forever rising, must be—has got to be, no doubt about it—as strong as our ancestors and twice as fierce."[11]

The heat of this more direct statement has been shared by many other artists who work in relationship to other communities also under attack. The ecofeminist proclamations of Rachel Rosenthal call the community to a more conscious relation between the individual and the planet. Guillermo Gómez-Peña's complex and fluent performances challenge the public assembled to confront the racist implications of monolingual culture. The visceral cries of Karen Finley pull us to own the fucked-up families we come from and to create our new families by gathering these "black sheep" together. Performer Dan Kwong leads us through his personal history as a Japanese/Chinese American, providing audiences a model for moving through internalized oppressions.

How does a performer follow the creative impulse and locate the voice to make this address to audiences? Judy Grahn notes that the audience must agree to enter the theater's second world; may we not also assume the audience can agree that certain issues are worthy of being addressed and may even require addressing? For an audience of lesbians and gay men, these issues will probably include (though not be limited to): sex, homophobia, AIDS, coming out, body image, family. This agreement is not static or concrete and probably depends on certain acts of faith. For an artist, it requires believing that there do indeed exist certain potential messages that may be received by certain identifiable groups of human beings, and that these particular messages will be of interest, even urgency, to some members of this group. Most human communication of any sort relies on a similar sequence of "acts of faith"; the process is just more apparent in the ritualized communications that take place in the theater.

In the creation of my most recent full-evening performance, *Naked Breath*, I made a leap into a topic that carries a lot of tension in my community of queer men: sexual intimacy between HIV-negative and HIV-positive men. I felt called to this subject because my own life demanded it. I was finding myself in a variety of intimate relations with men who are positive or are people with AIDS. I was required to sift through my feelings and fears around this intimacy in my own life. Because I teach a great deal within my community, I was seeing the same subject come up again and again in the performance workshops that I lead for gay men.

It became clear to me that my own deepest need to claim sexual connection in the face of the AIDS crisis was a necessary subject both for me and for my tribe. This called the piece forward.

I told the story of a boyfriend of mine in New York City who is HIV-positive. I told about our meeting on a street where a lover of mine who had died of AIDS, the performer John Bernd, used to live. I shared the complexities of eros and fear that accompanies all our acts these days. I made the manifesto that we can and should safely claim our desire with each other. That we can confront our fears and be in this time fiercely: "Cross that line! Take the scariest chance and seize the slippery day. Whatever it takes, do it! Like your life depends on it. Which it does."[12]

Performance artist, heal thyself. By sifting through my own sense of deep need, as it speaks to my observations and participations in community, I identify a hot spot. I explore the feelings surrounding this theme. I propose some plans of action that address my own needs and might possibly be of use to others in my community. I desire to convert our private and communal fears into the courage to connect with each other, to convert the anxieties we face in these troubled times into a deep commitment to face the challenges in our daily lives.

IV.

I am open to conversion. I am willing to allow myself the possibility of being disciplined into other people's fantasies, ideologies, performances. It doesn't always happen. Something to do with the chemistry, I imagine; the alchemy is sometimes off. Lately, I have been interested in expanding the field of my theatergoing and exploiting the infinite pleasures promised by performance. I ask myself: Why foreclose? I even went to see the Broadway revival of *Damn Yankees*; the alchemy was off, but at least we tried. I left the theater singing "You Gotta Have Heart"—for weeks. I didn't realize I liked the song. Is this conversion?

I go to great lengths to see everything directed by Joanne Akalaitis—Genet's *The Screens* at the Guthrie in Minneapolis, *Henry IV Parts I & II* at the Public in New York City, *'Tis a Pity She's a Whore* at the Goodman in Chicago—because I think she's a brilliant director. I'm always engaged, always enthralled by her work, even if, on occasion (Buchner's *Woyzeck*), she misses the mark. Is this conversion? Blind faith? In the summer of 1993, I flew into New York City from Seattle to see her production of Jane Bowles's *In the Summer House*. I was on a theater run; a binge really. Of course, I was there to see friends, but I spent most of my time in New York running in and out of the theater, some would say, indiscriminately. Friends know that I am a generous theatergoer, some of them tell me I am too much so. They know, since I always tell them, that I will usually find something worthwhile about the production. Have I been converted into an uncritical love for performance? If so, when did it happen? Was it Martin Sherman's *Bent*, featuring Richard Gere, on Broadway which I saw when I was a queer teen? Does this explain why I giddily keep returning to the 1994 revival of *Carousel* at Lincoln Center? Or why I saw *Jeffrey*, at the Minetta Lane, dare I admit it, twice? Is such promiscuous theatergoing queer?

During that 1993 New York City summer theater run, I ended up one Monday night at Dixon Place, Ellie Covan's living room performance space, south of Houston Street on the Bowery. Dixon Place is a very casual performance space, a place where artists perform their works-in-progress. Generally, performances are closed to critics: no reviews. Tickets are under ten dollars. Instead of theater seats, there are couches, lounge chairs, love seats. Dixon Place is quite small; seating for maybe sixty people, if that. This is a neighborhood performance space, not specifically queer, but unequivocally supportive of queer artists. I arrive with my friend, Bob; we are here to see Holly Hughes perform her latest solo piece, at the time provocatively titled *Snitches from Snatches*. Now it tours as *Clit Notes*, no less provocative. Bob and I are resting on a couch in the very front of the stage. Holly Hughes enters and, facing us, sits on a chair in the very front of the stage, too. If I wanted to, I could touch her. Instead, she touches me.

I have been a big fan of Holly Hughes for some time. I teach her work in my classes on lesbian and gay studies, U.S. theater and performance, and on "minority" discourse, and I teach many of the essays and reviews written by feminist and lesbian performance theorists about her plays and solo performances. The bibliography on her work is considerable; the critical assessment of her work ranges from the near disdainful to the near reverential, and this wide scope of opinion arises from her lesbian theorists.[13] I tend to align myself on the side of the near reverentialists. I admire the way that she is able to finesse humor and charm with difficult personal and cultural material (I'm thinking especially of *World without End*) and the way she has been able to help forge a new, and at times hotly contested, lesbian aesthetic (I'm thinking especially of *Well of Horniness*). *Snitches from Snatches*, now *Clit Notes*, is quite humorous, filled with charm and charisma, bears witness to important social issues, and contains many of the qualities I have come to expect from her work. But, in truth, nothing has prepared me for the sermon on shame that she will deliver tonight. *Clit Notes* is her first new solo material since the infamous summer of 1990 when her solo performance grant—along with the grants to Karen Finley, John Fleck, and Tim Miller—was rescinded. The last time I saw her perform was in Los Angeles in 1991, *World without End*, on a special bill with new work by Tim Miller and John Fleck.

Performers like Holly Hughes are always accused of preaching to the converted. But what does this really mean? Holly Hughes is a community-based lesbian playwright and performer, a product of WOW Café; since the early 1980s, she has been a vital and vibrant contributor to New York City's East Village performance scene. Her plays are produced in theaters throughout the United States and she herself tours her solo material widely. At Dixon Place—and on every other night I have seen her perform this work since—the performance enters into my body and moves me. I am not sure that I can explain it any more clearly, but I will try.

Clit Notes is essentially three stories: the first has to do with her father, his cancer, and Hughes's relation to both; the second concerns her early experiences with feminism and with the theater; and the third is about her relationship with her lover then, the lesbian singer and artist, Phranc. These stories are prefaced by a two-pronged prologue composed of her personal experiences with presumed authorities on sexuality (Dr. Reubens, the author of *Everything You Always Wanted to Know about Sex*), and art (John Frohnmayer, the former Chairperson of the NEA), or on both (her lesbian critics).

In all these stories, Hughes professes a vulnerability. Is she a victim? Is she a martyr? Is she a lesbian? Is she an artist? Of course she is; that's the easy part. It's not difficult to arrive at these conclusions. The proof of the pudding, as Brecht claims, is in the eating. For me, these questions miss the point. Instead, I wonder, in the wake of the NEA fiasco, what stories will she tell? I am here at Dixon Place for one reason only. Okay, maybe two. I want to support her work. I arrive as the converted. In part, I am here because I find that I still need to locate us within some mythic idea of queer community. But I am also here because her work seems to always resonate in the deep caverns of my queer psyche. I wonder, which queer nerve will she strike tonight?

Clit Notes is a performance about shame. Hughes tells stories of how she's been shamed—by her father, by other lesbians, by the government, by random people on the street. Shamed for being a lesbian. Shamed for being shameless. From this, the queer paradox: shamed our entire lives, we are accused of being shameless. Holly Hughes: "I wish I had no shame! Sometimes I think that shame is all I got."[14] She performs a profound exploration of shame in all its insidiousness and contagion, describing in brief breaths how shame has formed her sense of self. Eve Sedgwick: "Shame, as opposed to guilt, is a bad feeling that does not attach to what one does, but to what one is."[15] The piece is about shame's effects and her attempts to transform shame or, at least, learn to live with it. Here is a section from the third story. It begins with a reflection on Phranc's butchness, which I won't quote, and concludes with an anecdote of a trip to San Diego, which I will:

Don't you hate it when people ask you what you are? As if you had any idea? All I know is that I am a woman who loves another woman who most people think is a man and that once we were in San Diego together, ok?

We checked into the best motel, the Hanalei. Polynesian from the word go. Outside a pink neon sign announces: "A Taste of Aloha." You can taste it before you even check in. There's Styrofoam Easter island heads everywhere. The bed's a volcano. Every night there's a luau. It's free, it's gratis.

So of course we go. And I love the way they slip those pink plastic leis over your head. I just love that! I love the thought of those day-glo flowers blooming long after Jesse Helms is gone. I hope.

I look out on the astro-turf. Kids chasing each other around. Folks sipping Mai-tais and Piña Coladas out of plastic pineapples. They've got a helluva show at the Hanalei. Hula dancers. Fire eaters. A Don Ho impersonator that's much better than the real Don Ho.

Nobody cares it's not the real Polynesia. It's all the Polynesia they could take. It's the one we invented.

During "Tiny Bubbles" she starts kissing me. Everybody's looking at us. But you can only see what you want to see. And what these folks want to see is not a couple of dykes making out at their luau. So that's not what they see. They start translating their reality. What they think they're seeing is Matt Dillon making out with a young Julie Andrews. A young Julie Andrews. Before Victor/Victoria.

I don't mind. I'm not in the closet! I'm so far out of the closet that I've fallen out of the frame entirely. They don't have any words for us, so they can't see us, so we're safe, right?

I get confused. I forget that invisibility does not insure safety. We're not safe. We're never safe, we're just . . .

You tell me.

Holly Hughes concludes her performance with these words, a window that opens up *Clit Notes* from the deeply subjective to—well, the deeply subjective. I'm not sure whom she's addressing at the end, or if it even matters. Who's the us, the you, and the me in these final moments? I feel implicated in all the terms. And so, I play the parts. I want to answer her, but I, too, now want to know. What are we?—

"we're just . . . You tell me." I want to fill in the ellipses, answer the call, but I get stuck in the window. She's brought me in, her stories resonate with some of my own. Funny how solo performance is either understood as someone preaching or someone confessing. For me the best autobiographical solo pieces are windows into a world that is both my own and not my own.

So what is she preaching here? I leave New York thinking about her performance incessantly. I am stunned by her artistry, how she is able to sit in a chair and transform personal crisis—the private and the public shamings—into a lyrical reclamation of identity. But it's the sermon on shame, and not her individual journey with shame, that forms a residual haunt in my head. I wonder how shame has formed my own identity, how it shapes my sexuality. When I was very young, my mother started claiming, in varying tones of voice and with distinct effects but always only in Spanish, her first language, that I was *sin verguenza*. I had no idea what she meant by this, it simply became for me my Homeric epithet, what my mother put on me. She never delivered the phrase in any way that would demand from me a specific response other than the recognition that her words were a type of naming. *Sin verguenza*. Years later, I figured it out. Without shame. These days I wonder if my mother, who always pulls through for me, was offering me some kind of power, a gift that in its expletive performance was meant to be a hope. This may be too generous an interpretation.

Eve Sedgwick speculates that "for certain ('queer') people shame is simply the first, and remains a permanent, structuring fact of identity: one that has its own, powerfully productive and powerfully social metamorphic possibilities."[16] Sedgwick's prototype for all this is Henry James. But she could easily be describing the work of Holly Hughes. Did anyone ever accuse Henry James of "preaching to the converted"? Everywhere you turn reviewers are claiming that Hughes is preaching to the converted: What does this dyke have to say to me, they demand; and where's the shock? I can't answer these questions for them (or for anyone else for that matter). Who knows? Maybe they are right: nothing at all. But I can tell you this. I left Dixon Place exhilarated—shocked, I guess you could say—by the power and nakedness of her performance. A few stories were told, queer parables; something happened, a window was opened. "You tell me." I hear these final words as yet another performative stance of her vulnerability, an invitation (or is it a concession?) to interpretation, expropriation. But I also hear a summons in her closing lines that asks me to tell my own story, to preach. Overidentification? Perhaps. Sometimes I go to queer theater and overidentify. I write myself into the plot. Or, I want to be Bottom. I want to play all the parts: "Let me play Thisby." "Let me play the lion too."[17] I want to be in the representation, help produce or perform it, sometimes revise it.

Queer theater, like all theater, is about conversion and transformation. Bottom's journey in *A Midsummer Night's Dream* is the queer one; through him we can see the trajectory of queer performance. Set against the nuptials, queer performance is mocked and derided, shamed by the critical authorities in the very process of its performance: "It is not for you. I have heard it over, / and it is nothing, nothing in the world; / Unless you can find sport in their intents" (5.1.77–79). Shame's performance, however, is metamorphic. Queer performers preach this metamorphosis, and queer audiences are invited to preach it too. "You tell me." And so it is that we assemble and disperse. Gather and disband. Of all the illusions produced by performance, for me the most immediate is the illusion that performance can accommodate all my desires at once. This is the lure of performance and, of course, its failure. And yet, like Bottom, I still go for whatever I can get.

V.

The "preaching to the converted" dismissal surfaces often for community-based artists, and while its specific charge to lesbian and gay gatherings beckons forth and is symptomatic of a larger cultural anxiety around queer issues, queer artists and audiences are not the only people who must confront it. Most political artists from marginalized communities are vulnerable to this dismissal. The dialectical tension between the assumption that political artists are preaching a type of ideological redundancy to a group of sympathetic supporters and the possibility that community-based performers and audiences are participating in an active expression of what may constitute the community itself, obscures the fact that these very marginalized communities are themselves subject to the continuous rhetorical and material practices of a naturalized hegemonic norm. Hegemony's performance forces its subjects to a conversion into its alleged neutrality, its claims to the true and the real. Political performers who practice what Cornel West so aptly identifies as "prophetic criticism" expose these coercive attempts to maintain the hegemonic norms that govern and discipline our daily lives.[18]

The persistent attacks on the emerging multicultural agenda in this country have created a kind of battle fatigue. The nascent consensus that we must engage in hearing other people's stories, myths, and images has frayed severely. The "preaching to the converted" slap can be an easy out for some people to detach from the necessary and difficult work that is required to bring forth cultural equity. It can be a technique to devalue specific voices. What people are often really saying when they drag out the "preaching to the converted" critique is: "I'm tired of having angry black men, scary women, and shameless fags disturbing my posttheater dinner!" Even more dangerously, within the byzantine workings of oppression culture, this dismissal can also be a method—for members of any addressed community—to silence the heat and danger of a message that just maybe hits too close to home. We believe that the work of those who commit to the "new cultural politics of difference" will unsettle the force of the systems that sustain the regulatory regimes of power which insist on positioning us as marginal, abject, and in light of AIDS, disposable.

Community-based and community-identified artists and audiences offer each other necessary opportunities to rehearse the constitutive reiteration of our own identities in light of these facts, and a direct, proactive resistance to, and defiance of, hegemony's own unending production of what does and does not constitute, in Judith Butler's phrase, "bodies that matter."[19] Thus the "preaching to the converted" dismissal conceals yet a second, related agenda: when conservative critics dismiss community-based art projects on the grounds that this art is only propaganda, they also attempt to undermine the social movements which engender these art projects. The right's attack on progressive culture in the NEA crisis and the movement against political correctness (to name the most obvious examples) effectively positions the arts as a low casualty. Efforts to stifle the arts are, in essence, efforts to stifle the transformative cultural movements and social actions with which community-based arts see themselves in direct relationship. At the very least, these artists reclaim the once-long-standing alliance between performers and spectators as members of community who, in the enactment of communal ritual, give individuals the power to gather and perform the necessary constitutive rehearsal of identity.

But maybe here, in this essay and with these words, we too are only preaching to the converted. And yet, writing for readers, first in a journal dedicated to the theater in a special issue on lesbian and gay theater, and then in a book devoted to the subject, about the ways by which queer theater is derided and dismissed, doesn't in itself secure a readership sympathetic to these concerns. One could say, for example, that we either presuppose a converted readership which accepts queer theater as a legitimate, authorized area of concern—and therefore we are preaching to the converted. Or, that we set out to help legitimate and authorize queer theater as an area that should be critically engaged—and therefore, we are preaching to convert. Most likely, we are vulnerable to charges that question the combined effort of both these supposed strategies.

Nonetheless, by naming the subscribers of *Theater Journal* (and then, purchasers of *The Queerest Art*) as a community, we hope to put forward the idea that a community does exist, however disparate we are to each other. We also make a call to remember that no named community exists in isolation. Each reader, like each member of any audience, moves in a complex series of connections and engagements that can amplify and enlarge any discussion that begins in a publication or a performance venue. All our voices grow immeasurably in discussions with friends, colleagues, students, and coworkers. For those of us engaged in the collaborative process of creating, considering, and teaching community-based theater and performance, a momentary pause to honor the work we have dedicated our lives to seems warranted, even necessary. In acknowledging our venue, we acknowledge our audience. And from these acknowledgments, we locate the positions from which we speak, profess, and preach.

Notes

Reprinted by permission of Johns Hopkins University Press from *Theatre Journal* 47 (1995):169–88.

1. Tim Miller, "My Queer Body," in *Sharing the Delirium: Second Generation AIDS Plays and Performances,* ed. Therese Jones (Portsmouth: Heinemann, 1993), 326.

2. A notable recent example of the "preaching to the converted" argument is Arlene Croce's refusal to review choreographer Bill T. Jones's *Still/Here*, which was performed in New York City at the Brooklyn Academy in December 1994. *Still/Here* was inspired by a series of workshops Jones led for people with life-threatening and terminal illnesses, including AIDS. But for Croce, *The New Yorker's* leading dance critic, Jones and his audiences are "co-religionists in the cult of the Self" and the performance—which she has not even seen—"victim art"; see "A Critic at Bay: Discussing the Undiscussable," *The New Yorker*, 26 December 1994–2 January 1995, 54–60.

Croce's attempt to insert herself into the cultural wars succeeds, in part, because of the venue of her writing; the amazingly blatant racism and homophobia of her position is seemingly occluded by *The New Yorker's* position as a reputable periodical of the arts. Moreover, Croce's dismissal of Bill T. Jones seems permissible since the magazine printed it only a few weeks after publishing a celebratory profile of the choreographer by Henry Louis Gates. The nearly sequential pairing of these two essays suggests that

The New Yorker needed to counter Gates's intelligent appraisal of Jones with Croce's stinging rebuttal of him in the spirit of allegedly balanced journalism. For intelligent responses to Croce's condemning rhetoric, see Richard Goldstein, "The Croce Criterion," *The Village Voice*, 3 January 1995, 8; Deborah Jowitt, "Critic as Victim," *The Village Voice*, 10 January 1995, 67; Frank Rich, "Dance of Death," *The New York Times*, 8 January 1995, A19; and last but not least, letters from Tony Kushner, bell hooks, and others published in *The New Yorker* itself, 30 January 1995, 10–13.

3. Don Shewey, Introduction, in *Out Front: Contemporary Gay and Lesbian Plays* (New York: Grove Press, 1988), xi.

4. See Richard Owen, "Of the People, By the People, For the People: The Field of Community Performance," in *High Performance*'s special issue on community-based performance, 16.4 (1993):28–32.

5. The bibliography of the critique of a lesbian and gay community is enormous. Michael Warner's introduction to, along with the essays in, his anthology, *Fear of a Queer Planet: Queer Politics and Social Theory* (Minneapolis: University of Minnesota Press, 1993), is perhaps the best place to start, given its survey of the issues and its substantial bibliography. See also *Radical America*'s two-issue focus on "Becoming a Spectacle: Lesbian and Gay Politics and Culture," 24:4 (1993) and 25:1 (1994).

6. And, of course, varying degrees of homophobia. See Alisa Solomon, "Art Attack," *American Theatre* (March 1992): 18–24 and 57.

7. Susan Bennett, *Theatre Audiences: A Theory of Production and Reception* (New York: Routledge, 1990).

8. Fletcher Collins, Jr., Introduction, in *The Production of Medieval Church Music-Drama* (Charlottesville: University of Virginia Press, 1972), 6.

9. Tim Miller, "Jesus and the Queer Performance Artist," in *Amazing Grace: Stories of Lesbian and Gay Faith*, ed. Malcolm Boyd and Nancy L. Wilson (Freedom: Crossing Press, 1991), 57–66.

10. Judy Grahn, *Another Mother Tongue* (Boston: Beacon Press, 1984), 226–28.

11. Brian Freeman (with additional material by Eric Gupton and Djola Bernard Branner), *Fierce Love Stories from Black Gay Life*, unpublished performance script, ©1990 by the authors.

12. Tim Miller, *Naked Breath*, unpublished performance script, ©1994 by the author.

13. See Kate Davy, "From *Lady Dick* to Ladylike: The Work of Holly Hughes," in *Acting Out: Feminist Performances*, ed. Lynda Hart and Peggy Phelan (Ann Arbor: University of Michigan Press, 1993), 55–84, for a history of Hughes's career and a bibliography; and see also Hughes on her own work in Cindy Carr, "No Trace of the Bland: An Interview with Holly Hughes," *Theater* 24.2 (1993):67–75.

14. Holly Hughes, *Clit Notes*, unpublished and unpaginated play script, ©1994 by the author.

15. Eve Kosofsky Sedgwick, "Queer Performativity: Henry James's *The Art of the Novel*," *GLQ: A Journal of Lesbian and Gay Studies* 1.1 (1993):1–16.

16. Sedgwick, "Queer Performativity," 14.

17. Shakespeare, *A Midsummer Night's Dream*, in the *Riverside Shakespeare* (Boston: Houghton Mifflin, 1974), 1.2.51 and 1.2.70.

18. Cornel West, "The New Cultural Politics of Difference," in *Out There: Marginalization and Contemporary Cultures*, ed. Russell Ferguson, Martha Gever, Trinh T. Min-ha, and Cornel West (Cambridge: MIT Press, 1990).

19. Judith Butler, *Bodies That Matter: On the Discursive Limits of "Sex"* (New York: Routledge, 1993).

12   Queer Theater, Queer Theory

Luis Alfaro's *Cuerpo Politizado*

José Esteban Muñoz

Mapping Downtown: The Space of Memory

In November 1996, I presented a paper at a Latin/o performance conference at London's Institute of Contemporary Art that included theorists and performers. I was to deliver a paper on Luis Alfaro and Marga Gomez. One of the major stress points of having an archive such as mine is that many of the performers and artists that I work on are very much alive and are often interested in engaging with critics who evaluate their work, and in this instance that stress was palpable: Alfaro was in the audience. I asked him to join me onstage to read the performance monologue I was discussing.

That moment turned out to be quite interesting and powerful. Standing with me at the podium, Alfaro was no longer the "object of inquiry" but the coproducer of knowledge. I have always sensed that writing about artists like Alfaro was something of a collaboration and not simply advocacy criticism. Yet the centrality of this collaboration had never manifested itself so cogently to me before. Indeed, Alfaro is never merely an object of study, but an interlocutor, for he is a theorist in his own right, a thinker who helps me imagine theory and practice.[1] His work helps me intervene in queer social theory because his performances themselves carve out space for social theory making through their analysis of heteronormativity.

Alfaro presents us with views of the intersecting worlds that formed him as a queer, working-class, urban Chicano.[2] His memory performances help us not only imagine a future queer world, but also actually achieve a new counterpublic formation in the present through lived performance praxis. Thus Alfaro's work offers an important corrective to queer theory's failure ever truly to queer its theory. That is, though queer theory's early alliance with activist movements like Queer Nation and ACT UP promised that theory making would include activism and political performance, the "theory" end of the formulation has remained rigid and traditional, adhering to predictable modes of intellectual production. Performance, though—particularly by artists who stand at multiple points of antagonism in relation to racial, class, gender, and sexual hegemonies—can function as a productive site for producing theory. The work Alfaro presented during that London conference—*Cuerpo Politizado* (Politicized Body), a cross section of his solo performance work to date—is a compelling case in point.

I walk into the theater at the ICA in London and immediately notice the song that is playing: Petula Clark's "Downtown." The song paints an idyllic picture of a utopic urban sprawl, recalling a moment when downtowns were hubs of excitement and progress. Today, in the age of financially depressed commercial zones, the song's lyrics and soft pop melody seem rife with irony. As the houselights lower, I lose myself in thought about this song and what it means today. My reveries are interrupted when a video called *Chicanismos* is projected onto the screen.

The video begins with slow-moving sweeps of downtown Los Angeles, which then accelerate. The sound track jumps like a scratchy car stereo from station to station while the visual montage flashes shots of low riders gliding down crowded city streets, a man in a Mariachi outfit getting off work, Chicana home girls with heavy makeup leaning against a street pole, homeless men with overgrown beards, and graffiti that reads "Shy boy is crazy." Four times, the intense visual bombardment is interrupted by Alfaro who, playing four different characters, delivers brief video monologues between sections of the montage.

These characters—four manifestations of "Chicanismo"—all belong to the rich ensemble of social types that constitute Los Angeles. The first figure, a bearded and disillusioned Chicano Studies professor, represents faded nationalism. He is followed by a teenage mother who, despite her love for her baby, stands for youth in crisis. Then, a hyperassimilated Gap employee inadvertently reveals the situation of young people trapped within the service industry, and finally, an undocumented maid who identifies with her employers and declares that the United

States is her home, demonstrates how the most economically vulnerable are compelled to sacrifice their own nationality. These social players map the different
horizons of experience that delineate the space of contemporary Chicano L.A.
More than inhabiting space, these four characters are bodies that create space—
the space of Chicano Los Angeles. This is a complicated relationship, as Elizabeth
Grosz suggests:

*Bodies and cities are not causally linked. Every cause must be logically distinct from its
effect. The body, however, is not distinct, does not have an existence separate from the
city, for they are mutually defining. . . . there may be an isomorphism between the body
and the city. But it is not a mirroring of nature in artifice. Rather, there is a two-way linkage which could be defined as an interface, perhaps even a co-building. What I am suggesting is a model of relations of bodies and cities which sees them not as megalithic total
entities, distinct identities, but as an assemblage between subject and form linkages, ma-
chines, provisional and often temporary sub- or microgroupings.*[3]

Bodies and cities define each other. The bodies represented in *Chicanismos* are
the city of Los Angeles, which is to say that one cannot abstract them from the social matrix of that city. In setting the scene with the song, "Downtown," Alfaro
invokes a pointed irony: The song's idealistic lyrics, "Downtown, it's a beautiful
day . . ." contradict the downtown that Alfaro presents—one of faded dreams,
poverty, self-hatred, and social subordination. But Alfaro's citation of the song
reads as more than simply ironic. The song also evokes a memory, a dream that
was never achieved, a lost ideal. For Alfaro, then, the song is a passionate act of remembering, a strategy to conjure up the romanticized images of a world that
never really existed. Thus an unfulfilled dream from the past is read in relation to
a reality in the present. Alfaro starkly juxtaposes these images from two eras and
realms to call for a new temporality, a new moment, one of social transformation
and activist politics. Through critique of a false past and an embattled present he
lets the idea of a future emerge.

As the video concludes, the houselights go up and a man sitting in front of me
speaks loudly from his seat. He gets up and slowly walks toward the stage. He is
Luis Alfaro, in the flesh. When he emerges from the audience after having been
one of "us," our sense of tranquil spectatorship is displaced. The leap from performances "contained" within the video and the live body of Alfaro produces a
stirring shock effect.

The houselights begin to dim again as Alfaro reaches the stage. The monologue
he has recited since he began his migration from the audience to the stage is

entitled "On a Street Corner." It tells the story of a heterosexual couple walking down Broadway in downtown Los Angeles. The man says to the woman, "Shut up bitch." She complains about the beatings he inflicts upon her, and he threatens to leave her. She pleads for him to stay by saying: "Aw, no baby, you're the only thing I remember." The woman is so deeply immersed in this relationship that the man has overwhelmed her memory. Alfaro then accesses his own memory testimony as he reaches the center of the stage and says: "Because desire is memory and I crave it like the born-agains in my mama's church. But it's hard to be honest sometimes, because I live in the shadow of the Hollywood sign. Because on the street corner known as Pico and Union, my father made extra money on pool tables, my mother prayed on her knees."

Alfaro continues to transform downtown into a narrative series of childhood vignettes. He talks about the time when Sonia Lopez slaps him after he forces a kiss on her and he concludes that this must have been his introduction to S & M. He recalls Bozo the clown at the May Company on Broadway, tossing presents to a throng of kids that he is part of. When a board game hits another boy in the eye, Alfaro becomes terrified that the clown will throw something in his direction.

He then slips out of the directly autobiographical register, offering other memories laced with violence. He paces around the stage as he tells the story of a woman who dances in the projects and of the husband who beats her, about the drunk from the bar who staggers home, about the man who rides the Pico bus and slides his hand under women's seats, about the glue-sniffer on Venice Boulevard who watches the world in slow motion. Alfaro's pace and voice quicken as he concludes the monologue with an incantation that recalls memory and summarizes the piece: "A man got slapped. / A woman got slugged. / A clown threw toys. / A drunk staggered. / An earthquake shook. / A slap. / A slug. / A shove. / A kick." The stories condense into acts. And these acts conjure up bodies that collide with the image of a city. Indeed, these slaps, punches, and so forth *constitute* the social realm.

Clearly, memory is a central theme in Alfaro's work. It is structured through the violence and pain that inform much of urban Latina/o reality. Memory recalls and indexes both the affective world of U.S. Latinos—that is, their ways of being in the world that are organized through feeling—and their communal and collective construction of *latinidad*. The term *latinidad*, a theoretical catalog of different modes of Latina/o self-fashioning, demarcates a set of affective performances that help delineate Latina/o particularity. *Latinidad* is not about race, region, nation, gender, language, or any other easily identifiable demarcation of "difference." Rather, it is an antiidentitarian concept that nonetheless permits us to talk about

Latinas/os as having a group identity, which is necessary for social activism. Thinking of *latinidad* as antinormative affect offers a model of group identity that is coherent without being exclusionary. Through performed memory, a deployment of rehearsed and theatricalized Latino affect, Alfaro negotiates two different temporal narratives of the self: the migrant child and gay man of color, two affective registers of Latino experience that interrogate each other through the performer's theatrical mixing.

Alfaro has described his work as a series of combinations, "mixing gay life with Chicano life, street life with Catholic life, *cholo* life with my life."[4] This mixing resonates with the kind of cultural layering that queers of color often need to enact if they wish to maintain simultaneous memberships in queer communities and communities of color. Memory is not a static thing for the queer of color; it is an antinormative space where self is made and remade and where politics can be imagined. While memory is not static for anyone, it is always "in the making" for the minoritarian subject who cannot perform normative citizenship and thus has no access to the standardized narratives of national cultural memory. This dominant culture that projects an "official" history that elides queer lives and the lives of people of color necessitates a counternarrative that memory performances supply.

The memory performances that interest me are decidedly antinormative, which is to say that they are deployed for the purposes of contesting affective normativities that include, but are not limited to, white supremacy and the cultural logics of misogyny and homophobia. The queer of color's performances of memory transmit and broadcast affectively charged strategies of minoritarian survival and self-making, carving out a space for resistance and communal self-enactment. Their memory performances thus work as calls intended to solicit responses.

Those affiliated with Latino communities and queer communities know the ways in which so much has been lost—whether through the dismantling of civil rights discourse, the routinization of the AIDS pandemic, or in other social battles. Many of us take periodic refuge in the past: the time before the AIDS pandemic; before the state and the ideological forces of dominant culture had decided with renewed enthusiasm that Latinos and Latinas, along with other migrant communities, are the cause of all the nation's ills; before affirmative action was dismantled in California; before Proposition 187 in effect legalized the treatment of taxpaying undocumented workers as an underclass. Memory performances call forth an affect that predates current attempts to dismantle the citizen status of minoritarian subjects.

We need to remember this prior time not as a nostalgic escape, but to enable us to critique the present. Performances of memory remember, dream, recite a self, and reassert agency in a world that challenges and constantly attempts to snuff out subaltern identities. Memory performances deploy affective narratives of self, ways of being from the past, in the service of questioning the future, a future without annihilating epidemics, both viral and ideological. Alfaro's work demonstrates the importance of memory for the politics of the present and the future. Alfaro's memory performances are the dreams of a subject who falls out of the narrow confines prescribed by the state, the law, and other normative grids. They are the frames around subjects whose affect is deemed excessive, wrong, or simply off. Such performances amplify and transmit these recitations of dreams and contribute to a project of setting up counterpublics—communities and relational chains of resistance that contest the dominant public sphere.

Between Two Virgins

Alfaro walks into a circle of light after "On a Street Corner" and prepares to tell a family story called "Virgin Mary." He commences by explaining that "We used to have this Virgin Mary doll. Every time you connected her to an outlet she would turn and bless all sides of the room." A cylinder of light contains Alfaro, as though he too were in a glass case. The performer goes on to recount the story of the Virgin Mary's origin, how she was purchased during one of his father's surprise drunken trips to Tijuana when he would come home from the racetrack around midnight and load the entire family into the station wagon. Young Luis offers the Virgin as a gift to his Tia Ofelia when she is suffering from breast cancer.

Young Luis explains how Tia Ofelia, like everyone else in the family, was a grape picker from Delano, California. She lived on the top floor of a two-story wooden home that was flanked by high-rise projects. The bottom floor was occupied by *cholos* from the 18th Street Gang. After Luis's aunt passes away, the rivals of the 18th Street Gang, the Crips, come looking for them and firebomb the house, killing the *cholos* and destroying the house, along with the Virgin Mary.

Years later, Alfaro recounts, he meets a man who will become his first love. The man owns a rotating Virgin Mary doll that he bought in Mexico. Alfaro describes him as having white skin, eating broccoli, and talking like characters on a TV series. He was "every Partridge Family/Brady Bunch episode rolled into one." This white man teaches the young Alfaro how to French-kiss, lick an earlobe, and dance in the dark. The young Alfaro's fascination for this man has much to do with the way he embodies a normative imprint that dominates North American culture. In part Alfaro desires his whiteness, which itself constitutes his normative way of being in the world, but also his taste for broccoli, his sitcom voice, and his way of dancing that mark this way of being. Alfaro is crushed when this lover leaves him and he once again finds himself surrounded by family who let him know that "*Aye mijo*, don't you understand? Blood is thicker than water, family is greater than friends, and the Virgin Mary, that old Virgin Mary, she watches over all of us." The relationship fails, in part, because Alfaro cannot perform normative white affect, and he is comforted by his past world, a world of ethnic affect. The affect of an ethnic past is thus a storehouse of resources for the minority subject who strives to fabricate self in hostile normative climates.

Alfaro uses the rotating deity to forge a connection between these different layers of experience and affect. The life Alfaro describes, positioned between a straight ethnic past and a predominantly white queer present, is the kind of reality that queers of color often negotiate. One way of managing such an identity is to forsake the past, to let go of it altogether. But for Alfaro the cost is too high. Instead, he calls upon memory performance to manage identity and in doing so, he invents a theater of memory.

While the coherent self is most certainly an exhausted fiction, a "self effect," as Alfaro knows, is necessary to make interventions in the social and political realm. Minority, diasporic, and exiled subjects recalibrate the protocols of selfhood by insisting on the radical hybridity of the self, on the fact that a self is not a normative citizen or even a coherent whole, but instead a hybrid that contains disparate and even contradictory associations, identifications, and disidentifications. Coming to power, coming into self, for such subjects requires that they write themselves into history. Alfaro does so by historicizing the self through theatricalizations of Latino affect that index personal memory and collective memory—the personal memory of a family of migrant grape pickers from Delano, and the collective and spatialized memory of Chicano Los Angeles.

The Moo-Moo of History

In a valuable reading of Benjamin's angel of history, the Judaic scholar and ethnographer, Jonathan Boyarin, writes:

Part of the importance of Benjamin's image is the lesson that we are always once again being driven out; in some sense we have always just lost paradise, hence we are always close to it. The ongoing state of emergency Benjamin also speaks of doesn't just mean we are always in imminent danger, but also that something precious is eternally being lost.

This reading of the storm from paradise, which emphasizes the howling gap between us and the past and the past's proximity to us, suggests the need for a "double gesture" toward our past. We need constantly to be interrogating and recuperating the past, without pretending for long that we can recoup its plenitude. This double gesture, this contradictory movement of new recognitions and new distances between the present and the past, may be most easily articulated in a juxtaposition of explicit traditional and postmodern figures of multiplicity, rather than modern identity.[5]

Boyarin's concept of a "double gesture" that recognizes the need to reclaim a past while also resisting the temptation to succumb to a nostalgic and essentialized conception of it, is especially useful with respect to Luis Alfaro's memory performances. For the minority subject, the double gesture of remembering and not being lost to memory leads to a powerful emergence into politics. Memory is a catalyst; it assists in shoring up antinormative Latino/a affect and enables performances of the self that contest the affective normativity of dominant culture.

Alfaro's movement along this trajectory is especially evident in a segment of *Cuerpo Politizado* entitled "A Moo-Moo Approaches/A Story about Mamas and Mexico," in which Alfaro focuses on the figure of his mother. Moo-Moo connotes both his mother's large colorful dresses and her fat body, and Alfaro foregrounds his own body image as a fat man through this meditation on his mother. The segment begins with Alfaro walking up to a table of Twinkies and eating them one by one. As he literally gorges himself on dozens of Twinkies, a tape plays the story of the Moo-Moo. Alfaro's taped voice explains that when Alfaro's father first came to this country there simply wasn't enough for him, so he married Alfaro's mother, the Moo-Moo, who, with "hips as wide as a river [. . .] was abundance personified." The Moo-Moo's function was to signify the family's accruing wealth and to hide their actual poverty. But the children were embarrassed by the Moo-Moo, who attended every PTA meeting and Boy Scout outing, and inserted herself in altar boy affairs at church. She was there to remind the family "how good life was en Los Estados Unidos."

She served as a protector, even threatening to kill a neighbor who called her precious son effeminate. The Moo-Moo fended off burglars with a baseball bat, chasing a man who stole the family's small television set down to the corner of Pico and Union, though she was wearing slippers on her feet and curlers in her hair. She returned home whistling a happy tune as "blood dripped off the bat and onto the downtown pavement." In sum, says Alfaro about his mother, "The Moo-Moo was serious, gerl."

As time went on and Alfaro's father felt compelled to become "American" he decided that the Moo-Moo was too much. The Moo-Moo who once represented an abundant future now "was no longer desirable. The Moo-Moo of Mexico represented all the problems and setbacks we had endured in America. The Moo-Moo of Mexico was too big, too fat, too much. Too much for our new American sensibility." Then the Moo-Moo, like Tia Ofelia, lost a breast. She gave up her brightly colored moo-moos and began wearing simple dark dresses that she sewed on an old-fashioned sewing machine from the Deardens store on 5th and Main.

By the time the recording reaches this point in the narrative, Alfaro has eaten at least thirty Twinkies. He continues to stuff them down his throat in a violent fashion while the tape goes on with the story of the Moo-Moo's slow suicide courtesy of "Hostess Manufacturing," as the family home is overrun with cupcakes, Sno-Balls, lemon pies, donuts, and Ho-Hos. As this image of proliferating pastries invades his imagination, he reports that at night "far from the breast of The Moo-Moo, the nightmare that is the Mexico that I do not know haunts me. I clear the kitchen of all traces of my bicultural history: the Mexican telenovela and a sweetener called America. The nightmare continues, a Moo-Moo approaches."

That Moo-Moo is Alfaro's angel of history. Her face is turned to a past that is Mexico. The Moo-Moo would like to awaken the dead from a past life, another place and time, and make whole what has been shattered through relocation and migration. The forces that call the Alfaro family to assimilate are a storm blowing from paradise, coded as progress. Her back is turned to this paradise, her eyes are focused on a past that is being debased by those around her. She is tragic like history's angel insofar as she has lost control of herself. She is coming toward Alfaro like a house lifted by a tornado. She represents the nightmare that is his history and his bicultural queer body shakes at the thought of her. He performs a ritual reenactment of his mother's slow suicide by consuming the table full of Twinkies. In doing so he inhabits her abjected form. This effeminate queer son who was once protected by this Moo-Moo mother becomes her in an effort to rehabilitate a body and an image that has been battered by progress and assimilation. Through his performance of the Moo-Moo, Alfaro finds a place for himself in this nightmare. He identifies with this tragic Moo-Moo *and* with his father's will toward assimilation. His performance is an attempt to redeem what has been lost.

It is important that the vehicle for this return to the past is a powerful and embodied relationship to the gendered Moo-Moo and not to the genderless angel. Assimilation and progress are typically coded as male, and the past, ethnicity, and heritage are represented by an abjected maternal body. Alfaro metaphorically steps into the maternal position, thereby documenting this queer male activist-performer's debt to female embodiment. More than a queer cross-identification with the female body, it is in fact a call to disengage from masculine gender in an effort to rethink the social from within an expansive political frame, one that understands the structuring force of gender within the socio-politico realm.

Primitive Latino First Aid: The Double Gesture of Memory Performance

The double gesture described by Boyarin, with its impulse to invoke the past for a politics of the present, is evident in another moment in Alfaro's performance, when he returns to the scene of a heteronormative childhood. In this section, entitled "Abuelita," Alfaro stands behind a podium in a single, ominous spotlight, wearing a black slip, which the production's prop list describes as "a cheap JC Penny slip, size 18 or up." He holds one small finger up in the air as he recalls having cut his finger jumping through his mother's rosebush—in an effort to avoid his grandmother—when he was eleven years old. In the first half of the piece, he explains how he despises his grandmother more than his fifth-grade teacher, revealing the shame this second-generation Latino felt because of his grandmother's refusal to assimilate into North American culture. Abuelita insists on maintaining the quotidian reality of a Latin American woman who reads Vanidades and makes everyone hush when she watches her telenovelas (soap operas).

Emerging from the rosebush Alfaro discovers a wound:

I rise out of the rosebush
and immediately plunge into
the other Latino dramatic effect,
the painful
ay yai yai.

There's a gash on my finger
and it starts to bleed
pretty badly.

Abuelita turns on the hose
and runs my hand
under the water.
Inspecting my finger she laughs,
pinches my cheek,
Thanks the Virgin
for the minor miracle,
does a sign of the cross, and applies
Primitive Latino First Aid.

She looks at me,
smiles, raises a bloody finger
to her face.
Closely inspecting
my afflicted digit,
she brings it up close
to her eyes.

I can't tell
what she is looking for.
As if holding it up close
she might find
some truth,
some small lesson
or parable
about the world
and its workings.

Her eyes canvass the finger,
probing her vision
slowly and carefully.
And then quickly
and without warning,
she sticks it
inside her mouth
and begins
to suck on it.

I feel the inside of her mouth,
wet and warm,
her teeth
lightly pulling
equally discomforting
and disgusting
at the same time.

Being in that womb
feels as if I am being eaten alive
on one of those
late night
Thriller Chiller movies
Vampira, Senior Citizen Bloodsucker.

But it isn't that at all.
This is the only way
that abuelita
knows how to stop the bleeding.

The narrative then shifts from the past to the present:

See this finger?
Cut it at work. .
Making another pamphlet
critical of those
who would like
to see us dead.

The long gasp.
Four Gay Latinos
in one room
Four long gasps.

Afraid to touch my wound.
Would prefer
to see it bleed
and gush
than to question

mortality
and fate.

Could go on
about being tested,
but it seems
so futile.
As if we
don't know
that one little test
could have been wrong.

Hold the finger
in front of me
Stick it
close to mouth
Drip, drip, drip
all over the desktop
from Ikea.

Hold it close
to face.
Quickly
and without
warning,
stick it in my mouth
and I begin to
suck.

Tears roll down.
Salty wet
tears.
Down my face.
Can feel my teeth
lightly pulling
and I wish,

I wish for an abuelita
in this time.

This time of plague.
This time of loss.
This time of sorrow.
This time of mourning.
This time of shame.

And I
heal myself.
I heal myself
with abuelita's
Primitive Latino First Aid.

The prevailing tone of the poem's first section is that of shame. But the double gesture of interrogating the past while not collapsing under the gravitational pull of nostalgia helps us grasp its importance to the formulation of a politicized self in the here and now.

We also see a deep desire for a space of identity formation here as Alfaro calls forth a rehabilitated and reimagined Latino family, one that is necessary in the face of a devastating and alienating pandemic. Memory performance reinvents the space of *familia*, the *familia* made from scratch that Cherríe Moraga has described. It is a hub of identity consolidation that is reinhabited through the auspices of memory performance.

Family has been much criticized in contemporary queer theory as an oppressive totality. But such a characterization, from the perspective of queers of color, is deeply reductive. On the one hand, it is true that not all families of color affirm their queer sons and daughters. On the other hand, the generalized gay community often feels like a sea of whiteness to queers of color, and thus the imagined ethnic family is often a refuge. It is a space where all those elements of the self that are fetishized, ignored, and rejected in the larger queer world are suddenly revalorized. Alfaro's memory performance attunes us to those enabling characteristics.

Queer Theater and Social Theory

Michael Warner's introduction to his groundbreaking collection *Fear of a Queer Planet* is one of the most important interventions in queer social theory. In it, Warner produces a sharp critique of social theory's "heteronormativity," and calls upon queer studies to engage with the material social and political world. He notes that "the energies of queer studies have come more from rethinking the subjective meaning of sexuality than from thinking the social."[6] Warner contrasts *ethnos* and *eros*, arguing that, as experiences of identity, sexuality and ethnicity are fundamentally distinct: "People tend not to encounter queerness in the same way as ethnic identity. Often the disparity between racial and sexual imperatives can be registered as dissonance."[7] This is certainly true for Alfaro. In *Cuerpo Politizado* he theatricalizes this dissonance, considering it as part of queer experience.

Warner takes pains to show the way in which ethnicity and sexuality are not corresponding experiences. While I agree that these categories need to be differentiated, I would suggest that his reading of the differences between queers and people of color in relation to family requires more elaboration. His reading of the role of family is informed by a particularly white queer experience. He writes:

Familial language deployed to describe sociability in race- or gender-based movements (sisterhood, brotherhood, fatherland, mother tongue, etc.) can either be a language of exile or a resource of irony (in voguing houses, for example, one queen acts as "mother").[8]

In Alfaro's work, the family is more than just a site to run from or a source of irony. While for queers of color, family can often be a place of conflict and potential violence, it is also one where ethnicity and cultural difference are produced and nurtured. Indeed, Alfaro's work returns to the space of an ethnic past in order to formulate his identity as a queer of color. In the "Moo-Moo" and "Abuelita" sequences he specifically turns to his mother and grandmother to draw energy and critical force. While the majority of white queers can more easily fashion a break (an exile) from their childhood in heteronormative culture, since the queer community is a white normative one that would not dislocate them from their cultural formation as white people, the queer of color who cuts ties with his or her familial past is often also cutting ties with his or her ethnicity and/or race.

Alfaro emphasizes this risk in the last section of *Cuerpo Politizado*, "Orphan of Aztlan." Still clad in the black slip from the "Abuelita" segment and standing behind a music stand as if it were a pulpit, Alfaro literally preaches this last monologue, taking on the voice of a charismatic minister, one who might be preaching at his mother's church. He invokes Aztlan, the imaginary homeland that is a central organizing principle of Chicano nationalism, though his status as orphan (or exile) from this nationalist community foregrounds Chicano nationalism's inability to claim queer sons and daughters. But Alfaro expounds a more nuanced political position at this point in his performance. He sounds a militant political note in relation to liberal queer politics:

241

There has been no power-sharing
so we are power-taking
empowered
to march with a million
because I am
sick and tired
of seeing straight people
kiss and hold hands
in public

while I am
relegated to
a T-dance
at Rage

Fuck that shit!

The artist's rage rejects the politics of gay ghettoization and instead calls for a larger queering of the social realm. Alfaro calls on queers to take power and insert themselves within the national body, instead of waiting for liberal inclusion. For him, Rage is not a club holding a T-dance, but a politics.

After speaking in general terms about queer politics Alfaro locates himself within Chicano politics. He reintroduces the biography that we are familiar with from his memory performances:

I am a Queer Chicano
A native in no land
An orphan of Aztlan
The pocho son of farmworker parents

The Mexicans only want me
when they want me to
talk about Mexico
But what about
Mexican Queers in L.A.?

The Queers only want me
when they need
to add color
add spice

like salsa picante
on the side

With one foot
on each side
of the border
not the border
between Mexico
and the United States
but the border between
Nationality and Sexuality
I search for a home in both
yet neither one believes
that I exist.

Alfaro beautifully captures the liminality that characterizes the experience of being queer and of color. His work brings these concerns into the foreground but does not stop there. He calls for social change:

Blur the line
take the journey
play with the unknown
deal with the whole enchilada
Race
Class
Sex
Gender
Privilege

Arrive at the place called possibility
Try once again to create a language
a sense of what it means
to be in community

I am fast forwarding
past the reruns *ese*
and riding the big wave
called future
making myself

fabulous
as I disentangle
from the wreck of this
cultural collision

Alfaro's performance and its insistence on the whole enchilada is a challenge
to a range of minority communities. Warner produces a critique of what he calls
"Rainbow theory" and its weak multiculturalism. In his call to "break the frame"
of a slogan-oriented politics that presupposes the interchangeability of sexual and
ethnic differences, I read the implication that any subject can disengage him or
herself from this "frame" with equal ease, and that the mandate to critique such
a position is equally relevant for all queers. I would argue that queers of color do
not have the privilege of this analytical edge because different vectors of identity
are mapped on their bodies and comprise their horizons of experience. The connections are thus materially valenced for the working-class lesbian of color, for instance, in ways that an affluent gay white man may not be able to grasp. He can
dismiss the "Racism-Sexism-Homophobia-grasp the connections" bumper sticker
with relative ease since the connections that are suggested are to some degree ab-
stractions for him. When queer critique calls for an atomizing of "the whole enchilada," the white normativity at the center of queer discourse becomes visible.
I agree with Warner when I posit that queer politics does need a social theoretical
base. Yet to stand firmly on one, we need to call attention to just what experiential archive informs such a social theory. If queer politics is ever to acquire political efficacy, the experiential and affective archive that it accesses must not be
tainted by the false universality of white normativity.

My critique of the white normativity in queer theory might lead to a misread-
ing that I would like to head off at the pass. Whiteness is not monolithic. For
many white people *ethnos*—and therefore the ethnic family—is important; for
them, ethnicity cannot simply be trumped by sexuality. Italian-, Irish-, and Jew-
ish-American experiences, for example, complicate any monolithic understanding of whiteness. Furthermore, there are other nonethnicity based forms of difference, like class and region, that represent "difference" *within* whiteness. Yet all
these differences are occluded by *white normativity*, that is, by the assumption of a
universal whiteness. While it is important to stress that I am not interested in
making whiteness monolithic, I *am* interested in calling attention to the workings
and ruses of "white normativity."

Warner opens his introduction to *Fear of a Queer Planet* by invoking Karl Marx's definition of critical theory: "the self-clarification of the wishes and struggles of the age." This definition applies to the queer theater work of Alfaro, whose memory performance, with its focus on the production of hybrid selves and space, is in and of itself a mode of queer theory making that also functions as social theory. Another turn to Marx is helpful in further describing Alfaro's project. In the *Theses on Feuerbach*, Marx offers an aphorism on the difference between philosophy and praxis: "The philosophers have only interpreted the world in various ways; the point, however, is to change it."[9] While this aphorism is well-worn it nonetheless speaks to the complicated relationship between theory and praxis within actually existing queer cultures. Struggles between theory and praxis are central to the question of queer theater's (or any other mode of queer practice's) relationship to this enterprise called theory. Etienne Balibar has suggested that even though Marx was very young when he wrote that aphorism, "nothing he wrote afterwards ever went beyond the horizon of the problems posed by that formulation."[10] By this Balibar means to call attention to the ways in which the concerns outlined in that early text haunt the relationship between philosophy and politics. Balibar's reading ultimately marks the ways in which praxis becomes philosophy and vice versa. By invoking *The German Ideology's* rewriting of this formulation, a rewriting that stresses the interrelation between praxis and production, Balibar suggests that theory is the production of consciousness. Taking my direction from Balibar, I would suggest that the relationship of queer theory to queer theater is similar to the relationship between the critic-theorist and the performer, the relationship between Alfaro and me standing together at that podium in London. In both cases, both sides of this divide contribute to a specific mode of production, one we might call *the production* of queer consciousness.

Alfaro's *Cuerpo Politizado* contributes to the production of queer knowledges, queer possibilities, and queer consciousness by exploring the wishes and struggles that inform a transformative politics. In the course of the piece, the audience witnesses his migration from his past in Tia Ofelia's burned-out lot to his present—and presence—in the performance space. There, Alfaro's audience feasts on a "delicious spectacle," a performance that engenders queer Latino possibility where it could not flourish before. Queer Latino selves are called into existence through *Cuerpo Politizado*. Social space is reterritorialized through queer theater's demand for change.

Notes

1. A similar case is made by David Román who looks at Alfaro's work as a contribution to Chicano Studies. See his *Acts of Intervention: Performance, Gay Culture, and AIDS* (Bloomington: Indiana University Press, 1998), 177–201.

2. Luis Alfaro grew up in the Pico-Union district of Central Los Angeles, as the son of farmworkers. While working as a custodian at a theater where LAPD, the Los Angeles Poverty Department, worked, Alfaro met director Scott Kelman, who became his mentor. He later went on to study with playwrights Maria Irene Fornes and Tony Kushner. Alfaro has worked as a member of different artist collectives and as a solo artist.

3. Elizabeth Grosz, *Space, Time and Perversion: Essays on the Politics of Bodies* (New York: Routledge, 1995), 108.

4. Quoted in Doug Sadownick, "Two Different Worlds: Luis Alfaro Bridges the Gap between Gay Fantasies and Latino Reality," *The Advocate*, Issue 568, January 15, 1991, 6–63.

5. Jonathan Boyarin, *The Storm from Paradise: The Politics of Jewish Memory* (Minneapolis: University of Minnesota Press, 1992), xvi.

6. Michael Warner, "Introduction," in *Fear of a Queer Planet: Queer Politics and Social Theory* (Minneapolis: University of Minnesota Press, 1993), x.

7. Warner, "Introduction," xvii.

8. Warner, "Introduction," xix.

9. Karl Marx, "Theses on Feuerbach," in *The Marx-Engels Reader*, ed. Robert Tucker (New York: Norton, 1972), 145.

10. Etienne Balibar, *The Philosophy of Marx*, trans. Chris Turner (London: Verso, 1995), 13.

13 When We Were Warriors

Brian Freeman

My "Act Black" T-shirt, a black queer parody of "Silence=Death" iconography—
ACT UP/ACT BLACK—has been put away now, like my sister's bridal gown, which
my grandmother finished hemming in the limo on my sister en route to the service. (Queerness may or may not be hereditary, but drama queenness most definitely is.) Like my sister's bridal gown, a souvenir of a romantic moment in time,
that T-shirt has been cleaned and pressed and wrapped in acid-free paper and put
away, stored for the day when my rent-controlled San Francisco flat is filled with
children, or how do you say it in a sort of black way—*chillun*—or *the* children, the
next generation of queer, homo, or whatever moniker the next generation of lesbian, bi, trans queer playwrights, video makers, directors, performance artists, et
al. decides to operate under.

We'll sit together there in the shade of the peach tree that overhangs my deck.
I'll serve alcohol-free blue whales, keeping a little nip bottle in the pocket of my
caftan with which to spike my own. I'll put out my house music CDs, my Ultra
Naté, my Double Exposure. They'll roll their eyes and laugh. "You danced to that
stuff?" I'll lift my caftan and show them the steps, and when we're good and silly,
they will turn to me, now the griot of sorts, the village elder, and they will ask:
"What was it really like in the nineties?" And I'll reply: "Your Uncle Marlon, Uncle

Assoto, your Auntie Danitra, and I—we were once warriors. No, children, not Mandingo warriors." The essentialist and problematic nature of our Afrocentrism will have been well documented by this point in time, Kente cloth relegated to retrokitsch much as plaid polyester is today. "No, my lovely little gays. Come close and I will tell you of the time when we were cultural warriors."

The truth is, I've already had this moment, played this scene. I was invited to speak to Queer Nation four years ago when there actually was a Queer Nation. I was put on a panel of *elders* with other lesbian-gay-slash-performance artists over thirty. I thought it was pretty rude, too. My thoughts then were much the same as they are today: Rumors of my impending farewell, swan song, grand exit are greatly exaggerated.

For the moment, I'm enjoying the hiatus from black queer super spokesmodeldom, as the original Pomos's ensemble scatter, each to our own horizons, or as Ntozake Shange says, "In search of our own rainbows," no longer containable under one collective consciousness. If the Supremes of black queer performance break up—I always loathed that analogy with the obvious implication as to who is the real Diana? Let me tell you today: We're queer theater and we are *all* Dianas on this bus. And if any of you have ever worked in a collective queer theater, how well you know. I think more to the point is, we grew up.

Times changed. Strategies changed. Tradition brings reflection, but these past few days here seem more about looking at the past, recent and not so recent, than envisioning the future. I wonder if we're too scared. I question the concept that queer cultural production is sandbagged at the moment by an age of melancholia. What a strange word. It sounds like what Miss Thing comes down with in *Camille*. I live in San Francisco, a small city, and I'm quite familiar with that sensibility, and I know that finding the space—the *space* as we Californians like to say—to even speak to that sensibility, is so limited by our need to continue, to fight, to educate and entertain, to take care of our own, to take care of ourselves.

When we avoid saying the words publicly—"I miss him," "I miss her"—not because it's true but because we risk calling up everyone's ghost, I wonder sometimes if it's like those old Palmolive commercials. "Melancholia? Really?" "Yes! You're soaking in it!" Are we all soaking in it? Was it, or is it within this constantly disclaimed thing we call "community"? The Black Nations/Queer Nations event, another CLAGS conference in March 1995, was not soaking in it at all. It was bursting at the seams with theorists, activists, fresh cultural production, and more. The opening night of the conference was like a banquet of black queer video and music—Lavender Light, Toshi Regan just rocked the house. And I performed and I like my work.

But my favorite was Harmonica Sunbeam, which sounds kind of like a Northern California thing almost. Harmonica Sunbeam is a fierce, fierce, fierce drag performance arts person who began that evening in a blonde wig and a kind of country dress, doing Dolly Parton's version of "I Will Always Love You," which transitioned—when the dress ripped off—into Whitney's version of "I, I Will Always Love You." And I'm just jealous that she thought of it first.

How did we get here? I wonder if you're familiar with the work of Marlon Riggs, and if you're not, it's out there on video. And a yet-to-be-released work, "Black Is, Black Ain't," will be playing soon at a theater near you. Marlon, my friend, my sometimes collaborator, my sometimes competitor, the bitch narrates the film, from a hospital bed. How can I top that? She works it. It's quite fierce. Did you see Assoto Saint's work in the anthology, *In the Life*? Did you see his performance pieces about black gay men when they were performed here in New York City in the late seventies? That thick Haitian accent, a legacy of his home, would probably declare, "Pomo Afro Homos was *not* the first black gay performance company," and of course he'd be absolutely right.

Danitra Vance and the Mello White Boys with its groundbreaking lesbian satire that was clearly not ready-for-prime time during her short stint on "Saturday Night Live." Did that fabulous work ever tour through your college, city, town, or queer-friendly performance space? I call their names today to let you know, I didn't get here by myself, that my girl-group of black queer identity, the Pomo Afro Homos did not pop up from some hermetically sealed container, fully formed, like Venus from the head of Zeus.

We evolved from a moment, from a black queer arts movement, separate and distinct from queer/les/gay theater and performance, yet absolutely linked to it. For my community emerged in groups like Black Gay Men United in the Bay Area, or the Black Lesbian and Gay Leadership Conference in Los Angeles, or Gay Men of African Descent here in New York City. Han Ong, a theater and performance artist, in his *Symposia in Manila* refers to the curse of multiculturalism as putting us in a constant state of emerging—never quite there. And recently a black lesbian filmmaker whose work I find quite exciting, declared: The black gay male art thing is over. Over! It's time for the black lesbian thing to happen.

In this strange orbit of cultural consumption, where whole communities of people are skinned, sipped, and exhumed, where we are dined on for a moment, then tossed away like chicken bones—you know, "The Latino gay thing? We did that two years ago. And they were too angry." In this strange world, it is, of course, long past time for the black lesbian thing to happen, and to happen big. But to her, and to all of you in our assorted queer, kind of queer, transqueer, or en-queerying communities, I have news. Our ranks may be decimated, our funding no longer the fashion, our presence on the scene no longer *courant*. But I think we have indeed emerged—like Mister George C. Wolfe, like David Rousseve, like Isaac Julien, Reggie Jackson, Joan Jett Blakk, Bill T. Jones, we're still here. We're still big, black queers. The space that our art takes—demands, really—does not diminish her own. It feeds it. Get used to it.

Why do we *other* each other so in a community of others? I see you, I do. I sleep with you sometimes. I sex you. You sex me. You like it. I like it. It's a mutual re-spect for a mutual nasty thing. Depending on the moment. I live next door to you. I really do. Marlon abandoned the Castro. I'm still at 17th and Sanchez, where I celebrate being in the twelfth year of a relationship—with my rent-controlled apartment. I watch your plays, your performance pieces, your films and videos, though I rarely see myself in them, and when I do, I often don't like what I see. I often wonder if you know me at all. I've marched with you for twenty years now, and like good friends or long-term lovers, I sometimes think I know you better than you know yourself, yet I often feel like an enigma in your eyes. Do my sto-ries matter to you?

Are they of interest only if I heighten the performance and give you fierce drag? And I love fierce drag like I love what little Armani I can afford, I just don't always want to be featured in that. Must I wrap black manhood in the razzle-dazzle of Mandingo memories, before I become interesting to you? I know you listen if I'm talking about you. The only thing worse than being dissed is being ignored.

So, I know you'll be there for my rapier "reads." You'll wince. You'll cry. You'll hurt. Then you'll thank me for telling you about yourself, then ask me to do it again. Yawn. Was that good? Yeah. It was good for me, too. Yeah. You want to put that on Visa or Amex?

What happens if I show you, tell you, dramatize, perform, even dare to act out for you those parts of my collective community self that are ambivalent? Can you tolerate it? Can I tolerate you seeing it? That hurts, sometimes. The part that doesn't feel very black, sometimes. The part that doesn't feel very gay, sometimes. What happens if I reach down, down, down? As Maria Irene Fornes says, down there, down there to the very core of my being, and comes up with something like Jewelle Gomez's *The Gilda Stories*, black lesbian vampire stories, soon to be a major motion performance piece by the Urban Bush Women? Are you down with that? Are we still in the same tent? What if I dare to tell you about selves inside the selves of me, and what that feels like sometimes? It's not Sybil, trust me. What if I reach down in there and what pops out are my parents?

Back when I was a Boston teenage show queen—as opposed to the featured-on-Donahue San Francisco performance art fag I am today—my wish-we-were-middle-class parents subscribed to a Best of Broadway series, to which I more often than not tagged along, getting a single in the balcony or standing room at the back of the orchestra, swallowing every note of a *Dolly, Fiddler, Follies, Purlie*. Every pregnant pause of Claire Bloomish sort of-but not really-English dramas: "Really? Are you really? But really? Are you, really?" Every bad joke of sitcom star vehicles and every "right-on" moment in the occasional "Up-against-the-wall-honky" Negro-problem play.

One winter evening, I took a break from avoiding doing my homework by memorizing show tunes I would never be called upon to perform, and wandered downstairs in our Dorchester duplex to discover my parents polishing off a couple of highballs and donning their going-to-the-theater drag, that is, going without me. Why wasn't I told? I threw a big hissy fit. I started early. They take practice. But this one failed. As Dad headed out to warm up the car and chain-smoke Pall Malls, Mom pulled on her faux fur-lined vinyl gloves and offered the stoic consolation, "It's not a musical. It's about homosexuals. Now, Brian, you wouldn't want to go to *that*, would you?" Did any teenager in the early seventies want to hear his mother utter his name and the word "homosexual" in the same breath? Silence. I watched from my bedroom window and pondered my sexuality and their possible awareness of it as Dad puffed and Mom coughed and their smoke-filled maroon Impala skidded through the slush toward Boston's theater district and the fabulous possibilities onstage they were about to behold. I punished my parents by locking them out of the house that night. But that's another story.

By the time I finally saw *Boys in the Band*, I was out and out of the house and it was a rep-house movie. Its portraits of New York queens sitting around bitching over who's got the lowest self-esteem even then seemed archaic to this nineteen-year-old disco diva-slash-gay activist who was participating in Gay Activist Alliance zaps of a Philadelphia furniture store using a TV pitchman with limp wrists and a long lisp—Mr. Furniture, or, I should say, Mithter Furnithur. (I don't even lisp very well for a faggot)—Mr. Furniture, to peddle crushed velvet sofas and chrome coffee tables to working-class Italian housewives. He'd come on the screen and he had this number: "In your home, fabu!"

Seeing *Boys in the Band*, even in the campy film version, was the first time I saw gay people in popular culture—us—talking about our lives in our own vocabulary. But then and now, there is that not-so-fabulous question: Who is us? Black queer artists, my guys, my community, and me? I think our voices are moving toward more intimate stories. Yes, we'll fight the church. Yes, we will claim our space in the larger black nation, whether folks like it or not. But you will hear stories that speak to individual experience instead of collective community consciousness. Have you seen the recent novel *B-Boy Blues* by James Earl Hardy? I think it's a witty, fascinating example of the next movement.

It feels like the tip of an iceberg to me. There's a black theater conference happening at the same time as this over in Brooklyn today, at Medgar Evers College. And this afternoon there's a panel on sexual issues in black theater. Someone had to decode that for me: That means *us*. I'm not sure if I want to go to that or not. Sometimes I have a lot of anger with my community, my black community. Sometimes I think of Rodney King. What was his thing? People, why can't we all just get along? Sort of like, People, why can't we come on along? The bus is not only leaving, the bus has left the station like fifteen years ago. Jump on a fast train and catch up.

How do we share this big tent that everyone here keeps saying that we don't want to be in? I've never been to a conference before where everyone keeps saying, "I'm not really a queer playwright, a queer director. I really don't belong."

So do any of us really belong? Maybe none of us really wants to be in that tent. I don't know. At the Black Nations/Queer Nations conference, Urvashi Vaid, the former chair of the National Lesbian and Gay Task Force, proposed that those of us in communities of color, not try and replicate the structures of the white lesbian/gay community in building institutions, in creating space for ourselves. We don't have the money. Simple as that. We do not have the economics. The way we construct community at times is different. She suggests that we instead develop models of shared space with each other. This theater that we sit in today looks like a damn good example of that to me. How do we keep everyone in the tent? It's sort of the problem with coalitions. They work for a while. Perhaps this tent should remain in flux, constantly shifting to accommodate shifting identities and moments and sometimes maybe you just don't want to be up there in the tent with everybody, period.

San Francisco has boomed in the last year with a multitude of teeny, tiny storefront, predominantly dyke or queer or dyke-owned performance spaces, spaces for little baby dykes to explore, spaces for young queers to get it out in and get it on in. The new Caffe Cinos? The lifetime of these spaces will probably be brief, but I suspect their legacy will be enormous. Perhaps in a couple of decades or so, the by-then former proprietors of Dora's Red Beard or Luna C or 848 Space or Marvin White's FBP—it's called For Black People—an Oakland-based black and queer performance series, perhaps at some point in time all these folks will congregate in the shade of a peach tree overhanging the deck of some old queen in San Francisco. They will gather their own gaylings and dykelings and Miss Things at the hem of their own caftans. They'll wheel the old queen out. She'll look good. She'll be a little weary from her last tour, but she'll listen quietly as her younger friends tell of a time in the late nineties and the new millennium, when they too were once cultural warriors.

14 The Kids Stay in the Picture, or, Toward a New Queer Theater

Randy Gener

When I first met Prudence Browne, she showed me some skin—a bounty of soft, black, capacious, fleshy skin. She was onstage, performing in the Joseph Papp Public Theater with other young urban queer members of School's OUT: The Naming Project, a multimedia video and performance group for lesbian and gay youth in New York City. Standing in front of abstract undulating video images, Prudence slowly took off loose clothing and then put it back on as she intoned, "I'm obsessed with my body, and I'm obsessed with your body. The way it moves, the way it sits there in the audience staring back at my body." Devoid of rage, grief, or whiny petulance, her voice cooed in warm, trancelike tones until she was interrupted by shouts from offstage: hurtful words full of mocking and ridicule, slung like daggers at the big beautiful body she was courageously revealing to us. Unperturbed, Prudence paused, finished speaking, and then walked calmly offstage. No special pleading. No melodrama. She acknowledged that words can sting and leave behind a painful residue simply by being heard, yet through her steady presence she warded them off. After she left the stage, her absence turned our attention to an indelibly comforting and evocative video image: water cascading over abundant flesh.

Performance art is a door that opens the self to its artistic potential, and at a young age, Prudence Browne had already learned how to turn one of the genre's most fundamental cranks—the ability to hook the audience through physicality and intensity of voice—with the ease and confidence of an old-timer. But this is hardly the extent of her accomplishment. In the experimental tradition of theatrical video performances that began in the early 1970s, Browne integrates video art with a feminist and political aim in conjunction with her queer-themed performance. By placing dreamy video images, which she shot and edited herself, side by side with her fierce live performance, which she wrote and developed, she confronts, analyzes, presents, and poeticizes thorny questions about body image, erotic desire, and sexual harassment. Onstage, she's open-faced and direct, even overwhelming in her honesty. While there's no doubting the raw, hurt feelings beneath the balmy surface of poetic restraint she projects, Browne's performance conveys an aura of celebration and self-possession: She looks sexy and beautiful. For like her other School's OUT friends, she proves herself to be a cogent artist stuck in the body of a teenager.

In School's OUT, young urban queers get silly, smart-alecky, heavy, elegaic, and in-your-face. Breaking out of the confessional modes of commodified performance art and veering away from traditional coming-out narratives, the troupe's theatrical and video projects rip apart paternalistic media cliches about tormented adolescents, subvert cultural biases about sexuality, and throw a wrench into the works of a society that labels, circumscribes, stereotypes, and pigeonholes. Bright, outspoken, and gutsy, School's OUT members talk, leap, dance, act, and react, carving out self-scapes that tenderly portray their adolescent lives.

A project of the Dance Theater Workshop's Public Imaginations program, in conjunction with the Youth Enrichment Services program of the Lesbian and Gay Community Services Center, School's OUT is a watershed event in the lives of these New York City lesbian, gay, and bisexual artists of color, who range in age from sixteen to twenty. The program provides a supportive group experience in which its participants can deal with the process of growing up queer and explore the thistly themes in their young lives—coming out, race, loneliness, sex, dreams and fears of the future, homophobia, racism, AIDS—through the creation of art. The program brings queer teenagers together with professional artists to create original performances out of real-life experiences, and in some cases, to build long-term mentoring relationships. In a country where economic, social, and political constraints have conspired against the inclusion of arts education in public school curricula, School's OUT is remarkable, too, in influencing youth programs in other cities to affirm queer orientation, sexual liberty, and celebration in the face of despair and death. Though School's OUT is in touch with stark reality (suicide rates among queer teens remain high), and the project can look like social work, its primary function is to teach specific skills and to instill a professional sense of artistic craft. The program mixes workshops for thirteen students in creative writing, video production and editing, and performance art techniques. Six students are then chosen to make a performance together.

The video-maker Mary Ellen Strom, the founding director of School's OUT, describes her effort to enable young artists to create art from "a real place of clarity, to find a location where one can be fearlessly one's self." Strom guides the students through improvisational games and yoga and mime exercises, and presents theoretical, historical, and practical material about performance, the visual arts, and independent media. But she often leaves the teens on their own to sketch ideas. "I want them to learn to create work out of real-life experiences," Strom says, "to find art from the daily activities and symbolic actions of our lives." Strom adamantly refuses to claim the position as School's OUT's guiding head. "I am just the adult furniture who organizes things and helps support what their interests are," she says.

Finding creative ways to understand what queer teenagers are growing into (which is constantly changing), using art as a means of problem solving to address the complex questions involved in coming out—from how queers have sex to what constitutes community—School's OUT is, in sum, by, for, and about queer teens. Form matters here: Performance art is individuality in action, so by its very nature and substance, School's OUT has been a lynchpin for growth. Instead of spreading the primitive myth of tribal togetherness, the project offers young queers a stronger, more authentic foothold through the master of performing arts. It teaches them the rigorous, disciplined study and practice of art forms, principles, and methods in order to create their own art as well as understand and evaluate art forms created by others.

The crux of School's OUT is a series of retreats in New Hampshire, where the participants develop ideas for their annual show at the Dance Theater Workshop. In preparation for a project in 1998, Andres Montoya, then nineteen, worked on text and video about an issue that had been bothering him since he was six: his anxiety over his sexual attraction to his father. "There's a lot of ambivalence about how I felt," he explains, "exactly because it was something romantic and wonderful at the same time it was something society does not exactly accept as romantic or wonderful. I came out of the retreat not as ambivalent as when I went into it." Now an HIV activist, Montoya uses School's OUT not as therapy, but as a tool for creative exploration.

In the provocative video-performance piece that resulted, Montoya recounts, in explicit and tough-minded detail, how as a young boy, he touched his father's penis while they were lying naked on a bed one punishingly hot summer afternoon. In a soft-spoken monologue delivered in front of a wildly abstract video, Montoya speaks in the voice of young Andy—shy, confused, fearful of retribution, but endlessly curious. His narrative starts over again and again as he tries out phrases and metaphors to describe his tremulous thoughts, confused feelings, perilous sensations, and erotic interest. One thing remains constant: his wish to tell the story with respect for himself and his dad, and his insistence on not being read as perverse.

Remarkable for its wide-eyed evocation of inner turmoil, Montoya's self-consciously stoic performance calls forth the stark recognition that defines queer identity as much as anything else—the recognition Frank Browning describes in *Culture of Desire*: "There's an unmistakable queerness in realizing that the emerging story of your internal desires has little in common with the tales of straightforward desires recounted in dimestore novels. By its very absence, the queer plot tantalizes." Teasing out the tantalizing, yet sustaining a tone of innocence and sexual discovery, Montoya uncovers a far from unique desire that men rarely admit to each other. Still, while Montoya says that he is always tempted in writing "to make it general, to comment on the cultural aspects of it," it's the focus on the particular that gives the work resonance. Performance art, after all, is the form best suited to young queer exploration because it offers no closets to hide in. Unlike performing a character in a traditional play, performance art atavistically seeks to erase the metaphysical boundary between the dancer and the dance. "The personal is the one thing the audience can't deny," Montoya says.

Candor trumps fear in performance art. That has an especially powerful meaning for young queers, whose fears are legion and legitimate. As a form, performance art allows them to recontextualize real-life narratives without relying on fictional clichés and outside certification. In effect, School's OUT members benefit spiritually and artistically by coming out twice—first when they open their souls to friends and family, and second, when their video and/or performance works assert their public selves.

Unlike other theater programs for youth—the Young Playwrights Festival or the 52nd Street Project—School's OUT is not teaching playwriting per se. "My background is nontraditional theater," says Mary Ellen Strom, describing her organizing influence and explaining how the project is not interested in rearing little gay Neil Simons or perky lesbian Wendy Wassersteins. "We do a lot of readings about performance. We talk about the issues gay and lesbian youth face. We help people to get in touch with themselves because it helps them make art from a position of clarity. We discuss everything ad nauseum."

Despite the endless group discussions and the sense of family the members develop as these young queers show up week in and week out for themselves and for each other, each participant shapes her or his own project. And though when staged together, they add up to connected, compelling performances, the individual differences in style, tone, angle, and content are vast. In the troupe's 1996 show, for instance, family is a common theme, seen from a variety of perspectives. Browne presents "the mad women" who haunt her: women overwhelmed by child rearing who slowly seem to disappear. Jason Newland, chain-smoking and watching TV, recalls the child abuse he says his mother inflicted upon him. Sadie Rodriguez narrates childhood capers. And as a sort of emcee, Diana Casillas describes her upbringing in rap/hip-hop numbers. A glitzy not-quite-mock fashion show binds the evening, with each performer offering an exaggerated image of perceived perversity. As Cyberboy, Newland vamps across the stage in a space-agey black vinyl outfit that he wears at dance clubs. Montoya walks down a runway in a white priest's collar, holding a Bible; then he turns into a sex slave with a leash and his butt is spanked by the holy book. Browne wears a stack of books as headwear.

Throughout this pageant, a white size-10 tafetta, polka-dot, spaghetti-strap dress hangs on one side of the stage, fluffy with several petticoats, laces, and feather boa. It is the dress Nelson Rodriguez wore in the previous year's show at DTW, performing a hilarious drag piece inspired by Michael Jackson and Bette Midler, in which he delivered a monologue from "Designing Women." Rodriguez, one of the original members of School's OUT, became a legendary figure in the youth community of the YES Program for being daring and forthcoming, harrowingly investigating his sero-positive status in his art. (He also gave a memorable performance as the frenzied queer boy waiting by the phone in Maria Maggenti's film, *The Incredibly True Adventure of Two Girls in Love*.) He died of AIDS in 1997. In the last two years of his life, Strom recalls, "Nelson became committed to making work that had incredible depth and clear messages. That was an inspiration for everyone. There was a point when he knew his years were numbered, and he changed his work to deal with the loneliness and grief of being HIV-positive. On the other hand, his drag work was filled with great joy and celebration."

258

Formally pluralistic, intensely collaborative, and theatrically experimental in its loose pulling together of various forms and media, each intermedia project strives aesthetically to create a group portrait. By refusing to follow the Interstate 80 of plots, the interdisciplinary pieces ask us to make a leap of faith and imagination because what's suggested or implied is often more revelatory than what is actually said—these are dramas not of crisis, but of open spatiality. Often the dramaturgical point is brought home through the liminal interactions between bodily presence and video image. Juxtaposing video representations against physical reality puts quotation marks around the onstage roles performed, allowing us to see them clearly. In both Browne's and Montoya's pieces, the actor's physical presence substantively mediates the plastic image on the video screen. One might even go so far as to say that the performance colonizes the queer self that is presented. Browne presents an erotic archetype, yet her revealed female body is also the place for washing away guilt and shame, self-loathing and self-hate, repression and feelings of inferiority. As her own hands explore and caress her body, time passes—and then she leaves, as quickly as she had shown up in front of us. There's no denying who's in control here, nor any denying the emotionally direct challenges her theatrical self presents against our image-saturated, media-numbed, highly sexed, deeply puritanical, blatantly narcissistic culture. Performance reinvests Browne's body with mystery and we can begin to see it anew, to understand it as a kind of undiscovered country.

School's OUT pushes the envelope from within, along two different tracks. From the perspective of practical sex education, it differs radically from a majority of the nation's youth programs by placing the study of sex and sexual definition in the positive context of loving relationships. The radical nature of this attitude cannot be emphasized enough: Though homosexuality may be more widely accepted in America than ever before, America continues to discuss sex primarily in terms of risk. High school sex education is usually an exercise in fear-mongering, focusing on risk and pushing condoms and abstinence, but seldom addressing the pleasure and growth young adults find in exploring their sexualities.

From a performing arts perspective, on the other hand, School's OUT actively looks for a language or shared aesthetic that shows what cannot be described by words alone. By allowing every young voice to speak in whatever medium s/he chooses, and by fostering community survival through workable consensus, School's OUT evolves a new way of looking at queer theater, one that, anachronistically perhaps, recalls the predictions of the legendary stage designer Robert Edmond Jones. Jones complained of a theater that was "strikingly out of date" in comparison to other arts, and called upon theater artists to create a new theater art by incorporating film and other developing technologies. More than half a century later, School's OUT is unselfconsciously answering Jones's call with its synthesis of live performance, video, and computers.

But what does it even mean to call a theater project "experimental" at the turn of the new century, especially when speaking of queer theater, when so much of the lesbian and gay work of earlier decades has yet to be acknowledged as part of even a queer repertory? As a philosophical concept, experimentation feels quaint because it plays directly into long-held myths of unimpeded American progress. In this model, queer theater, as Charles Ludlam once said, is considered "the re-search-and-development department for the culture at large," a marginalized studio or lab where actors, directors, designers, and writers get to play around until they graduate into something more sophisticated. In an industry-based culture that actively seeks and takes from the cutting edge or alternative scenes in order to quickly feed (and thus neutralize) alternative practices into the maw of the mainstream machine, all the official organs of artistic power (schools, newspapers, galleries, museums, not-for-profit institutions) fall over one another to endorse, and claim credit for discovering, the new. In today's theater, there is neither an avant-garde nor a rear guard. Everyone is simply on guard. Against the futility of experimentation itself, where does an experimental queer theater position itself?

School's OUT doesn't preoccupy itself with such questions; it just does the work—for *all* of us. It takes up the forms available and engaging to its young practitioners not so much to make an artsy statement about experimentation, but to enable them to express what they must. Patricia Nell Warren has written, "No community has a future if it fails to ensure that its children can flourish physically, emotionally, mentally and spiritually." School's OUT is then, most of all perhaps, about fostering queer futures. As the project develops, bringing new groups of young people into it, predicts Strom, "School's OUT will shape itself differently. The goals will change. The models will change." And so are the lives of the young queer artists inescapably, irrevocably altered—as they master the art of being gloriously themselves.

15 Goodnight Irene

An Endnote

Carmelita Tropicana

Memories from the corners of my . . . With that song in my heart that is how my first play began. A play written with Uzi Parnes with an all live-girl cast from WOW. Memories of theater, memories of the CLAGS Queer Theater Conference of April 1995. My memories are like Xeroxes. I take one out to look at from my memory bank, then the next time I take one out I am remembering the memory of the memory, and then it's the memory of the memory of the memory. Every time I take one out, the sharp focus softens and gets fuzzy like the outline of an erect morning glory cup when it is pierced by the bright rays of the sun goddess.

When I look back at the CLAGS conference two images come to mind, the mirror and backstage drama. I missed the opening eloquent speech of Jill Dolan (but I read it) for I was at another conference doing research for my new piece on Sor Juana, a nun who was the seventeenth-century combo of Emily Dickinson and Madonna. I could tell the Sor Juana conference was not a queer conference because there was no panel discussion on Sor Juana's proclivity—butch, femme, top, bottom—and as a nun who wrote love poems to another woman, did she or didn't she? could she or couldn't she? At the conference, I met the formidable Madame du theater, playwright-director and mentor to almost all the Latino playwrights in the East and West Coasts, Maria Irene Fornes. We cabbed it to the Judson Memorial Church where she was going to serve as a panelist.

On the steps of the church stood David Román, Alberto Sandoval, and José Muñoz chatting postmodernly, but when I joined in and put my arms around them, we felt like chorus girls, Rockettes. Gonzalo Aburto, of Homovisiones cable TV, held out a mike for the *la lucha continua* contingency. Inside the church, Maria Irene looked around and reminisced. Judson Church held many theater memories for her. I imagined voices echoing through the hallway.

To be . . . to be . . . or . . . or . . . not. This is where she began to do theater. She said the Judson Church is to her what WOW is to me.

WOW. In 1982 I went to the Women's One World Festival celebrating women's, mostly lesbian, culture. It was there that I saw Split Britches, Deb Margolin, Peggy Shaw, and Lois Weaver perform their title piece and like many Wowettes I was smitten by the play, and by the girls on- and offstage. I thought I had died and gone to girl heaven. Here were girls who were fun and funny, who wore all kinds of outfits, not just battle fatigues, girls who came in all sizes, shapes, and colors. As I watched the play, my mouth hung open and stayed open laughing. Here was theater that touched my innermost core and Cubana corazón. This was a slice of Americana, a portrait of three women in Virginia, a girl's *Waiting for Godot*. For these three women it was biscuits, for my great-aunts in Cuba it would have been *pan con cafe con leche*. I had found a jolly matriarchy. I had been longing to throw myself into her heaving bosom, though I didn't know it at the time. When people ask me can art change your life I think of that play *Split Britches*—how it acted as a magnet for a bevy of girls like myself. The magnetic pull was great. It was at WOW that I was born and baptized Tropicana; it was at WOW that Holly Hughes traded her paintbrush for the mighty pen; it was at WOW that the Five Lesbian Brothers met and started singing "We Are Family." And those are only three of a million stories in this naked city.

I went to WOW to meet girls, talk art, and celebrate the holidays at WOW rituals like the X-Rated XMAS, The God Ball, The Debutante Ball. It was fate that with such balls, we would turn thespians and make theater the dominant art form. But from the perspective of a loose girl collective, when we examined the art form, we saw that there was a hole, a void in the variety and amount of theater offerings with lesbian overtures. We looked in the mirror and asked the primordial question: *Mira*, Mirror on the wall who is the fairest of them all? The answer was a triumphant queer theater, especially lesbian. And like good lesbians who have a need to fill holes, we tried.

We've come a long way baby. In the eighties we performed at clubs like WOW, 8BC, and Chandelier, and now as we enter the new millennium we perform in academic conferences like the CLAGS Queer Theater Conference. I was honored when the conference organizers asked me to do a panel recreating "Cheet Chats with Carmelita" at the old club Chandelier, even though it had to relocate to the Joseph Papp Public Theater.

Uzi Parnes, my collaborator, ran club Chandelier on Avenue C. One of the most memorable events at the club was the LOISAIDA (Lower East Side) Beauty Pageant. The late Ethyl Eichelberger presided over the contest, and in five-inch heels, was and will always be the reigning Queen. Her sidekick, the late Rita Redd won Ms. Congeniality when she/he unfurled out of the American flag she was wrapped in and brought the house down with her piquant smile. And though the competition was tough, I won the title, $25, and all the beer I could guzzle. With such success, Uzi was inspired and created the "Cheet Chats with Carmelita," a lesbian faux variety talk show. The shows had themes and guest stars who could address them. The theme for one was, who were the greatest women in herstory? Among the greatest were Lois Weaver as country western singer Tammy Whynot, Lisa Kron as anthropologist Margaret Mead, Holly Hughes as Lady Godiva, and Yolanda Hawkins as Saint Joan of Arc.

In bringing "Cheet Chats" to the CLAGS conference, I followed the format and chose my theme: "To Niche or Not to Niche" with performers who straddled different art forms: Eileen Myles, poet-performance artist; Jennifer Miller, performance artist-circus amoker; and Lucy Sexton and Annie Iobst (DANCENOISE) performance artists-dancers. I opened the show with the history of the "Cheet Chat," and was followed by Jennifer Miller who delivered her Xenobia soliloquy while juggling knives that looked like machetes. As she dropped the machetes close to the audience, and defiantly stuck one in the marley floor of the Public Theater, I as the host cowered, and the audience, like the NEA, trembled at the dangers of performance art. Then Eileen Myles addressed the state of Lesbian Theater and the dearth of producers for such oeuvre. When it came time for DANCENOISE, we didn't know whether they should perform onstage alone, or we should join them. We decided to take part as spectators sitting on our talk-show set. Loud rock music played. Annie and Lucy appeared on opposite sides of the stage. They mirrored each other in their wigs. We looked at them. We mirrored the audience in front of us. A beautiful mirror image was created with the spirit of spontaneous combustion that is part of performance art. Guns and buttocks were exposed as these girls cavorted onstage. Both audiences watched Lucy and Annie, two naked girls in wigs, kiss on the lips. Their kiss brought bittersweet memories of the eighties, a kiss too homoerotic for the NEA, but not for us others, in the U.S.A.

We artists have two lives. The one mortal of flesh and bones, and the other soulful, immortal, the artistic life. The CLAGS conference could not escape the impact AIDS has had on our artistic community. This is where the backstage drama began.

I hosted the closing performance/party show of the conference by default. Harvey Fierstein could not make it, so I, the understudy, got the part. It is true we are always up for the same parts in Hollywood and it is always a choice, Harvey or Carmelita. So there I was with Ellie Covan of Dixon Place backstage exchanging notes on the performers' bios and setting the order for the show. She told me Frank Maya was performing, but he was sick. Very sick. We didn't know whether to encourage or discourage him from performing. Frank showed up in a baseball cap and jacket. I didn't recognize him at first, he was so thin. I remembered meeting him years ago at the Wah Wah Hut run by DANCENOISE. He was very handsome then with his green eyes, big grin, and gold-painted ears. He told me he was Latino. Say what? Come on, Frank. But it was true. Frank and Vanna White, both Latinos.

When I leaned over to kiss him hello at the CLAGS performance, I felt him burning through his jacket. He said he had a fever. Ellie sat down with him and I went out to start the show. It was packed at the Public, the crowd clamored for a Queer show with flagrant abandon. The first performer was Lisa Lerner, Cowboy Girl, who sang a lascivious "Number 69" dinner-for-two song. I returned backstage and Frank asked me if I remembered that benefit for DIFFA we did some years ago. It was held at a midtown club. The noise from the DIFFA crowd was deafening. They walked, talked, drank—while we tried to get their attention. It was one of those shows that made you wish you had a day job. Frank did his stand-up gay routine and like a trooper did not cut his set. We agreed the show was hell.

I went to introduce Brian Freeman of Pomo Afro Homos and when I returned I saw Ellie and Frank intimately engaged in conversation. I couldn't hear what they were saying, but it seemed urgent. I thought of Ethyl Eichelberger who reminded me of Frank, both consummate performers. Ethyl had AIDS and chose a dramatic exit, suicide. The news of her suicide spread fast. It was a shock to all of us who knew her. But then I couldn't imagine her not treading the boards. Such a commanding operatic performer so sick she could lose her concentration and energy onstage: It was hard to imagine. I looked over at Ellie; she was Frank's audience of one. Ellie and I acknowledged his high fever and Frank finally gave in and admitted it would probably be better if he went home and rested. "Carmelita tell them I'm touring," Frank said. Ellie and Frank disappeared into the elevator. I went out to do time, patter, something so common for a comedian like Frank. The audience was in great spirits. I looked around and saw familiar faces, the Five Lesbian Brothers sitting on the side and then some new faces, unlined ruddy cheeks of a new generation of gay boys who lusted after my white bunny wonder bra. I modeled my latex gloves showing them I'm always ready, hoping they will be too. Nicky Paraiso took the stage. I saw Ellie getting out of the elevator sad, teary-eyed. She had to give Frank money and put him in a cab. He'd walked out with a couple of dollars. It was raining out. I imagined her giving him wrinkled wet dollar bills. I tried to console her and suggested we end the show with the song she always sings. We asked Nicky to play it on the piano. The audience joined us as we dedicated it to Frank. "Good Night Irene, Good Night Irene, I'll see you in my dreams."

As I walked home I thought of Shakespeare. "Good night sweet prince. May flights of angels sing thee to thy rest." Sweet tender words. Then I thought of Frank's routine. He hated the tender sweet image of white helium balloons flying up to the sky in memory of those who have died of AIDS. He was angry, he wanted something loud, an uzi, a bomb to explode. I continued Shakespeare: "Speak loudly of him. Take up the bodies, Given a sight as this becomes the field, But here shows much amiss. Go bid the soldiers shoot."

Frank Maya died four months after the conference, joining many whose artistic lives have been cut short. We are left with the sorrow of a promise and work unrealized. We admire those who struggle with disease and devote every moment hurrying to write that book, finish that play. If theater is the mirror where our queer visions are reflected, we theater practitioners must make a pact with queer-friendly academics and stand guard as sentinels so that the mirror does not shatter like the mirror in *Citizen Kane*, and our queer reflections smash into smithereens and get sent flying into oblivion. Let our queer, lesbian, gay, bisexual, transgender, and any other future gender images be reflected beyond our lifetimes into queer infinity. Let us march into the new millennium echoing the words of the French Revolution: Liberté, Égalité, Homosexualité!

Contributors

Maureen Angelos is one of the Five Lesbian Brothers. She has been a member of the WOW Café since 1981. She is an Aquarian and her hobbies are baking, bicycling, and agitation toward the dismantling of the patriarchy.

Jill Dolan holds the Zachary T. Scott Family Chair in Theatre and Drama at the University of Texas, Austin. She is the author of *The Feminist Spectator as Critic, Presence and Desire: Essays on Gender, Sexuality and Performance*, and *Geographies of Learning: Theory and Practice, Activism and Performance*, as well as numerous essays and articles on feminist and lesbian performance.

Susan Finque is an actor, director, administrator, and educator based in Seattle, where she was the co-artistic Director of the Alice B. Theatre for nearly nine years. The recent recipient of an NEA/TCG Career Development grant for directors, she has also worked at such companies as The Group Theatre, Umo/Small Hand Open Fist, the Langston Hughes Cultural Center, Dixon Place, and Pomo Afro Homos. Her movement-theater work on transsexuality, *T.S./Crossing*, has toured to critical acclaim.

Brian Freeman is a San Francisco-based writer, director, and performer best known as the co-founder of Pomo Afro Homos (Postmodern African-American Homosexuals), the award-winning black gay male performance group. He recently completed a year as Resident Director at the New York Shakespeare Festival/Joseph Papp Public Theater, and is currently Artist-in-Residence at Yerba Buena Center in San Francisco. He also served as Associate Producer on *Tongues Untied*, the groundbreaking documentary by the late film maker Marlon Riggs, and is the recipient of the 1999 Cal Arts Alpert Award in Theater, which helps him divide his time between San Francisco and New York City. His recent play, *Civil Sex*, explores the politics of race and sexuality in the life and times of Bayard Rustin, the organizer of the 1963 March on Washington.

Randy Gener is a writer, cultural critic and theater director. He is senior journalist and theater columnist for BroadwayOnline.com and critic-at-large for *New York Theatre Wire*. His features, criticism, and essays appear in the *New York Times*, the *Star Ledger, Stagebill, Lambda Book Report, American Theatre*, and the *Village Voice*.

He has directed at La MaMa E.T.C, Dixon Place, Grove Street Playhouse, Theatre for a New City, Asian American Writers Workshop, and HERE Arts Center.

George E. Haggerty, Professor of English at the University of California, Riverside, is the author of *Men in Love: Masculinity and Sexuality in the Eighteenth Century, Gothic Fiction/Gothic Form,* and *Unnatural Affections: Women and Fiction in the Late Eighteenth Century,* and a range of essays on same-sex desire in the eighteenth century. He coedited (with Bonnie Zimmerman) *Professions of Desire,* and the *Encyclopedia of Lesbian and Gay Histories and Cultures.*

Holly Hughes, according to former National Endowment for the Arts chairman John Frohnmayer, "is a lesbian and her work is heavily of that genre." Her most recent solo performance piece, *Preaching to the Perverted,* directed by Lois Weaver, played to packed houses around the country. She is the author of *Clit Notes: A Sapphic Sampler,* and coeditor of *O Solo Homo: The New Queer Performance.*

Ania Loomba is a Professor of English at the University of Illinois at Urbana Champaign. She is author of *Gender, Race, Renaissance Drama* (1989), *Colonialism/Postcolonialism* (1998) and coeditor (with Martin Orkin) of *Postcolonial Shakespeares* (1998), and *Shakespeare, Race, and Colonialism* (2002). She is currently working on representations of the East in Renaissance theater.

Cynthia Mayeda, currently the deputy director of the Brooklyn Museum of Art, worked for the Dayton Hudson Foundation, one of the largest corporate giving programs in America, for twelve years, serving as Chair of the Foundation from March 1990 until her resignation in October 1994. She served on numerous NEA Theater and Dance panels over the past decade and as Director of the NEA Dance Program for an interim period. She has been a Senior Advisor to the Andrew W. Mellon Foundation and with Garland Wright, initiated the gathering that led to the Twin Cities' Arts Over AIDS. She was also midwife to the birth of the NEA's AIDS Working Group.

Tim Miller is a solo performer and Artistic Director of Highways Performance Space in Santa Monica, California. He is cofounder of P.S. 122 in New York, and author of *Shirts and Skins.*

Framji Minwalla is Assistant Professor of Theater and Women's Studies at Dartmouth College, where he teaches theater history, performance and queer theory, and popular culture. His work has appeared in *Theater, Theater Three,* and *Ameri-*

can Theatre, as well as a number of anthologies. He presently is at work on a book negotiating the connections among performances, politics, and pedagogies.

José Esteban Muñoz teaches in the Department of Performance Studies at the Tisch School of the Arts, New York University, and is the author of *Disidentifications: Queers of Color and the Performance of Politics.* His articles have been published in the journals *GLQ, Screen, Social Text,* and *Women and Performance* as well as several anthologies of critical theory. He is the coeditor of *Pop Out: Queer Warhol* and *Every Nightlife: Culture and Dance in Latin/o America.* He has also coedited special "queer theory" issues of the journals *Social Text* and *Women and Performance.*

Lola Pashalinski is a founding member of Charles Ludlam's Ridiculous Theatrical Company, and won two Obie Awards while with the company. She has since gone on to work with Anne Bogart, Richard Foreman, JoAnne Akalaitis, Robert Wilson, Lee Breuer and Mabou Mines, and in many regional and Off-Broadway theaters. She is coauthor and costar (with Linda Chapman) of the play *Gertrude and Alice: A Likeness to Loving.*

Everett Quinton is the Artistic Director of the Ridiculous Theatrical Company. He has performed in more than forty productions.

David Román teaches English at the University of Southern California. He is the author of *Acts of Intervention: Performance, Gay Culture, and AIDS* which received the 1999 ATHE Award for "Outstanding Book of the Year," and is coeditor with Holly Hughes of *O Solo Homo: The New Queer Performance.* His most recent project is *Downtown and Elsewhere: A Luis Alfaro Reader* (2002).

David Savran is Professor of Theater at the Graduate Center of the City University of New York. His books include *Breaking the Rules: The Wooster Group, Communists, Cowboys, and Queers: The Politics of Masculinity in the Work of Arthur Miller and Tennessee Williams* and *Taking It Like a Man: White Masculinity, Masochism, and Contemporary Culture.* He is an associate editor of *Theatre Journal.* His current research involves an investigation of the positioning of theater as an institution in the Unites States and drama as a particular form of cultural production.

Deb Parks-Satterfield, a poet, playwright, and performer, is the founder and Artistic Director of the fat African American lesbian comedy group, Four Big Girls. She lives in Seattle.

Laurence Senelick is Fletcher Professor of Drama at Tufts University. His most recent books are *The Chekhov Theatre: A Century of the Plays in Performance* which won the Barnard Hewitt award of the American Society for Theatre Research for the best theater book of 1998; *Lovesick: Modernist Plays of Same-Sex Love 1894–1925*; and *The Changing Room: Sex, Drag and Theatre,* which was awarded a Freedley prize of the Theatre Library Association as one of the best theater books of 2000.

Don Shewey has published three books about theater: the biography *Sam Shepard* (1985); *Caught in the Act: New York Actors Face to Face,* a collaboration with photographer Susan Shacter (1986); and *Out Front,* an anthology of gay and lesbian plays published by Grove Press (1988). He writes feature articles for the *New York Times* and theater reviews for the *Advocate.* His articles have also appeared in the *Village Voice, Esquire, Rolling Stone,* and other publications, and his writings have been included in various anthologies ranging from *Contemporary Shakespeare Criticism* to *Best Gay Erotica 2000.* He grew up in a trailer park on a dirt road in Waco, Texas, and now lives in midtown Manhattan halfway between Trump Tower and Carnegie Hall.

Ana Maria Simo is a playwright and activist. She is a cofounder of Medusa's Revenge, Dyke TV, and the Lesbian Avengers. She is the author of *The Table of Liquid Measure,* a radio play about the 1992 firebombing murders of Hattie Mae Cohen and Brian Mock, as well as of such films, plays, and radio plays as *How to Kill Her, Passion,* and *The Opium Wars.*

Alisa Solomon teaches at Baruch College and the Graduate Center of the City University of New York, and is the author of *Redressing the Canon: Essays on Theater and Gender,* winner of the George Jean Nathan Award for Dramatic Criticism.

Valerie Traub is Professor of English and Women's Studies at the University of Michigan. She is the author of *Desire and Anxiety: Circulations of Sexuality in Shakespearean Drama;* coeditor of *Feminist Readings in Early Modern Culture: Emerging Subjects;* and *The Renaissance of Lesbianism in Early Modern England* (2002). She has written several essays on early modern sexuality, particularly homoeroticism, in such journals as *Shakespeare Quarterly, History Workshop Journal, Feminist Studies,* and *GLQ.*

Carmelita Tropicana (Alina Troyano), a Cuban American writer and performer, has written plays in collaboration with Uzi Parnes, a screenplay with Ela Troyano entitled *Carmelita Tropicana: Your Kunst Is Your Waffen,* as well as solo performance pieces. Her plays, prose pieces, and solo work can be found in *I, Carmelita Tropicana: Performing Between Cultures.*

Paula Vogel's play, *How I Learned to Drive,* won the 1998 Pulitzer Prize for drama. Her other plays include *The Baltimore Waltz,* which won Obie Awards in 1992 for Best Play, Best Director (Anne Bogart), and Best Actor (Cherry Jones), *Hot N Throbbing, Desdemona, The Mineola Twins, Meg, And Baby Makes Seven,* and *The Oldest Profession.* Recipient of fellowships from the National Endowment for the Arts, the Pew and Guggenheim Foundations, Vogel has been commissioned twice by the Actors Theatre of Louisville. Her plays are published as *The Mammary Plays* and *The Baltimore Waltz and Other Plays,* both by TCG. She is Professor-at-Large at Brown University.

Doric Wilson was the first playwright at New York's legendary Caffe Cino—his comedy *And He Mad A Her* opened there in 1961. A participant in the Stonewall riots, in 1974 he started TOSOS (The Other Side of Silence), the first professional theater company to deal openly with the gay male experience. A recipient of the Rober Chesley Lifetime Achievement Award, his plays *Street Theater, The West Street Gang, Forever After, A Perfect Relationship,* and *Now She Dances!* are staples in the queer theater canon.

Stacy Wolf is Visiting Associate Professor in the Department of Theater and Dance at the University of Texas, Austin. She is the author of *A Problem Like Maria: Gender and Sexuality in the American Musical,* forthcoming from the University of Michigan Press.

Index

Latinidad, 227–46
Lavender Light, 249
Law, 60–63, 78
Lee, Nathanial, 113, 114–18; *The Rival Queens*, 113, 114–17, 119
Lerner, Lisa, 264
Lesbian and Gay Community Center, 255
Lesbian Avengers, 140
Lesbian identity, 183–202
Levin, Richard A., 101
Levine, Laura, 13
LGTBQ Youth, 254–60
Libertine, 109
Lochrie, Karma, 92–93
Love, heroic, 119
Ludlam, Charles, 125, 131–32, 133, 134, 137, 138, 144, 150, 260; *Anti-Galaxy Nebulae*, 131; *Camille*, 131, 146; *Caprice*, 138, 144; *Eunuchs of the Forbidden City*, 145; *Hot Ice*, 138; *Punch and Judy Show*, 131; *Stage Blood*, 131; *The Ventriloquist's Wife*, 131
Luther, Martin, 79
Lyly, John, 40, 41, 44; *Gallathea*, 26, 40

Macdonald, Robert David, 34, 36–37; *Camille*, 36; *Chinchilla*, 37; *A Waste of Time*, 36
Mabou Mines, 159
Madonna, 164, 261
Maggenti, Maria, *The Incredibly True Adventures of Two Girls in Love*, 258
Mahabarata, The, 213
Mailman, Bruce, *The Off-Broadway Book*, 130
Male femininity, 110
Manhattan Theater Club, 3
Mann, Klaus, *Anya and Esther*, 32–33
Mapplethorpe, Robert, 155
Margolin, Deb, 6
Marlowe, Christopher, 26–27, 109, 114, 115, 117; *Edward II*, 109, 111, 114; *Tragedy of Dido, Queen of Carthage*, 26

Martin, Billy, 189
Marvell, Andrew, 79
Marx, Karl, 245; *The German Ideology*, 245; *Theses on Feurbach*, 245
Massinger, Philip, 47; *The Renegado*, 47
Maya, Frank, 264–65
McCarthyism, 29, 157
McClintock, Anne, 49, 53; *Imperial Leather*, 53
McDonald Amendment, 16
McNally, Terrence, 152, 159, 168; *Love! Valour! Compassion!*, 2, 125, 156, 158, 159, 160, 166, 168, 175
Medusa's Revenge, 133, 150
Memory, 6, 227–46, 261–65
Mercer, Kobena, 7
Metz, Christian, 12, 162
Meyer, Moe, 25
Michigan Women's Music Festival, 196
Mickee Faust Club, 188, 193
Miguel, Muriel, 142
Milhouse, Judith, 119
Miller, Jennifer, 263
Miller, Tim, 2, 177, 191–92, 193; *My Queer Body*, 203; *Naked Breath*, 216
Montez, Maria, 137
Montoya, Andres, 256–57, 259
Montrose, Louis, 74, 81, 89–90, 103, 104
Moraga, Cherríe, 240
Mullaney, Steven, 94
Mulvey, Laura, 162
Muñoz, Jose, 262
Musical theater, 171, 176, 191, 217, 218, 220, 251; *Annie Get Your Gun*, 140; *Auntie Mame*, 136; *Carousel*, 218; *Damn Yankees*, 217; *Fiddler on the Roof*, 142, 251; *Hair*, 143; *Miss Saigon*, 176; *My Fair Lady*, 171; *Oklahoma*, 124; *Pacific Overtures*, 144; *Peter Pan*, 144, 191: *South Pacific*, 171
Myles, Eileen, 263

Nagy, Phyllis, 179
Naked Truth, The (Apple Island), 190